GETTING OUTSIDE

GETTING OUTSIDE

A Far-Western Childhood

Michael Waterman

ISBN-13: 978-1530929344

In any weather, at any hour of the day or night,
I have been anxious to improve the nick of time.

Henry David Thoreau
Walden, 1854

It's my regular grinding
Gets me by in this world.

Jimmie Rodgers
Blue Yodel No. 10
February 6, 1932

Contents

Preface

Writing this book began with a breakdown. Health, financial, and emotional breakdowns have often jarred people in new directions. My water pump blew out on the downgrade to Adir in Eastern Oregon. At one time Adir was named Lonely; in 1995 it consisted of a gas pump, a shack with a plywood bar, and a telephone booth. Eventually the vehicle was towed back to the town of Lakeview and the one-man garage, T-Model Tom's. I then spent five days in a motel run by a South Indian who tried to persuade me that I should move to Lakeview. He had done so well there that his family no longer cleaned the rooms themselves, and he was adding on another building. After a visit two years earlier to my family's ranch on the Oregon Coast, I had written "Road War" and that sad minor comedy was on my mind. Back in my motel room I made a list of topics, turned on my portable computer, and started typing. Words came like flood waters rushing down a New Mexico arroyo after a violent thunderstorm. The first draft of one-third of the book was written in that room. Nine months later it was approximately in its present form. The time to write this was nine months or thirty-five years, depending on how you look at it.

In my view this is also some of the narrative of the American West, a tiny portion of an undramatic story of hard work and discomfort that was over almost as soon as it began. The land of the Native Americans was transformed, and today tourists can swiftly drive by wondrous scenery in an air-conditioned automobile to stay in temperature-controlled rooms. Every small piece of geography, every tiny watershed that they pass by, has a history that would yield at least as many artifacts as the ones I have collected here. During my years on Four Mile Creek we went from horses to tractors, and I have tried to describe that now vanished life. Today Four Mile Road has evolved to Fourmile Lane and Four Mile Creek to Fourmile Creek.

Many of my debts and I hope much of my gratitude are described in these chapters. When we lived in Hawaii, Sandra Douglas urged me to "write it down" years before I (or she) had any idea what "it" actually was other than it had to do with Four Mile, Oregon. My daughter Tracey was my closest confidant while I was working to shape the manuscript. She has her own complex relationship with Oregon. Henry Antosiewicz was the first to read a complete draft, and he encouraged me to finish it, to publish it, not to stop writing. MG Lord read the manuscript and made many useful suggestions, Jonathan Kirsch gave me advice about legal issues, and Sylvia Vance helped see the work into publication.

Various material came my way while I was writing this, mostly from my mother who was the family historian. My grandmother Mabel Waterman's diary of the wagon trip across Oregon returned to Four Mile about the time I thought I was finished writing. This frightens me, that I might have gone to my grave without reading her strong sweet no nonsense optimistic account. The pioneers' apple orchards that remain still bloom in the spring and the fruit of their dreams drop from the trees in the fall to feed the animals, domestic and wild alike. They won't last much longer.

1 Out West

I grew up on a livestock ranch at Four Mile Creek on the southern coast of Oregon where my family raised sheep and cattle. While Europeans discovered Oregon and Europeans moved in and across it, the settlement of our part was not begun until the 1890s. Native Americans lived on this land for centuries, and a few remained by the time my family arrived. My grandparents Charlie and Mabel Waterman came to Four Mile in 1911, so my family has lived there during most of the time the country was converted from what was considered wilderness to civilization. This transition is the subject of these chapters, the transformation of the primal landscape and of my family. I write of what we did to the land but also of what the land and we did to ourselves; these things are not easily disconnected.

My people made a life on the edge between civilization and the wilderness, in that scrubby border between the cultivated fields and the unsettled regions. And that shows up in their actions: my great-grandfathers went straight to the frontier where they scraped out a living. All four sets of my great-grandparents and some of my great-great-grandparents settled in various foothills of the Blue Mountains, that formidable obstacle on the Oregon Trail. My grandparents continued to go West, but there was no land west of Four Mile. My parents had been brought to the edge of the continent and did not know what to do next, so they stayed by the ocean and saw the transition from timber to scrub land to suburbs. While my grandfathers were nostalgic for the wilderness and what could be taken from it by hunting and fishing, the next generations are resentful of the controls of civilization. They are mad as hell, so the saying goes, but they can do nothing about it except to resent others who seem to have more and who make rules they now must follow.

If the paths of my family moving from home to home across the West are traced onto a map, it looks like a tangle of telephone cord tied by itself into knots with loop ends stapled to the Blue Mountains and southwestern Oregon. It seemed as if Four Mile was at the end of the road, the promised land. My great-uncle Leo went to Alaska to work construction in summers and spent rainy Oregon winters spending his wages, but he did not stick to the North. Other countries were mentioned, Australia, New Zealand and Canada, but imagination or energy or courage failed us, and we stayed put. The air and water and earth of Four Mile made up the molecules of our bodies. We ate it, we drank it, we breathed it.

Those tangled traces marking the pathways to Four Mile Creek conceal a central fact of my family's existence: its intense insularity. We were so isolated that Bandon, 10 miles away, was a big city and Coos Bay, 15 miles more miles distant, a metropolis. Anything beyond that was Outside, as in "I hear Jack Crook went Outside last week. What was *that* for?" He might have gone to the Willamette Valley, several hours drive. Most of what I have written is about that vanished inside world. Growing up on Four Mile Creek it was difficult to believe there was any other reality.

2 Roots

This story begins with land, before Asians crossed that narrow bridge to populate a true wilderness, before Europeans found the American continents for themselves. Land. Rock and earth and water; plants and animals and microbes; evolution and co-evolution, millennium after millennium.

There is a strip of plain along southern Oregon next to the Pacific, a mile or two or three wide in generous places, shrinking to rocky cliffs in others. The wind blows so hard and relentlessly that on this plain the trees are stooped and stunted, dramatically sculpted by the constant stress. Limbs grow swept back from the trunk toward the north, pushed that direction by winter winds. Some stunted branches may reach tentatively to the south, so that the trees look out of balance. Less violent summer winds come from the opposite direction, the north. Small pine, fir, and cedar grow close together and hold off the weather. Back nearer the hills, there are hemlock and spruce growing in thick clusters. The sand and peat soil supports moss, ferns, clever species of grasses, and a host of bushes. Madrone and manzanita trees with their purple-hued trunks live only on this sandy ground and do not penetrate far inland. Huckleberries and thickets of salal up to six-feet in height grow in unforested regions. The delicate ground-cone, looking exactly like a large pale fir cone sitting upright, is a parasite of the salal.

Rivers and creeks come out of the low, steep mountains that rise quickly out of the plain. The length of most watersheds is short, and the run is quick until the fresh water meets the tides of the Pacific. There are rivers, the Rogue to the south and the

Umpqua to the north, that cut deeply into the coastal mountains. With these boundaries, this land is boxed in and isolated by ocean, rivers and rugged mountains. The meeting of rivers and sea creates the coastal plain, and sand dunes and small lakes, both fresh and salt, dot an uneven landscape. Relentless winds scour the sand down to the water table, creating bodies of water an inch or so deep. Some fertile land is built up near the streams from winter floods which carry silt and debris down from the hills, floods that pulse with the tides. The tidewater regions support a wide variety of creatures: crabs, salt- and fresh-water fish, ducks, geese, hawks, eagles, mink, otter, beaver, coyotes, ringtail cats and raccoons.

Back toward the hills, the streams cut their way into steep little valleys, valleys with benches of rich fertile land quickly bending up into hills away from the stream. The stream banks are covered with alders, willows, and berry brambles. Skunk cabbage and horse-tails grow in boggy areas. Away from the banks are smaller trees, small because streambeds that change course every winter do not allow them to get too large. Elegant myrtle trees grow on the valley floor; garden snakes make scraping sounds as they work through the dry leaves looking for food. Then on the hills, the trees become large and then even larger. Squirrels and mountain boomers dig up the occasional opening. Red- and white-fir, red- and white-cedar, and vine maple. Spruce and hemlock. The Douglas- or red-fir become dignified in their old age of a few-hundred years; diameters of eight-feet are not uncommon, the furrowed bark a foot thick. And the Port Orford or red-cedar are also awesome: they grow to twelve-feet and more in diameter, two-hundred feet high. The primal forests are thick with forest litter; fallen trees with huge root wads jutting upright, lines of new trees growing on the century-old decay of fallen giants, jungles of the wiry vine maple, and ferns and moss covering almost everything.

This is a temperate zone, a cool fertile rain-forest. A current from Asia running fifty miles off the Coast usually keeps temperatures above freezing, while in winter storms blow in layer after layer of cold rain, hammering the plants and rocks and anything else that is exposed. It is a dry winter that only has sixty inches of rain, and winters with one-hundred-and-fifty inches are easy to locate. Winds of fifty miles-per-hour come with mild storms, and gales of over one hundred occur with regularity. The seemingly endless rains cease to reveal dryer summer months. When the temperature exceeds 70 degrees, cool dense fogs are drawn in from the Pacific Ocean, lifting up the watersheds, blanketing the scrub, wreathing through the timber.

Heavy stands of Douglas fir collect moisture from morning fogs that is later released as a steady mist, a light summer rain while the bright sun shines above the forest canopy. The ferns underneath collect this moisture and bend from the weight of it. A deer or elk moving along a trail releases the now larger drops, creating a dark-green swath as it goes. The bears, beavers, deer, ducks, and salmon adapted to this terrain as surely as did the cedars, firs, alders, and vine maples.

In the 1850s gold was discovered on the southern Oregon coast. The rim of forest and mountain shielding this country from settlement was penetrated by rough roads by 1885, and opportunity presented itself: settlers swarmed over this scrubby country, all looking for their own place in the world. They came from lines of ne'er-do-wells who were unlucky or lazy or criminals, flung West by disaster, calamity and ambition; this was their opportunity for a piece of land, something none of their ancestors had possessed. The Homestead Act was their ticket, and they did not let this last chance slip by them. The frontier was coming to a close; there was only ocean to the west; it was now or never.

The names the pioneers gave to their landscape are direct and descriptive. Two Mile and Four Mile are distances along the shore from the Bandon harbor. There is Beaver Creek, Buck Creek, Bear Creek, Elk Horn Creek, Elk River, Buzzard Butte, Gobblers Knobb, and Panther Mountain. We have Slide Creek, Rusty Creek, Blueberry Creek, Rock Creek; Burnt Ridge, Coffee Butte, Watchers Butte, Tent Prairie; Calf Ranch Mountain, Round Top Mountain, Sand Rock Mountain, and Anvil Mountain. My favorites are Euchre Creek, Dead Man Creek, Pistol River, Devils Backbone, Whiskey Run. And Drowned Out Creek. It would be a mistake to infer that Gold Beach is named for sand shining from a rare sunset. Instead it is named for the gold that miners removed from those sands in the 1850s. They built sluice boxes in the surf and used the cold waves to run the boxes. The Oregon Coast is not a place of the imagination.

3 Dehorning

It is a cloudy cold day of early winter 1951 and I am at the barn my father built on a bulldozed flat above our farmhouse. My father tells me "Go get the cow." As I was milking two cows, a yellow Jersey and a mixed breed brindle called Goggles, I didn't know if he meant both or a specific cow. If I asked he'd get angry for me not knowing what he meant, if I brought the wrong one it would be worse. So I drove both cows to the barn. Ray exploded. "What the goddam hell are you doing with the other cow? I WANT GOGGLES. Get that one outta here. You. God. Damn. Lazy. Stupid. Kid."

My father had decided to dehorn Goggles. Usually this is done to younger animals, and if the animal is large, it should be secured in a cattle chute that holds the entire body immobile. It is a serious operation. My father was in a rush and mad at Goggles, so he just put her in the stall where we milked. The stanchion had vertical boards that shut onto the cow's neck in a V shape, stopping much motion to the right or left but leaving up-down and front-back motions somewhat free. My father did not securely tie down her head. Then he got the device used to cut horns. Imagine one of those axes with a curved blade used to behead people in the Middle Ages. The dehorner had a matched pair of these blades, and three-foot-long handles to give the operator mechanical advantage. He got the first horn off, not without a tussle, and then Goggles went crazy, threshing about, falling down, making an anguished series of sounds. Blood was everywhere, coming out of her head in spurts, and foam was coming from her mouth and nose. She did not plan on having the second horn cut off. This made my father, who was already angry and who hadn't done the job right in the first place, even more angry, angry at the cow and probably angry at himself, something he hadn't much practice at. The dehorning went on and on, Goggles doing a valiant job of fighting off the assault on horn number two. Finally my father finished the job but not without getting banged up. Then he tried to stop the bleeding, and even after application of bone-oil, our universal remedy for all stock injuries that was smelly runny tar, the blood kept jetting out of Goggles' head from twin fountains. The old cow survived this, and she never was calm around my father again. I think he sold her to keep from being reminded of this event.

Usually we had Jersey milk cows, but Goggles with her long ivory-colored horns, came with the purchase of the Wilson Place that spring. I had two cows to manage then, and we had extra milk. When Goggles was brought to our home ranch, she displayed an uncanny ability to open gates with her long horns. She concentrated on getting to the grain barrel, and the gates she opened allowed other livestock to get into forbidden pastures. While my father blamed me for not closing gates and doors properly, that did not stop the cow. That was why he decided to cut her horns off.

In 1951 my father bought the Wilson Place. He made his bargain, shook hands, and when later in the week he went to town, he stopped by the Bank of Bandon to tell them of his purchase. He returned later that afternoon after buying some feed and wire, and the papers were already drawn up. This was a huge expansion of my world; abruptly my life's potential doubled. Now I would see the mysterious origin of Mrs. Wilson who had walked across our ranch and had almost daily talked with me. Before we bought the Wilson Place, I was restricted to stop at the gate on the boundary fence between the ranches. Now there was no such barrier, and I had new territories to explore.

I was eight-years-old when the purchase was made in the spring. The summer of 1951 held no drizzling June rains. The sky cleared, and the grass dried yellow and sweet, ripe seeds bending the stalks. As soon as school was out, I had a new duty added to my regular chores. After my day's work, either before dinner on an easy day or after on the usual long work day, and in the mornings, I milked our cow as usual. Then I walked the half-mile to the Wilson barn and milked a big brindle cow there, her distinct dark streaks a standout from our usual Jersey milk cows. She had big, almost black circles around her eyes and I decided to call her Goggles. She was the only animal other than horses to be named. She had long ivory horns, and I liked this handsome good-natured animal. Her tall husky calf used a lot of the milk, but the couple of gallons I carried home in the pail was a welcome addition to our cooler.

This was a great new job. Twice a day I went off, free of my father for those hours, unsupervised, uncriticized, to walk from the Home Place onto new land, then off the road the Longs used, down a hill toward the creek where the trees came up to and crowded over the road, across the creek on a shaky little bridge, up a steep hill to the barn. Finding Goggles was never much trouble, because she liked her calf and showed up to feed him and to eat hay and the dollop of grain I put into an old dynamite box sitting in the manger. I liked the barn which tall and mossy stood against a stand of Douglas firs which I prowled about when I had time. On a bench there was a set of antelope horns, truly exotic on the Coast, and I tried to understand where they were from and why they were so different from blacktail deer antlers. For all I knew, they could have come from Africa. Part of the barn had already fallen down, and this just made it more fun for me, why I am not sure, pitching hay out of the open into the covered manger for the cow.

Once I noticed the grain was going down in the barrel faster than I was dishing it out to Goggles, and I set a trap. I caught a rat, the largest rat I had ever seen and it was difficult to kill. Big and strong, this animal set my idea of what a large rat was. Only years later did I realize that I had caught a possum, an animal I had never heard of in 1951, weighing pounds more than the largest rat. Even in New York City as an adult, watching rats scurry across subway tracks at 1:00 AM, I had the thought that they were hardly larger than a healthy mouse.

Beyond the barn were the ruins of the old log cabin that the original homesteaders built. I made up tales about this building, trying to fit it to the stories about Daniel Boone I checked out of the school library. The house where Mrs. Wilson and her family had last lived was down the hill and up the creek from the barn and was almost consumed by termites. It was held up only by ivy, the entire structure covered by luxuriant ivy, so thick that it did not look like a house until you were close and could see a door in the green. Inside it smelled of decay and urine. My father turned the house into a shelter for the livestock, pulling the doors off and letting the stock use it for shade. It stood for years serving as a thin shelter of ivy against the weather, a green ghost.

Many of my explorations were up and down the creek that flowed through the ranch. In those days the creek was surrounded by heavy stands of alder, willow, and fir, and it had a clean steady flow. The timber had been sold but not yet cut until that first summer, and even then near the creek was not logged until later. I took every chance to look the pools over and to fish if I could get my stubby pole and some worms nearby. Eventually I found the most exciting part of the stream. Beyond the decaying log cabin there were hills that came down steeply, almost making a canyon. Where this began, the creek cut through a sandstone formation. This came in a series of pools. First was a big pool, with the water coming into it in a chute, which contained a number of small trout throughout the summer. Then, after I carefully crawled along the mossy hillside above this water, there were a couple of small pools, the stream beautifully flowing along benches of sandstone. A smaller pool upstream was made by a falls of water coming from a long stretch of water contained in a shoe-box of sandstone walls, the head of which was formed by a cascade coming down chutes swirling into and out of small dishes made by all this flow. I never was successful catching fish in this last place, probably because of my inability to cast with my equipment. Above, I lay on flat rock to watch the nimble insects we called skippers skate their dimpling way right over the trout's hold.

And I was amazed that flowing water could literally carve rock. It was beyond my imagination, but the fact of it was splashing in front of me. How long did that take? Far upstream near the boundary of the Mitchell Place (a ranch my father bought later) the stream ran through another sandstone narrows.

Back down the creek, just above the bridge I walked over to get to my cow, was a small stream flowing off John Long's Place. It was clear and sparkling over rocks and gravel, and the summer sun was not blocked by large trees as it was in the main creek. The Longs sent their sewage almost directly into the stream, as did everyone else. At their barn were manure piles standing on the stream bank which must have added a few more impurities to this water. These matters were of concern to no one.

"A stream renews itself every one-hundred yards of free flow," my mother often quoted from some source, perhaps belief or just hope.

Still we took the water as pure, and bathed in it and drank it without reservation or ill effects. The Wilson Place had for me a sense of being at the edge of an endless wilderness that was pure and untrammeled. The devastation of logging had not yet occurred, and the watershed could have gone on forever except for the Long's ranch. Wilderness was an exciting illusion for me.

And at this magic spot along the tiny creek I spent whatever time I could. The pools formed below and around mossy boulders, and the bottoms were gravel and sand. These Coast streams were an incredible hatchery for trout and salmon, and a variety of fry hatched here and lived at least briefly in those waters. Cutthroat trout with vivid orange slashes under their chins, rainbow trout that spent their lives in fresh water, steelhead trout that were rainbows waiting to go to sea and become huge before returning to spawn, coho- or silver-salmon fry and finally chum and Chinook-salmon fry. Of course nothing is so simple; the trouts crossbred and perhaps the salmon did also. So there was a variety of tiny and slightly larger fishes, growing in this small water. If I walked down the trail to the bridge, by a fir and through the willows, out onto a small gravel bar, the minnows scattered making quick dashes for cover and deeper water, small flickers of light when they turned and then invisibility. So I crawled down around rocks and driftwood and berry bushes to get into position to spy on the fish. Even when they were not spooked, they were diicult to see, their backs and sides blending into sand and small gravel and the vibrations of sunlight and flowing water. Eventually they moved a little, and I could make them out. My intense desire was to get much closer. I deeply wished to know fish, to understand their beings, but that was not easily accomplished. The instinct to avoid being eaten was in full force; everything was after these fry: raccoons, mink, herons which flew up and stalked the trout when the water receded later in the summer, other birds including the bright kingfisher, and any fish larger than they were. So a clumsy, impatient boy didn't have much chance to get a fish to swim into his hand.

Then I made a discovery. The Crisco cans my mother emptied making fried food and pies and cakes had bright interiors. With one of these cans, I set a trap for the minnows, sliding it into the creek with some sand and gravel in the bottom to make the opening look like the creek itself and to keep the can from floating away. To the fish, it was a mansion of silver walls, a miracle of a world where no dangerous horizons loomed in any direction except from the opening itself. I set the can in the creek at a location where I could crawl up without being detected, now more easily done as fish in the can could only see out the opening. Still, when I spooked other minnows not in the can, the fish located in the Crisco can usually darted away too. But I did capture fish, tilting the can violently up out of the water, cutting off escape. Then I could sit cross-legged and stare at little fish swimming about in the can, their reflections flickering on the shiny interior. I watched them, planting the can into sand

and then later making small pools at the side of the creek and putting the minnows into pools from which they soon escaped back into the stream. Those bright days seem concentrated into silver cans of liquid and light and pulsating life.

The Wilson Place gave me only brief escapes from my father. Ray Waterman was always there, putting me to work, criticizing my efforts, telling me how lazy and worthless I was. Inside my mother's house things were different but daylight hours on the ranch I spent under orders from my father. I was desperate to get away from him. My grandfather Waterman who lived close by provided some relief and a longer view of life. And there was my grandmother Waterman who died before I became a worker on the ranch.

4 Long Hard Pulling

My grandparents Mabel Crooks and Charlie Waterman married August 1903 in Pomery Washington. And in 1911 with their daughter Leora they traveled by covered wagon from Huntington in eastern Oregon to the Oregon Coast. My grandmother kept a diary in a 4" x 7" notebook, and at the time of her death in 1945 a shoe-box of her things was taken away by my aunt Leora, her entire inheritance from Four Mile. The account of the trip returned to Four Mile Creek after more than fifty years. That diary is precious to me, my only tangible record of Mabel Waterman except for old photographs. Written on the brown cover in ink in her best handwriting appears

The Trip Across Ore., In A Prarrie Schooner
Sept. 16, 1911.

Ended Oct. 30, 1911 45 da. on road
Traveled 715 mi.
from Huntington to 14 mi. south of Bandon.
Frank Waterman
Leora Waterman
Mabel Waterman
Carrie W. Rowell
Roy Rowell

Sept. 17, 1911, Birch Creek, Huntington, Ore.

Their departure was from Huntington on the old Oregon Trial, not far from Farewell Bend at the eastern foothills of the Blue Mountains. Mabel called their journey to Four Mile Creek "a long hard pulling." These years later we are looking for details of pioneer life, while Mabel's focus was on the new and modern, and on the country she was passing through. All those cars! All that rich living! They could have gotten themselves and their goods to Oregon's Willamette Valley by train, but that was too expensive. Even if they had a car it could not have made the trip. They were lucky not to have been hit by more snow in the Cascade Mountains, but the mud and roads sound bad enough. They were tempted to stop and settle at several places along the way, especially at Bridge. But Roy Rowell would then bring out an often-read letter from Herm Delong that recounted the generous virtues of Four Mile Creek, and after some discussion they continued on to the Coast. Roy and his family settled on Bear Creek just east of Bandon. This diary was the first I heard of the terrible fire of 1854 which explains the patterning of old-growth timber I had long puzzled over. Although my grandmother was optimistic to think she could raise many strawberries in the short Coast summers, just as she anticipated Four Mile Creek was marvelous country for apple orchards.

At the close of her diary Mabel tallies up all the expenses of the trip and arrives at a total of $261.40. She includes the cost of two additional horses (one for $73.75 and old One-eyed Riley purchased in Riley Oregon for $60.00). The wagon to get them there was bought and outfitted for $82.20. She has every penny laid out in four pages, including five-cents for 2 pencils. The high living at the hotels in the Willamette Valley cost them $2.25 and picture shows cost 35 cents. I doubt my grandfather went without tobacco and whiskey but they are not mentioned. Either he had laid in a good supply or Mabel was just too shy to write those expenses down. She begins this accounting with the sentence: Had a good supply to start with, lots of fruit, honey &

eggs, and other provisions. They also had a good amount of certain other commodities which cannot be purchased anywhere.

Mabel Waterman, who was a tall long-faced woman, died in 1945 at age 64 from cancer. I barely recall her at the end of slow meandering walks with my mother from our house to hers. We picked blackberries along the way, one berry for my grandmother, one into my mouth, berries thumping into the pail never finished the half-mile trip, berries that Mabel only heard stories about. She was a tea drinker and used lemon drops for sweetener, drops she shared with me. In my memories Mabel floats in the shadows of her house in summer afternoons. And one clearer view in angled fall light where she stands at a chopping block, swinging a small double-bit axe, Douglas-fir pitch kindling flying. (Woman's work included chopping wood and butchering small animals, and marriage was different from what it is today. Neither of my grandparents could have managed without the help of the other.) Although I only knew my grandmother briefly, to this day I am certain of her deep love. My mother told of my sitting at her bedside while she was dying. When she asked for water which did not soon arrive, I shouted down the stairs to my aunt Leora, "Grandma wants her water! She wants it now!" Leora did not give me the swat I deserved, but she must have thought: Spoiled Brat!

My grandmother's grandfather was John M. Crooks, born in Indiana. He moved to Missouri, then to Iowa and finally Oregon in 1852 where he lived at the Dalles, a rapids on the Columbia River on the Oregon Trail. There he accumulated gaunt cattle from discouraged owners who could not face the last terrible push to the Willamette Valley. In 1862 John Crooks herded one-thousand cows from the Dalles to the Nez Perce country of Camus Prairie in Idaho where he was the first cattle rancher. His relations with the local Nez Perce Indians were excellent, perhaps based on the mutual respect between good stock-men. It was said "that no one was ever known to be bothered by the Nez Perce Indians if riding a horse with the brand of John M. Crooks." At some peril to himself he tried to stop the Nez Perce from their famous war with the Americans. My grandmother Mabel was born in 1881, the daughter of one of John Crook's twin sons. Both her mother and father died and eventually she was passed entirely out of her family.

Mabel Crooks was an orphaned child raised in foster homes in a rough frontier society. She emerged a social, generous, good-hearted woman, and was so far as I know undamaged by her childhood experiences. She met and married my grandfather; their 1903 wedding-day photograph shows a handsome couple. Although I am certain living with my good-time grandfather was not always easy, they had a solid and enduring marriage and found their apple orchard on Four Mile Creek.

5 Good Time Charlie

I grew up a half-mile from my grandfather Charlie Frank Waterman in the house my parents moved into when they married, the year before I was born. Until my grandfather died when I was fifteen, I visited him at every opportunity, after milking and dinner on weekend and summer nights and on those delicious days when it rained and I was not required to work. We talked about the things that concern a boy growing up far from other children among cows, sheep, horses and other animals. I took up raising game chickens which ran free around the barns, eating whatever they could find and roosting in trees to escape weasels and skunks which devastated the domestic Rhode Island Reds we kept for eggs and meat. My grandfather approved of this small wildness introduced into the tame currents of our ranch.

For his part of our rambling conversations, he told me of growing up in eastern Washington and northwestern Idaho, and what it was like coming across Oregon in a covered wagon with my grandmother, coming to this new land in western Oregon in 1911. Born July 24, 1875, he was 36 years old and ready for a change. Imagine his decision to leave, looking at a map in the light of a coal-oil lamp, running a work-hardened index finger down the Oregon Coast, stopping at the jut of Cape Blanco. You cannot go farther west in Oregon. They carried with them a new Edison windup record-player, one that took those heavy hollow plastic records that slipped over a silver cylinder. Edison Amberol Records, Four Minutes or Two Minutes, just switch on the machine and sit back. The Edison rode under the wagon seat, and they brought it out at night, listening to music after the day's journey. Some places were dry, and water was kept in a barrel and carefully rationed. Other times the road was muddy and almost impassable. The music gave them great pleasure and relief from the trip: dancing on bare earth in flickering campfire light, dreaming of the splash of surf and the clean sand at journey's end.

Hanging on his wall was a painting of the ranch on the Two Canyon River where he was raised. The ranch house was gone in the painting, but a non-native tree grew in a clearing on the narrow river valley, the river flowed unseen beneath cottonwoods across the picture, and steep ridges rose from a tight valley going away from the river. Unlike our part of Oregon, only part of the land was timbered, with about half the landscape clear, naturally clear my grandfather said. In western Oregon we had to work hard with axes and controlled burning to keep the land open enough to grow grass, so to me naturally clear land sounded like a gift. He told me about runs of salmon up the Two Canyon River. "We'd drive a team pulling a wagon down to a side-stream and fill the wagon bed with salmon just by forking them out of the stream. They were so thick in the water they could not escape. That's what happened," he said. And he pointed to a location on the painting, "And that's where it happened." There were large trout he caught in the Two Canyon River after he learned to use bullheads as bait. I loved to hear about the hunting too, on the high open ridges after snow was knee to waist deep. Those ridges were right there at the top of the painting. Aims were adjusted after seeing the misses marked by plumes of snow from the bullets. Our Oregon winters were rainy and muddy with land slides which closed roads and sometimes kept me out of school.

I learned decades later that, while I heard him say Two Canyon, it was actually Tucannon he had said. The stories were not all true; for example that side-stream turned out to be a steep dry gully. My grandfather moved everything to specific places on the painting to make them definite and real. And while by experience I know that bullets fired into snow do not create plumes, I carry that image still.

There were different animals in the Two Canyon country too, not just mule deer, but elk and animals such as the badger. This fascinated me, and I soaked up the tale of one of those yellow-gray animals with a white stripe up its nose and over its head. About twenty-five pounds and two-feet long, my grandfather said, with powerful claws to dig out rodents like mice and prairie dogs. Badgers live in deep dens. One took up residence in the bank of their road and covered the road with dirt from its excavations. It came out snarling and growling when a team went by, startling the horses and the driver. My grandfather told a long involved story of how hard they were to kill, of how strong and vital this animal was. Years later an Idaho rancher told me the same story about an eastern-Idaho badger. Apparently badgers do not depart from this world without making their tormentors do a lot of shooting and digging. I wished for badgers of our own, to eat our digger squirrels and to disrupt our lives.

I learned cribbage, a card game played using a board with rows of holes to keep score with small wooden pegs or match-sticks in the holes. My grandfather used hand-carved wooden pegs, and he was a master player. The game involves discarding, and then points are gained by laying the cards down sequentially against the opponent's cards and then by counting hands. Strategy and card counting were his specialty, and eventually I became good enough that he could play without deliberately giving away points. We played cribbage in the living room, which had a large rock fireplace, and in the kitchen. There were rainy winter days when we did not have to work, the rain pouring down outside, with my grandfather and I sitting at his kitchen table, counting our hands.

"Fifteen-two, fifteen-four, and a pair is six."

The fire in the wood-burning cook stove in the kitchen was allowed to go out. The heating stove on opposite side of the room required wood every hour or so, and I went out to the woodshed and brought it in. Keeping the fire going in my mother's house was a job; here the same task had romance: the damp chill of outdoors, the glowing fierce heat of the red-orange coals when I opened the stove's door. There was a cabinet next to the stove built into the wall so that bricks heated its interior. My grandfather kept his firearms in that cabinet: a Model 06 .22 rim-fire and an old 30-30, both Winchesters. The humidity was so bad that it was difficult to keep the barrels from pitting with rust. He brought the Model 64 30-30 from Washington where he had used it, hunting mule deer in that cold dry snow. It was a lever-action with a straight stock; the blueing had long since worn off the gun metal and gold-colored solder repaired broken metal near where a peep-sight had been installed. I listened to stories about life in other places and earlier times, punctuated by gusts of wind that reflected down the brick chimney shaking the stove-pipe and by the counting of cribbage hands. Fifteen-two, fifteen-four, fifteen-six and a pair is eight.

When my grandparents first arrived on the Oregon Coast, they lived in a tiny cabin on a butte above the Cope Place, in the forest just beyond the open prairie of the Indian Allotment. Each day my grandfather walked down to the Copes and worked in the dairy. The butter they made was taken to Bandon by buggy and from there it went to San Francisco by ship.

I located two post-cards he sent to his father and mother from Four Mile Creek.

Dear Father,

How are you getting along? They don't have any snow down here in the winter. [Brother] Frank and I will do quite a lot of hunting now that we have finished haying. I milk 2 cows now. I went for a swim in the Ocean the other day. it is fine but awfully cold. I wish you were here to take a dip in the ocean would do you good. Fruit is awfully plentiful. A person gets tired of fishing for trout with love, Frank.

Dec. 1915.

Dear Mother,

This is the next day after Christmas. Mabel and Ray making garden. Oh! Come on down you and father and spend the winter with us. We would sure enjoy it. We have plenty of room and lots to eat. If you put in a winter here you both would be willing to try a few more. How is C.H. making it mining? Hope he has the real dope this time for he sure deserves it. Your last letter telling of his find got my feet to itching. Hope to hear from you all soon, lovingly, Frank.

My grandfather purchased his property in 1916, and he built his house in 1917. He named his classic Coast homestead Tanglewood. Four Mile Creek ran through his land, and his buildings were on the arc of land at an oxbow in the creek. The early settlers built low down; this was for access to water and fertile land and to have the house out of the worst weather. Notably their structures were close to water but never flooded. In my grandfather's case, he built his house on the upstream side of the bow. The road crossed the creek at the center and deepest part of the turn, over a bridge. Toward the house, upstream and to the left, was a large garden, fallow in winter of course. Along the creek side toward the house were shrubs, some berry vines, and special plants including rhubarb, loganberries, and strawberries by the cedar foot-log which spanned the stream, just before reaching the house. The outhouse was near the foot-log, and more berry vines grew on the other side of the creek, high on the bank beside the foot-log. Adjacent to the house were ornamental bushes and flower beds. My grandfather enjoyed gardening. The road from the bridge was on the highest of this land and bisected the settlement. Just up the hill from the road's end was a chicken house. A path went to the left to the house. Right of the road was a level field, bounded by an impenetrable white-cedar windbreak, six-feet wide and fifteen-feet high. A large barn was just to the right of the road, at the base of the hills. This barn stood high in my eyes and held an enormous amount of hay. On the downstream slope beyond the barn was a shed, containing equipment for forging and blacksmithing which was no longer used in my time. There was a sandstone wheel for sharpening tools which I tried out but accomplished nothing except to further dull my axes, and equipment for rough blacksmithing included a big anvil. In the field toward the creek from the shed was an orchard. While orchards today are limited to a few varieties of fruit, in those days many more varieties, in this case apples, were planted. Many have been lost. My grandfather was skilled at grafting a branch cut from one tree onto

another, so even within one tree there might be three types of fruit. In some trees, he grafted a limb between branches to increase the tree's strength. These were places to climb, and in the fall, deer came into the orchard at night to eat the windfalls.

Beside the woodshed that was attached to his house was a strange tree we called the monkey tree. Its branches were covered by sharp spines which attracted hummingbirds with fiery red-orange throats. They whirred about on invisible wings to collect nectar. They built nests of spider webs, moss, and fine grasses in the thorny branches, and filled them with two tiny oval white eggs. When the new barn was built above our ranch house in the late 1940s, the glass windows so optimistically installed became dim with dust, mud, and manure. Sometimes hummingbirds tried to escape the barn through a pane of glass. They could die there, long needle-like beaks vibrating against the glass, wings never stilled. It took all my courage to rescue one of them, catching that creature — wings and sharp beak — in my bare hands, feeling its heart beating so fast that I thought it would die from fright, running through the barn to throw it into the air where it paused, defying gravity before whirring off. I thought that it was flying back to the monkey tree to tell its tale.

My father made improvements to the homestead. Running water came fairly late however, in the early 1950s. These modern additions were tolerated by my grandfather, but I do not think he cared one way or the other. An old iron hand-pump remained on the back porch. If I threw all my weight I could move the deeply rusted handle one stroke. When water finally splashed from the thick corroded spout into a bucket, it tasted so strongly of iron that it was hard to swallow. I loved to work the pump with its rusty squeaks and squawks, but I drank my water belly down on the smooth gravel of Four Mile Creek.

My grandfather had what he had always wanted and that was good enough for him. In fact he never even paid his property loan off. Strange as it sounds, he borrowed to buy the place in 1916, and finally the loan was paid off by my father around 1950, after my father married and purchased his own land. My grandfather deeded his property to my father in the 1940s; Leora, my father's sister who was Outside, received nothing. My father wanted his own father to say thank you for the improvements he made, but that never happened; my grandfather went along at his own pace. He didn't show appreciation because he knew my father was doing all that modernizing for himself and for what outsiders might think.

My grandfather never accumulated much property, in fact I suspect his journey across the West was to escape his own father's ambition and success. He didn't talk much about his father, nor about my father, his son, the man whom he worked for doing those odd jobs that never end on a ranch. He tied wool, kept a fire going for branding, mended fence, that sort of thing. It was his brand, a C with a W inside for Charlie Waterman, that we applied to the cattle, one of the earliest brands registered in Oregon, but they were not his cows or his land. He taught me to do things like sharpen an axe, because it was easier to work with a sharp axe so a man needed to know how to do that properly. I had little jobs early on and rocketed through them as I grew, doing a full-grown man's work by the time he died. He showed me how to do most of what I learned from anyone in that life.

In 1920 the road along the Oregon Coast was just a muddy buggy path. It was better than the road the pioneers came in on, but not by much. In the 1920s the road that is now Highway 101 was built. Teams were needed, and my grandfather was a good horseman with an excellent team of horses. So he went to work with his team using a big scoop called a Fresno to move dirt and create the level grade for the road. One day he had to do something else and asked a man named Dorlan to work the team in his place. After a hard morning's labour, Dorlan let the team drink its fill, and one of the horses foundered and died. This was a big blow to my grandfather. I grew up with the idea that my grandfather had built a good piece of Highway 101.

My grandfather wore old clothes; his loose Levis hung from wide suspenders, the sleeves of his cotton work shirts rolled up. Even in his seventies, he worked so much that the knees of the Levis went first, and they were always patched. There are people who can wear clothes with flair and style; he was the only family member with that ability. There were white threads showing the outlines of the round whetstone carried in his hip pocket and of his knife in his front pocket. He gave to me his pair of dragon cuff-links which once had sported diamond-chip eyes but still had gold-edged wings. He smoked, rolling cigarettes using Prince Albert and other cut tobaccos. I loved to watch him roll and to smell the initial burn of tobacco. The cans were a perfect pocket size, made of metal and opening with a hinge at the top. He saved the empties so that I could fill them with worms I dug from the manure piles to catch trout. They slipped in and out of my coat pockets easily, red cans against faded denim.

Copies of *Arizona Highways* arrived regularly at my grandfather's house. No one else had copies of this sensual brightly colored magazine, with its wonderfully reproduced photographs of pools of cool water under cottonwoods, long-needled ponderosas, and fleshy cactus in brilliant sunlight. He had never been to Arizona, but my grandfather resonated to that celebration of the American Southwest. Snow-covered cap-rock, right there on Four Mile.

In a corner of the barn among decaying farm tools were whiskey bottles, dusty empties just strewn about. I never asked about them but knew that my grandfather had emptied them. Above my grandfather's ranch on Stonewall Wilson's place was a still that my grandfather helped Stonewall run during prohibition. Copper pipe remains there, tangled in the brush. They ran the still at night when the smoke was not visible. At dawn they walked home tired and a little drunk to milk the cows. The whiskey drinking I knew about involved men standing by a truck passing the bottle at the end of a long day's job, one or two swigs each. That litter of dusty brown bottles in the barn represented something different. And I somehow knew that my grandfather liked women and played around. I don't recall anyone talking about this in my presence, but there it was, whiskey and women. There are two photographs, one of my grandfather standing before a Model A, wearing a suit with tie tucked into his shirt, his arms draped over the two women who stand beside leaning into him. The second picture taken later in 1938 has five women (young and old) sitting in a group with my grandfather behind them looking manic and devilish. "Your grandfather, he didn't want for anything," Aloma Gamble told me once. "He just liked to boogaloo."

My grandfather's main accomplishment was collecting rocks, rocks that he gathered on the beach or from the bed of the stream that ran through the ranch. He walked along Four Mile Creek and stacked rocks that took his fancy into piles along the bank, sometimes wrenching larger boulders from the streambed with a long iron bar and patience. Some years he hitched a horse to a sled and pulled a few rock piles to his house where he made rock walls and enjoyed them. A few undisturbed piles remain along the stream sinking back into the earth, overgrown with tall weeds until another land-clearing burn reveals them. Special stones went into the facing of his fireplace, the lower half laid before 1920 and the upper half with a wider spacing between the rocks laid in 1931, that date spelled out in agates and arrowheads. Another project was a wall of the front porch that was cement with mostly cut rocks embedded to create a distinctive pattern. When I found the ranch site on the Tucannon River that was the subject of that oil painting and the foundation all those stories, I fished along the stream, thinking as a joke that I might expect there to be hints of grandfather's presence in little mounds of rocks slowly sinking into the ground. Then on my hike into the adjacent wilderness area, late one night staring at campfire embers, I thought about my grandfather who would have loved my seeking out his home country. I repeated the joke I had thought up along the river about the small piles of rocks. Suddenly I knew why he had loved those Oregon stones. The volcanic origin of the rocks, of the entire region along the Tucannon, determines that they are a drab grey or brown. When he got to the Oregon Coast, he must have been amazed by the rainbow of colors made by the stones, so much so as to spend the rest of his life trying to gather in some of it.

My grandmother Mabel Waterman died in 1945 when she was 64. A year after Mabel's death, my grandfather married Edna, a woman from California. She died too a few years after that, and my grandfather did it again, finding another woman from California. He drove those stout tightly corseted ladies up on the hill, gestured widely and said, "There is the Waterman Ranch." They were on the hook. The second lady, Bertha, had a little Chevy sedan which frighteningly she drove onto Highway 101, frequently coming close to collisions of which she was entirely unaware. This woman had some spiritualist leanings and composed long accounts of past lives to the amusement and bewilderment of her audiences. I was a fresh soul while my brother had been around for many lives. The idea of my brother with lives of experiences was pretty funny to me even then, and I teased him about it. This was my first exposure to such whimsy, and it was odd, unrelated to the world I could piece together from my ranch experiences.

My grandfather cooked for himself when he was single. My parents fumed with anger after visiting him and seeing him frying onions and garlic. I thought the smell odd but wondered at how that could be such a terrible thing to do. Now I see that it went differently for each of them, my mother playing out her own mother's food morality and my father associating such food with poverty and failure.

I was eight, and left at home when my parents made a trip to buy or sell livestock. It was my job to do chores, and my grandfather's to see that I did them, and to have me down for my evening meal. The next day a young woman showed up with a roan mare.

"Get on and try her out," my grandfather said, and I did, trotting the mare until we came to a hill and she stopped. As it would turn out this horse had her own ideas about what she would and would not do.

"Like her?" he asked after I returned, and I said yes, my heart pounding. Then he wrote a check and handed it to the woman.

"It's yours," he told me.

I had been using the ancient work horses that used to pull plows and wagons; Babe and Bill were twenty-seven and thirty years old. This was incredible! Where did the money come from? My grandfather's total financial support came from my father who wrote him a small check each month. It was not out of line with the labor my grandfather put into the ranch, saving hiring outside help, but it was not intended for extravagances such as a horse. On being confronted on their return with the fait acompli, my parents became grim and silent, but as my grandfather and I both knew, there was nothing they could do about it.

The Edison player had been given to my grandfather's brother Leo, and as a consequence of Leo not taking it away, the player spent years in an attic in Bandon. In 1955 the Edison came back to Four Mile, but damp sea air had corroded the machine and it no longer played. I was interested in how it worked, and as my grandfather's fingers were not nimble enough to accomplish the repair, he and I formed a team, spending my free time of the winter of 1955-56 at his back porch workbench, trying to coax the Edison back to life. In the back porch we were high enough to see Four Mile Creek over the leafless thicket of willows and the large bare-thorned vines of the Himalaya blackberries. Drizzling and sometimes lashing rain struck the windows, dark floods swung by outside. Eventually the workings of the machine became clear to me, and I managed to clean some of the rusted parts. Outside the rain pounded away, and we talked while I strained with my tools at the mechanism. Finally I stitched a leather strap tightly enough that the cylinder actually turned. The speaker was a large horn, red with faded roses on the inside, hanging off a steel rod and connected to the cylinder by a hose-tape construction of ours. He had two boxes of Edison Amberol Records. The music was awful: pseudo opera and generally junk to my ears. (For example: Lily of the Prairie, P. Murray & Chorus.) A copy of Turkey in the Straw existed that broke later. I do recall a joke from a vaudeville routine.

"I just bought a farm that is a hundred miles long."

"Did you really?"

"Yes, and it's a half-inch wide!"

I was on the edge of puberty and discovered under my grandfather's work-table a stack of pornographic magazines. My limited knowledge of the details of female anatomy came from the Sears Roebuck and Montgomery Wards catalogs and by analogy with farm animals. This was heavy going for a naive boy, and was my first glimpse into the world of the sexually explicit. I was fascinated by magazines published on forbidden topics which were never mentioned. How did anyone learn about them? What else was out there?

Surely as a result of smoking all those years, my grandfather had a stroke and was taken to the tiny hospital in Bandon. Seeing him in bed wearing one of those hospital gowns made a big impression on me; he was sick and it was serious. His sex was revealed, hanging down from the short gown. He recovered and came home, but he was never fully well again. My grandfather and Bertha began to go to hard-preaching revival ministers, and one foggy night after work I went along to listen to the strange calls to Jesus. There were no miracles, and those late attentions to religion could no more save him than the white ghost shirts of the Sioux shielded them from soldier's bullets.

The stories I had heard for years mutated and came to their closings in confusing loops, as if my grandfather knew he had lost the thread. I had to restrain myself from correcting his accounts which I now knew better than he did. We played cribbage and I was the one playing hands incorectly so the game would be more even. His mastery at discarding just the right cards and making points as the cards were played had vanished.

Another operation was required, something that obviously would cost a good deal of money. A week before the operation was to occur, he told my father one evening to be sure I got the Edison. The next day he was at his kitchen table writing his brother Leo a long letter, breaking off, writing that he saw a stray dog and that he would go shoot it, customary practice on our ranch. Then he took the rifle that he had used to shoot mule deer on eastern Washington's snowy ridges and that he had brought across Oregon in a covered wagon to shoot the coastal blacktail deer and feed his family and for his son and grandson to use to make their first kills; he took that worn rifle and went out onto his back steps. So the family version goes: he saw the dog, cocked the rifle to shoot, and then stumbled, putting the rifle down as a crutch, shooting himself in the heart. It was an accident; no one ever spoke the word suicide.

When my brother and I came home from school September 17, 1957, my father was in front of the big barn, and he shouted up for us to go home, not to come down. That was, after all, exactly where we were headed; I had chores to do at home before I could visit my grandfather. Adults underestimate the reasoning ability and intuition of children. I knew that instant my grandfather was gone. Later I heard about the letter and the Edison and was certain how it had happened.

On the crumbling concrete of his back steps where just past the willows, water sounded as it slid along a long gravel run into the foot-log pool. My grandfather went down the steps and levered a bullet into the chamber. The hammer was cocked back. The steel rifle butt ground into the fragments of concrete as he propped the gun on the edge of a step and leaned down the length of the barrel to the trigger. Did he hesitate, or had he worked it out so completely that he didn't take that last chance to listen to the water running over the dark beautiful stones? Was Four Mile Creek part of his heartbeat or was he already beyond all that? Later rain washed away the traces of his passing that stained the steps.

His final wife Bertha was upset when she finally understood that none of the Waterman ranch was in the name of Charlie Frank Waterman. To recover from this blow, she planned to take to Los Angeles to sell the only thing she could get her hands on that was worth any money, the Edison player. In fact it was not worth much. Whatever his reasons, my father did not allow this and delivered the Edison to me as my grandfather had asked. I will always be grateful for that gift. Soon after this Bertha left Four Mile Creek—the small support that my grandfather received from my father halted with his death.

When he died, his rotting old house sat empty for a few years. I came home from college, married and working the logging woods, and lived in his house for three summers. This was the early 1960s and I played country Jimmie Rodgers, Woody Guthrie and Bob Dylan, cranked up high on weekend afternoons. I purchased one of those box collections of records that added orchestral and chamber music to the mix. Then my father found he could rent the house out and get some cash, and I never again lived on the ranch. Around that time a disease struck the white-cedar windbreak, and the removal of those trees left the resulting larger field naked and raw. Finally over ten years after his death, my grandfather's house burned due to some careless renters; sparks flew up the chimney and landed on the old mossy shingle roof which caught fire and burned like a torch. My grandfather's rock constructions stood charred in the ashes like monuments surviving a war. Soon after that my father took his bulldozer and leveled the fireplace and rock walls, burying the only things remaining that my grandfather had put his heart into, clearing away those stones to gain a few square-feet of grass. The monkey tree, set back into the border toward the creek, survived the bulldozer and grew taller, taking its sharp thorns higher, leaving a relatively smooth trunk.

6 Never Send a Kid

I puzzled and agonized over my father for most of my early life. He treated me with far less warmth than he did his stock dogs and certainly worked me harder than he did them. The only picture of him touching me is when I was a baby being awkwardly held by the new father, and my only memories of being touched by him are being shoved, pinched or punished. Aloma Gamble recalled when I was two years old at a Bandon beach gathering, had fallen as two year olds will, and was crying. Someone started over to pick me up, and my father would not allow anyone comfort me.

"Leave the kid alone!" he ordered in a loud voice.

"I have long since made peace with Ray," Aloma told me, "but my mother who saw that always referred to your father as *that awful man.*"

Whatever it was, something had a deep effect on me. I cannot recall a time as a child when I did not deeply hate him. He showed no affection or understanding, and used me as labor, again as far back as I can remember. Obviously he needed the help, with unending work in front of him at all times. He got up to it, pushed and shoved it along all day, and went to bed with at least as much left to be done as there had been that morning. If in the morning I did not get out of bed at first call (a thump on the floor of my room from below), he would rush upstairs and fling me out onto the floor, or worse yet, roughly shove a rag of cold water on my neck and push me out of bed. He was proud of the cold water torture and it was effective. I was like a shovel or axe, a tool to get the job done.

There was a complaint my father made when I had failed at some task I had been dispatched to do. "Never send a kid to do a man's job," he would mutter, "Never send a goddamn kid to do a man's job." Of course I wanted to ask him why he did send a kid, but as usual he meant something other than what he said. Another of his sayings has stuck with me. "You'll never learn any younger."

With his instructions, I might never have learned anything. Still another came when I was at work and made a mistake such as to dodge-gate an old ewe into the yearling's pen. "Wake up and die right." In spite of the source, I liked that one. If I was going to die, I definitely wanted to be awake for it. It had a good twist, and secretly I thought it was funny.

"Sit on damp ground and you'll get piles," he repeatedly told me. When I finally learned what piles were, I thought it to be an amazing connection.

How did Ray turn out as he did? Isolation may explain a bit of it. Born on June 1, 1913 in the house on the Cope Place where my grandfather Waterman had worked in the dairy when he and my grandmother first came to the Oregon Coast, Ray grew up about a mile-and-a-half down the road and then moved a half-mile back up the road when he married. Few days of his life were spent out of Four Mile's watershed. His twin sister died at birth and that might explain my grandmother's attention and softness regarding her son, something which may not have been too common in that time and place. Did he feel the loss of his twin? Did that eat at him? I doubt it.

I don't know much about my father's childhood. When he was quite small, playing above a large pool in the creek, he fell the ten or twelve feet into the pool. As he told it he did not know how to swim, but it was learn or die. His instinctive dog-paddle was about all the swimming he was ever to do, but in this story it saved his life.

School was close by until high school. The school house was on the main fork of Four Mile, and my grandfather schemed successfully to move the schoolhouse closer to their home, onto the Cox Place which my father was later to buy. The men jacked the square building off its foundation, lowered it onto wheels, and pulled it all that way with a team of horses. The children ran down the steep hills to the creek during recess; yelling, splashing, the boys throwing flat-sided rocks to skip across the water's surface for one-two-three bounces. Later they went to Bandon for high school, fully ten miles away. Ray rode a bicycle to Laurel Grove Store, a one-way distance of four miles. Then a small truck took him to Bandon.

There were never childhood friends about and no childhood stories. He told me that his grandfather instructed him to mix more with other people, something which clearly did not take. His grandfather regularly sent him presents, warm notes, elaborate handmade cartoons. His was another loving presence in Ray's life.

There is a story, communicated to me by my mother, that my father shot another boy when they were out with guns and the child died. His fanatical approach to gun safety is something for which I am grateful and it certainly resulted from this tragic event. Perhaps my mother was trying to explain her husband's behavior—did she think that was what made him so hard and inflexible? The records of deaths in the vicinity for those years are incomplete, just as are the excuses I can find for Ray.

Pictures survive showing my father with livestock, sheep and calves which he even showed at fairs. This herd was a gift purchased by his father and grandfather who approved of "blooded stock." At the road entering my grandfather's ranch was a large twenty-foot-tall fire-scarred old-growth stump, and one photo was taken there. My father is thin, staring intently into the camera. In most of these photographs my father is twisting and tugging at an animal to wrench it into some pose he had decided was required. They are pulling away. His two children would recognize his determination to shove something into a configuration known only to him.

The depression arrived constricting these lives. No one left the land, and there are no stories of bums or drifters coming by the ranch. But people now had no money instead of a little money. They had a small apple orchard, ate fish in the winter when the salmon came to spawn, ate all the deer they could shoot, and drank cow's milk throughout. In my own childhood, my father often ate a bowl of bread and milk, comfort food from his youth. His mother gave him the most and best of everything, even though he had an older sister, Leora, who in typical rural fashion was less favored. In reaction, Leora seduced a high school teacher and married him, moving away to the Willamette Valley. This was a scandal, and my grandfather always strongly disliked her husband. Then again, that man was a pompous windbag, someone who would never have appealed to my grandfather. I recall him following my mother around as she did her chores, droning on and on. But with her desperate act of escape, Leora took herself outside the family, leaving behind any claim on what the Watermans possessed on Four Mile.

There is a blank then from my father's high-school graduation until he married my mother when he was almost thirty, late for marriage on the 1940s Oregon Coast. He cleared land over the hill on the main Four Mile drainage on property he was later to own. The timber was dense and trees measured three to four feet in diameter. Logs were without value in that depressed country, and he was paid one dollar per day to slash in preparation for years of burning to obtain hilly pasture land. The logs have finally disappeared, but they were charcoal reminders of the original forest for fifty years. On the whole, my father seems to have been as inert as my grandfather, and he had not half so much fun. Then he burst into activity at thirty years of age, getting married and purchasing his first ranch. There was no stopping him then; he worked the daylight hours both on and off the ranch for decades without a noticeable break, decade after decade of grim, unending, joyless labor.

Just after his marriage, Ray joined the Masonic Lodge in Bandon. Rising through the levels took a good deal of memorization, and he had difficulty learning the material. An older man patiently helped him until he was finally a full member.

Ray travelled to Portland to take his Army physical for service in World War II. He went with men from Bandon who leapt from the train in Florence to buy whiskey. Because of his ranch work, Ray was given a deferment. On the trip back they left the train in Eugene for food, and when he returned, Ray found two young men sitting in the seat he had occupied from Portland. When they did not vacate the unreserved seat, Ray flung one of them out into the aisle like he was a sheep about to be sheared. "Then they left the car," he said with pride.

Paying for land with the proceeds from the land has not been easy for at least one-hundred years, and it was not in the 1940s. So my father sheared sheep, grueling repetitive work that had two essential features: it brought in much needed cash, and was scheduled around the ranch work. In earlier times, the wool was shorn from the sheep with hand shears; by 1940 shearing required an electrical generator, a Kohler plant operated by a small gasoline engine. There was no electrical infrastructure. No one on Four Mile had electric lights which were then common in cities. The equipment was pulled around in a little trailer and set up at each shearing site. The jobs were all over the southern Oregon Coast, and he sheared with a few people, mainly Willis Van Leuven and later Harley Hildebrand who were the only friends he was ever to have. The pay was by-the-sheep, and while it was not much, it was money that paid down the mortgage. These men worked long days, bending over the sheep in back destroying positions, shearing one-hundred and more sheep per day. On breaks they staggered away, dripping sweat and greasy with machine oil and lanolin, to collapse on full eight-foot-long bags of wool, waiting for the back aches to let up. Before starting in again they took long gurgling drinks from upended gallon jugs of water. About 1952 my father's back gave out. Then he could only shear one or two sheep before he was in severe pain, and he could not even shear the few-hundred head of sheep he owned.

Income from the ranch still would not do it though, and he soon found another type of piece work, falling timber. This was generated by the post-war housing boom, and the timber economy on the Coast lasted until the 1980s. Cutting down trees brought more than a dollar per day in 1953, and the skills learned during the Depression came in handy. Although this work was dangerous, it was not as hard as shearing. Not getting killed was the key part.

On rare occasions we went into Bandon to the movies, invariably one of two types. There were movies that I called "mommy" movies, sentimental and full of music and dance. I had never seen anyone dance to anything except country music and could not relate to the movies my mother loved to see. The other were Westerns, and I liked them with their own romantic stories of cowboys and Indians. The unreality of those Western movies was striking: there we were, as far West as you could get, our saddles mildewed and our hilly range boxed into smaller pastures. Movie cowboys drew six-shooters and hit targets farther away than a rifle could be reliably shot. I often was cheering for the Indians but couldn't say it because that made my father angry. Ray liked Westerns and approved of John Wayne with his brusk toughness. I believe that both my parents identified my father with John Wayne. A typical John Wayne character is a tough guy who is gruff and who appears hard and unfeeling. But underneath and hidden from view, except from the audience and the knowing love interest, is a warm, sensitive person who does not often show it, that not being the manly thing to do. This I believe was to explain my father to us; that this man really did care about us all. Except that in every John Wayne movie is that critical point of the plot when he is shown for his inner self, that ultimately caring and giving person. Well, he is that for a minute or two, at least. In our life on Four Mile Creek, such minutes did not occur.

Men did not occupy themselves with tasks such as rearing children (except for training them to work) or buying presents. Gifts appeared with tags reading "From Mom and Dad" but they were chosen and prepared by my mother. Indeed presents to my mother "From Dad" were always picked out and purchased by her. This even included anniversary gifts of jewelry.

My father carried the largest folding knife he could find, at least one was a Case. He would remove the monster from his pocket, lever it to its full bone-handled length, and cut. Cut a sheep's tail off against the Burdizzo's clamp, steel against steel, blood welling after. Cut up a deer's belly and remove its intestines, then reach far inside and sever the last remaining connections between intestines and the deer's body, then finally the windpipe. Cut white cedar shavings to start a fire for the branding iron. With a flick of the wrist whack off the heads of bull thistles so the bristled balls could not mature and sow their seed. Once inflamed by company from town I recklessly slid down a weathered 2" x 12" board and embedded a long sliver deep into my rear end. My terror at my father's knife was so great that I could not hold still for the cutting, and was taken to town to have a doctor remove the chunk of wood. Another family legend born. Remember when.

My nicks and scrapes came into a conversation many years later. I was living in New Mexico and was beset by an illness no MD there could diagnose. An administrator in Washington wanted me to work for him, but as I was not of much use in my condition, he sent me to the Princeton physician John Seed. John spent several days a week at a Free Clinic in the Bronx, and asked me to go there to see him. He gave me frightening subway directions; instead I drove a rental car through streets that looked bombed out and parked my car on brick rubble from a collapsed building. It was summer, hotter than hell, and fire hydrants had been opened by young blacks who were sitting in the spray. Finally in to see John Seed, he examined my body. "How long after your finger was broken did you have it set?" he asked. I've never had any broken bones, I answered. "Yes you have. And all these scars on your right hand?" Barbed wire, I answered. There were 37 stitches too, I quickly added. "And this one?" Barbed wire too. "This scar too?" No that was broken glass. "And this one?" A knife slipped when I was working sheep, I answered. (John was used to seeing the results of street-gang violence, and he was quietly skeptical of my explanations.) He was especially interested in a wide white scar on my leg. A knife slipped, I said. "I'll bet it did. Didn't you see a physician?" No, never, just for that little scar on my ass. My scars have faded over the decades and sometimes I wonder if they will disappear by the end of my life.

My father's definition of a man included knowing exactly what to do and when to do it, and never having any questions or doubts. You don't see John Wayne in a quandary asking advice, admitting he doesn't understand something. It was convenient and no accident that Ray lived his entire life on one small stretch of Four Mile Creek. Those things go some of the way of accounting for his inability to explain or articulate anything, but his complete lack of empathy and imagination sealed the bargain. His fury at my not knowing things automatically was only exceeded at the times I asked questions. Why did the posts rot most severely at the junction between air and earth and not uniformly to the bottom of the post? Why did alder smoke smell so different from fir smoke? How did animals know when the weather was about to change while we remained clueless? I kept my curiosity to myself when with my father.

We worked constantly even during the school year, mornings, nights, and weekends. My reaction to school was to treat it as a place to rest from the weekend. Often I did not recover until Wednesday or Thursday and then began to register what was happening in class. Still I do think it was how I became so partial to school. Thanksgiving, Christmas and sometimes Easter were the only days that were dependably holidays, the gatherings of my mother's family. Our birthdays were not of consequence enough for a break, and it is family legend that one year—I was perhaps eight or nine—it rained on my birthday, and haying could not proceed. I had received books and a box of candy, and as the story goes, I spent the rainy summer day reading. End of story. It was not the relentless nature of the work that was so painful; it was the domination and bullying by my father.

My dream was to be rid of him. I fantasized that he would have an accident and be killed. My hopes were highest when he was away shearing. All those crooked roads, perhaps exhausted he'd miss a turn. The next best thing, and much more likely I thought, was that during one of her hysterical screaming dish-throwing episodes, my mother would bundle my brother and me into the car and leave as she had often threatened. I do not believe I would ever have looked back except for my grandfather Waterman. I must confess that I thought of more direct ways to rid myself of him but did not have the courage—I do not believe that I avoided anything for moral reasons, I doubt that I had many morals. So I stuck it out, trying to get by doing a man's job with the body of a growing child. My own back had its problems, and I was in such pain that I went to chiropractors for treatment from the age of eight. Since my dream was to escape from my father's control, I counted the years until I was eighteen and could just say good-by. That seemed infinitely far away until I finally became ten. Then I saw two digits in my age, and somehow that gave me faith that I would reach eighteen and could leave Four Mile, faith that I would survive childhood and the ordeal would be over. When I did achieve that magic age, I went to college and my back problems disappeared.

Stories like this one often go as follows: and then I was twenty-five or thirty or some age, and then we understood each other, and so on. This never happened to me; I looked but did not locate much that I had not seen clearly when I was a child. I had to see things as they were to survive, and so later all there was left to do was to arrange them in digestible boxes. I see now that my father was enormously immature, just a spoiled child who had deep issues with his own father, and on top of that he was a natural-born bully. He felt deprived and humiliated that his own father Charlie Waterman—who loved nothing so much as a good time—had so little and was so irresponsible. When Ray became activated, he was trying to have enough stuff—sheep, cattle, and land—that people would not think he was a nobody.

While my grandfather Waterman was easy going and friendly, my father was always looking for insults which he'd curse about and then attempt to "get even with the bastards." He held grudges forever if necessary and they ate at him. Often he could make himself believe he was winning, as when "Jewing them down" to buy a car, but when his honor was injured he'd turn black. As it often happens, this dark bitter anger was one of his legacies.

"By gum, now it looks like somebody lives here. You betcha, by golly!" he often said when we did some work that was visible to someone who might drive by on our little travelled roads. It did not occur to him that no one else cared one way or the other.

My father's complete lack of imagination required him to accomplish his advance right there on Four Mile Creek where he understood what to do and what success was. What he was able to do collect in terms of acres and livestock is perhaps remarkable and admirable. How he accomplished it, with the costs to those around him and to himself, is another matter. Whereas my grandfather just deeded his land over to his son Ray with no compensation, Ray himself, except for his error of selling the Walker Place to his own son Charlie, never while he lived surrendered another square-foot of the land that he had so painfully secured.

Ray Waterman was deeply ashamed of and embarrassed by his family, of his good-time father and of his young sons. My mother escaped but he certainly was not proud of her. This man who created minor scenes trying to order in any eating place more up-scale than the counter at the livestock auction, who loudly cleared his throat and spit on the street, who would not have known what to wear if my mother had not laid his clothes out for him each morning, this man was ashamed of the rest of us. My guess is that deposits of such emotions are to be found in most families. In ours they ran wide and deep. When I look at photographs there appears to be a happy family, none of the anguish and torment is visible.

When Ray became older, he and my mother tried traveling but without much enjoyment for either of them. He wanted to see sheep and cows and grass and judged even those things as if they were on Four Mile, unhappy unless at home where they were his own sheep and cows and grass. He didn't find the differences in the world interesting; to him that made the rest of the planet inferior, automatically. He did show increasing interest in sex. I imagine he tried to suppress those urges in his younger days because of his shame about his father's womanizing. But there he was, repeatedly coming into the bathroom when his curvaceous grand-daughter was bathing and then parking his four-wheel drive where he could watch with his binoculars the sun-bathing wife of one of his hired hands. A decade later he invited that same grand-daughter to watch a porno movie with him. Men who take up the sexually explicit in their later years do it without much grace it seems.

7 Making Hay

On my father's first ranch, there was no creek-side fertile land, and we hayed in fields high on the ridges. There are photographs of me two-years-old in those hayfields, one shot with my mother beside a shock of loose hay and another high atop a wagon load of hay with my grandfather Waterman. Since the summer of 1944 I have floated there, circled by his strong hard kind arm, safe against his leg, the puffed white clouds just above us, the mortal horses and hay shocks far below. My grandfather drove the team of draft horses that pulled the wagon load of hay, unlike his son he had a way with animals. In 1944 my mother still went outdoors and took photographs to document the work. By 1945 she did not venture out except to bring food and drink to us.

"Just take a big bite. Damn good," my father said to a man standing in our hayfield wearing pressed slacks. The man was holding a round green fruit with half-inch fleshy bristles and he had no idea what to do with it. My father took one of the fruit, tore it open, and turning slightly away appeared to take a bite of it. "Sure is good," he said moving his jaws enthusiastically. The guy followed directions and then with wide eyes, spit and swore, spit and swore, finally almost running went back to his car. Wild cucumber grew in the brush at the borders of the hayfields. The vines spread over the terrain and had white flowers. It was also called man-in-the-ground because the root was bucket sized. My father fondly recalled the day he "got that city guy to eat wild cucumber."

Every year we put up grass hay. Even the early homesteaders had large barns, always much larger than their houses, that were principally for sheltering hay from the weather. Without a good supply of hay, the cattle and horses would not survive the winter.

The best land was used to grow hay. My grandfather's ranch had hayfields adjacent to the creek. The mower to cut the hay was pulled by the horses. There were snakes and mice in the grass, and occasionally they were sliced up by the mower. Most often they escaped to uncut regions, so that the last island standing was teeming with frantic mice that made a break for it. Young boys with three-prong pitchforks had great and futile sport of stabbing at the desperate escaping mice.

When the hay dried a little, it was raked into windrows. Someone sat on an iron seat, driving the horses with reins in one hand, periodically pulling with the other hand a lever that raised the ten-feet of curved tines which scratched along the ground and pulled the hay together. Lifting the tines up left a row of hay, and when the field was finished, it was geometrical with graceful lines of hay curving across the slopes. Next, when the hay was really dry, we came along and gathered the windrows into mounds or shocks of hay, which were two to three-feet tall. The odors of this work were fabulous. Fresh-cut hay had its own smell from the juice of the just-cut stalks. Then the hay dried, and there was a concentrated perfume, sweet scents that depend on the mixture of grasses and clovers. Shocking hay was lovely work, sweating away in the sun, working with a three-tine pitchfork to gather a few feet of the windrow into a shock. The construction was important; you had to layer the hay into a mound. You could get a regular swing to this work, and the hay just fell into place when you and it were both going right.

It is critical to put up hay that is dry. Wet hay will mildew and spoil; even worse, the heat from the chemical reactions can create a fire and burn down the barn, if hay is put up wet. Moisture came in the form of dew, and it was simple to wait until the sun dried off the hay. Heavy fogs were different. All summer it might be hot, or what passed for hot on the ranch which was any time the temperature exceeded 75 degrees, and when we drove the ten-miles to Bandon, it was like passing into another climate zone. There, the thick fog chilled us to the bone, and we came in from sweating in the Four Mile fields to pull on wool coats to survive Bandon.

Mark Twain is credited with the line "The coldest winter I ever spent was a summer in San Francisco," and he only left Bandon out because he had never been there.

A dense chilly mass of fog moved in and out of the Coast, and when it reached our hay fields, it was as bad as rain, and the hay was drenched. Some years the winter rains did not cease, and it was difficult to get any haying done with frequent light rain showers. Those years the grass and hay grew beyond expectations, and we could not make hay and did not have enough livestock to turn onto the fields to eat the grass.

After shocking the hay, the real work began. The wagon was pulled onto the field between rows of shocks. A man on the ground forked a shock and swung it up, onto the wagon. This is why the shock construction had to be correct. If it wasn't, the shock fell apart and the man on the ground had to take several swings to get the hay onto the wagon. There was always some hay left on the ground, and a three- or four-year-old boy could gather that and get it to the next shock. Ideally you had a man on each side of the wagon, and the person on the wagon arranged the hay as it was forked up to him. This was a job that my grandfather excelled at, building the load up with straight sides and with the shocks of hay layered over the wagon from about the center to one side. It had to bind together or the load would fall apart. Both the men on the ground and the man on top had harder work as the load was built up. The distance to throw a heavy shock up from the ground was steadily increasing, and it became necessary for the person on top to catch shocks midair and help lift them up.

Finally the load was as full as could survive the tilts and grades to the barn. We were out on some pretty steep land, and there was always a possibility of tipping the load over. Usually I rode on the hay to the barn, something I loved to do, the wagon swaying along, my grandfather urging his horses ahead, me ducking the limbs that could sweep me off the load. I burrowed down into the hay, sometimes getting stuck by dried thistles which had been gathered in with the hay.

Then we arrived at the barn, and the wagon was pulled directly under a section of roof that extended from the barn and was bracing for a system of cables. The cable and track assembly ran along the underside of the peak of the roofline. A draft horse was harnessed and attached to the cable at the opposite end of the barn, and when the Johnson hayfork was set into the hay, at a shout the horse was driven to pull the cable, and along with it, the large dollop of hay straight up into the overhang which then squeaked and squealed and swayed along the metal track on the underside of the barn's roofline. Another shout from the men in the barn and the wagon-man jerked a light rope which tripped the big fork. Then the hay dropped from the Johnson fork into the hay-loft. The horse was backed up so that the man on the wagon could pull the fork back and reset the fork for the next load. The men in the barn's mow worked the hay around, again so that it was layered and not rolled up in knots. This was important to whoever had to feed the hay out to the animals in the winter. Careless work at this point made it almost impossible to get the hay into the feeding stalls. There was even a big knife designed to cut such hay. We tried not to need it by doing the job correctly in the first place. Each year we spent a few weeks haying.

The downstream fields of Lower Place were almost against Highway 101, and I spent days working in those hayfields listening to the cars drive by, wondering where they were going, where they all came from, and how those people spent their days. This was our country—my grandfather had helped build that highway. But I wondered what was out there in the world, and who was able to spend the summer driving up and down 101.

I saw my first jet-plane streak overhead while sitting atop a load of hay coming up out of my grandfather's closest hayfield, just as the horses were pulling the load onto his road. My grandfather stopped the horses to look up at the jet's path in the sky. Progress came in a more tangible form when we bought a John Deere tractor. Horses were then used only to pull the hay up off the wagon into the barn. The tractor speeded the work up, and I remember being frightened that I would fall off the iron seat of that old hay rake when it was pulled by the tractor driven by my father. It really frightened me, and I could not hold on the seat and summon the strength to lift the tines. If I used both hands to lift, I was certain I would fall into the rake. My father, once again seeing me between him and getting the job done, was furious with me, and although the rows were crooked, we did get the hay raked. Not long after that he bought a side-delivery rake which did not require anyone to sit on it.

My father bought the Lower Place in 1946, and my grandfather sold him on a get-rich-quick scheme. There was a boom in Easter lilies, and the bulbs increased in value. My grandfather knew that the fertile land of the Lower Place could grow more than grass hay. So the Watermans went into the lily-bulb business. For at least two years, several acres of beautiful Easter lilies bloomed next to the homesteader's orchard, row after row of sensual white trumpets centered by yellow accents. The lilies must have required enormous work, but I only recall the bulb grading, the sizing with a board drilled with holes of specified diameters. There were sacks and baskets of lily bulbs with extra skins which flaked off and made a shuffing, hissing sound whenever the bulbs were moved. The bulb market crashed before we made much money, and we went back to what we knew, raising heavy crops of grass hay on the bottom land of the Lower Place. My uncle Ben Payne told me that the talk was that old-man Waterman had made a killing, and that all those who followed him into the bulb business lost their shirts. It was true except for the made-a-killing part.

At the Lower Place haying was done on fairly level ground. One year my father did not get the stock onto the fields, and the wet year produced a heavy crop of hay. The understory of this crop was subterranean clover, and that sub-clover was impossibly thick. The mower my father now had was operated directly from his tractor and could not handle this dense clover, which was knotted with thick twisted stems containing clumps of seeds just at the ground level. He cut a foot or so, and then the mower clogged up. Then with a pitchfork I lifted the hay so that he could back up the mower to get the blades moving again. Then we cut another few more inches of hay. It took a week to get once around the field. Even when we were moving slightly faster, the strip of cut hay had to be separated from the mass of hay that was still growing, still anchored to the earth. This was accomplished by tying a heavy rope to the mower bar, and attaching me to the rope. My job was to tear the cut hay apart from the uncut. We went around and around that forty-acre field, inches at a time. Hanging onto that two-inch rope with a braided knot at the end, pulling with all my strength to tear the clotted mass of hay apart, being jerked and tossed by the tractor as the rope-end once again disappeared into an unbroken seam. This was one grueling job that frustrated my father as much as it did me, and he looked back on those days with the same dark memories. I know we had trouble raking that crop of hay, but that blurs while the terrible cutting stays fresh enough to give me goose-bumps today.

8 Riding Horses

I am unconscious of a time before I rode horses. I was put on sway-back draft horses and set to driving stock. I rode the dusty clod-busting wooden sled pulled by one of those horses to prepare the garden plot. Horses were everywhere, and I loved them. The silken noses with large stiff hairs which poked me when I stroked them or fed them grain or apples. The slobbering snort of air and snot as they shook themselves into action. The flatulence which loudly punctuated their gaits, especially during uphill climbs. The satisfaction with which they ate hay, the hedonism with which they ate grain. Released into the pasture from a day's work, they lay, back down, legs up, twisting on the earth to relieve aches and itches. They were huge, powerful, warm engines with almost visible emotions.

There are images of me as a baby, born in June 1942, 31 years after my grandparents arrived at Four Mile Creek: the dangerous and difficult birth in Coquille; hanging in a basket from a nail while my mother milks the cow and awaits the Japanese invasion which never came; at six months old tied onto the back of the saddle while my mother helps drive livestock. Whoa! Tied to the back of the saddle with my mother riding the horse? She was hardly a competent rider a few years later. What was going on there? I believe this fable, and I feel more fortunate to have survived the saddle binding than the birth during which I almost died.

The backs of the work horses, Babe and Bill, were so wide that I had a hard time sitting up on them, spreading my legs wide enough. There was no saddle for me, but that was not a problem. I stuck with the horse, saddle or not. In the beginning, I was just stationed on a horse and told to shout when the stock came. If I had been on foot, I probably would have wandered off or been run over, but up on that immobile horse, I stayed in place and yelled at the stock when the time came. After I was little older, I was trusted to move the horse from one location to another, urging the horse to a slow walk. The old horses had been through a lot, and they did not pay me much attention. Around the age of six, I had emphatic instructions to turn one herd of sheep at a gate above the schoolhouse barn, and then, as soon as I possibly could, to go to another location down the hill. "God damn it, you head 'em back right here and then get yourself to the gate. The gate! Don't go off playing some damn place and hurry it the hell up." So there I was urging the horse, shaking the reins against her neck and clucking in that way people encourage horses. Suddenly a miracle: the old horse broke into a trot. I bounced up and down on the back of my horse, clutching the mane. Then she went into a canter and I was floating. It seemed as if the wind was whistling by my ears! I made it to the right place (itself a miracle) in time to do the next job of heading off sheep. The lives of our old horses were not easier after I discovered how to make them go faster.

When I was young, we kept a stallion for someone, and to the surprise of my family, a foal was born on the hillside above the barn the next fall. Just why this was a surprise remains a mystery to me. The colt was given to me, and I named him Dewey for his light-mottled color. I had dreams of riding this beautiful horse along the ridges, herding the livestock. The foal grew, and then it was necessary to neuter him. Castrating a horse is a different process from the routine jobs we made of male lambs and calves. I was still small when a group of men assembled to "fix" Dewey. It was, inexplicably, in the winter. I recall an overcast cold day, and the men getting ropes and long knives together. Unfortunately I was too young to remember much of the procedure. I know Dewey got up a couple of times after being tied down, and that the cutting operation was a difficult one. Perhaps none of them knew what they were doing. Certainly any prudent person would have called the castration off because of the weather, but for my father that would have been admitting an error. They finally completed the operation, and that night the weather became even colder. The consequence of this was an infection that almost killed Dewey. His disposition was never pleasant after that, and his penis hung hugely down, making him look even more dangerous than he was. My dream horse had become a monster, and I was permanently stuck with the old nags, which now seemed to move more slowly than growing grass.

My father's appendix was removed early one winter, and he was unable to work until after lambing. The cattle and sheep on the open range still needed feed. In the grey daylight hours of weekends, I covered as much country as I could. As winter deepened and darkened, I fed hay to the cattle, and from my father's horse, threw nibs to hungry sheep. The rangy gelding was strong but jumpy, looking for an excuse to buck. The summer before, I stood on the road before our house looking uphill toward the barn to see my father's upper body raise into sight and then drop out of view as his mount, invisible to me, bucked below him. On the third beat of this primitive drum, my father was gone, thrown to the ground, and I just caught a glimpse of twisting saddle. There I was in the same place with the same horse. And as much as I loved to ride, I did not have the time to be bucked off, and was frightened of it as well. So I was extremely careful not to spook the horse, and after a couple of hours he was tired enough to be safe to ride. Then I found a solution to this difficulty. After the horse was saddled and loaded with burlap sacks full of nibs, I led him to a nearby steep slope that seeped water all winter long. Swinging into the saddle, I kicked the horse in the ribs, and he jumped into the slope coming down stiff-legged, ready to buck. Instead he slipped on the mud and had to struggle to stay upright. I slapped him with the rein ends, keeping him generally pointed uphill. I loved that elastic first-leap, and our lurching, plunging assent. When we gained the top and more solid ground, the fight was out of my winded mount, and we were ready to ride the range and feed the stock. It was a long winter.

We came through the winter my father was laid up just as well as we had when my father made his winter-long quietly dramatic and completely grim production of work on the range. The weather was as awful as normal so that did not explain it. The feed was as short as ever, the animals as thin. I wondered then what he had been doing all those days, of which I spent five out of seven in school. Apparently my small fraction of the work that he normally put in had accomplished as much as usual. What did he do out there all winter long in the weather? Did all that doing actually need doing?

My grandfather rescued me from riding work horses, buying me a horse out of the pittance he received from my father. My parents were not pleased, but I was ecstatic. The horse came with an army saddle, with that wide crack down the middle, painful to sit on for the long days we spent driving stock, and without a saddle horn to wrap a lariat around. But this horse Berry saved me from the old nags. She was not what I expected. She was smart and lazy and mean. I knew to watch a horse's hooves and not to walk where they could kick. This was good training for Berry. She bit me, she kicked at me, she tried to crush me against the stall. One summer's day I was in bare feet, and she managed to step on my foot, leaning her weight onto that toe for endless time. This was not one of those horse-loves-man stories I had read. I was not getting another horse, and I had to get control of her. I found ways to handle her, from how to hit her hard enough to get her started to the strength to turn her in the resulting gallop. I studied her expressions; a horse's moods are signaled by the ears, and ears that are laid back mean trouble could be coming. When I was dismounted on the range, Berry loved to sneak away and run back to the barn. Once I put a heavy rope around her neck, dropped her reins, and while I was pretending to open a gate, I tied the rope to a heavy fence post. She hit the end of the rope without tearing the fence out, and I was beginning to make an impression on her.

And by this time I had a non-sentimental attitude toward animals. Why should a horse be so happy to carry us around on the hills? I can remember riding that tough little horse so long and hard that she couldn't move uphill at the end of the day. I dismounted and scrambled up the hill to turn the sheep back. Berry was so exhausted that she did not even turn toward the barn. She could hardly walk by then and just stood there, head hung down.

In the movies, the cowboys gallop everywhere on their horses. This is nonsense and wishful thinking, because in real life the horses would soon collapse. We never ran our horses unless necessary. During our usual sheep roundups, we seldom even trotted the horses. The rough, hilly country worked them so hard that we brought the stock in with horses dripping sweat that frothed around the cinches and saddle blankets and bridles. Even the reins slapping against the horse's necks were covered with a white foam.

Berry was sure-footed and got around on the steep hills without difficulty. Once when I was riding on a trail on the upper edge of a steep gully, some sheep tried to go down the ridge above me. I turned Berry toward the sheep. There was a small washout in the trail that both Berry and I had missed seeing. Her back feet went into the hole, and she lurched backwards. Her front feet were still on the trail, and she clawed at the damp dirt. This gave me just enough time to scramble off the saddle; she fell down into the gully as I rolled off. She went over and over, two-and-a-half times, and ended up on her back. I was afraid her back was broken because she just lay there, feet in the air. Fortunately when I went down to her and tried to push her over, she kicked and struggled and came up on her feet. I was incredibly relieved and had so much adrenaline that I walked, leading her up and down the hills for rest of the evening.

We had one pair of chaps made of heavy bull-hide. I wore them on cold winter days whenever my father didn't, and they kept my legs warm against the horse's ribs. They were also shield against the thorns and brush we went through. When I had to race my horse to turn the cattle in tight stands of alder, wild-cherry and greasewood, the limbs scratched and snapped against my leather-clad legs. I imagined myself a vaquero from one of my uncle George's paperbacks, running cattle somewhere in Texas. Working cattle on a horse is fun because cattle are both big and quick. Separating a cow from a herd takes a quick horse that can sense the cow's next move. Berry was only interested in herself, but at least I could try to read the cow's intentions. I practiced with Berry, turning her as fast as I could. It was the most fun in the mud, and one day she slipped and fell and rolled over as I slid her into a turn. I left a rubber boot in the stirrup as I scrambled over her rolling body. Fortunately neither my father nor my boot caught me at that reckless pleasure.

After I went to college, Berry was sold, and she terrorized the family who thought they were getting one of those lovable horses. She always caused trouble in a herd of horses. She kicked and terrorized them, and kept them running whenever anyone came into the pasture to catch them. We dealt with that, although getting her in after a month out in the fields was a real job. I do not believe her new owners ever rode her, and she made problems with their other horses. My belief was that she would be a terrible mother and probably kill her own foals. The new owners had her bred in hopes of getting something out of her, and to my surprise, Berry was a wonderful mother. She raised several excellent foals for them.

Horses were essential during the time I lived on Four Mile. But beyond that I loved horses and I loved riding horses, with the strong belief that if I had to dismount to do something — open a gate, dig a hole — it was a come-down, something I should have avoided. Today, livestock are worked from those little three-wheel all-terrain vehicles. Never mind that they are supposed to be dangerous, the horses might not have been too safe themselves. And these new steeds eat no grass, they are easy to catch, and they scare the sheep and cattle at least as much as the horses ever did. Horses have joined old-growth firs as tourist attractions.

I rode my last horse in 1971 on a visit to Four Mile. My brother decided to corral one of those crazy cows. The animal ran for a mile or so before we lost her in heavy brush and timber; she went straight through fences and thickets, over logs and hills, straight off small cliffs and right up the other side of the draws. Charlie and I went just as straight after her as fast as we could go, and I remember when we stopped, the horses blowing hard and covered with that white foam of sweat, thinking that I still could ride a horse. John Sinclair has a few sentences on this topic: "But I knew cowboying was over for me. I wanted to write. Incidentally, that was the last time I rode a horse, because I thoroughly believe that you don't ride a horse for pleasure; you ride a horse for either transportation or work."[1] Amen.

1. *A Cowboy Writer in New Mexico*, 82.

9 Messy Bessie

My mother was at the shed on top of a ridge where she stopped a grass fire, beating it down with a wet burlap bag. A neighbor was surprised at that. "What this ranch needs is more women," she told him. "One woman beats a crew of men."

Even this story requires a close look. She was outside working on the ranch but that didn't last long. All of time that I knew her, my mother disliked and ignored the outdoors. At the beginning of her marriage to my father she took part in the work. There are hayfield photographs of me at two-years-old taken the summer of 1944, with my mother by a shock of hay, then on top of a full wagon-load of hay with my grandfather Waterman. He has me on one arm, a pitchfork driven into the loose hay beside us, and he holds the long leather reins with his other hand. Two horses, Babe and Bill, are pulling the wagon. My mother was out there in the open, helping with the work. Then the situation between my parents changed abruptly and my mother withdrew into the house by the time I have any memories. She did not go outdoors, she did not ask about anything that happened outdoors, and she did not judge anything outdoors. There were only those hayfield photos, and a story or two to show she had ever ventured outside except to tend her garden.

A brief strained exception came at haying time when my father set the Johnson fork into the load of hay at the barn and my grandfather was in the barn's hay mow to spread the hay. Someone had to drive the team to pull the hay off the wagon and my mother was forced to do that task until I was six. It was tense and loudly shouted business as my mother never knew when to start or stop, either stopping the hay short of its destination or pulling it past to jam up at the far end of the barn.

Whether inside or out, I never saw either my mother or father touch the other for reassurance, let alone out of affection. There was a taut rusty-barbed-wire fence-line separating them. Her relationship with my father became so strained that she could not face who he was or what he did, to the ranch or to people. Her refuge was the house which became her house. Growing up there, working the daylight hours for my harsh father, the house was almost the opposite of life outdoors. When I went across the stoop, there was light from candles or a kerosene lamp, there was heat, and most important there was her love. Except in droughts, we always had running water and for years water was heated on the wood stove. I even associated being clean with the house, a contrast to the layers of dust, mud and manure I accumulated on the ranch. Still, scrub as hard as I could, I could not remove the stench of bone-oil tar on my hands from doctoring stock. The house was her area, her territory, her domain. The rest of us were just visitors.

My mother was born April 14, 1913 in Huntington, Oregon. Her life until high school was spent constantly moving around the West because of my grandfather Payne's work on the railroad. She and her siblings were railroad brats, much in the sense of today's army brats. My grandfather got another job or was reassigned by the company he was working for, and they packed up and moved the trunks to the train and rode the railroad to the next location. My mother, Mildred, Ben, and the youngest child Tommy; the sisters and brothers started at a new school and made friends. This apparently caused them no problems, at least I never heard one of them say anything negative about their experiences moving about. It should be remembered that this was a family that did almost everything undercover, that they were a bunch that let nothing hang out in view, so if anything unpleasant happened it might never have been mentioned.

When my mother was four years old, the Paynes moved into a large old house in the tiny Oregon town of Noti (west of Eugene). My grandparents had just returned from a trip to Salem where they purchased on time payments twin beds for Mildred and Bessie. My grandmother Anna was outdoors washing clothes in a big tub when the house caught fire and burned like kindling. The children survived the fire, but other than the garments they were wearing, their remaining possessions were the wet clothes in the wash tub and an iron bank of baby Ben's. Then they moved into a one room cabin in the woods and the people living in the neighborhood brought them everything from quilts to potatoes. Grandmother Payne came and mended the donated clothing. Amos and Anna had no insurance (as was the case with everyone at that time) and they even had to finish paying off the bed set. Not long after this they moved to Canby where the railroad was better established and the Paynes had an easier time.

It was the Davenport Hotel in Spokane (that exists today as a restored historical landmark), and the Payne family minus my grandfather was once again in transit. My mother and Mildred were left on a horsehair sofa while their mother took Ben away to clean his diaper. The daughters were dressed in their best which included small purses. My mother was swinging her purse and let loose of it; it sailed into a big brass spittoon. This could give her mother another reason to call her Messy Bessie. Mildred, prim and proper as usual, was superior to such events, and my mother went speechless. Just then, she told me, an elegant black man in a handsome uniform came up and said, "Don't you worry about a thing, little girl. Just you rest easy." And he vanished to reappear just before Anna Payne did with the purse spotless.

Brother Tommy died at ten-years-old in 1930 of complications from scarlet fever, and for that reason my mother resented doctors for the remainder of her long life.

"They should have done more," she would say. "They just should have done more. They could have."

Tommy was a Payne and Irish, and he loved stories. He had a favorite beginning for the tall tales he told: *And then they started out.*

It is hard to imagine a better way to kick things off. His father Amos carried on an endless contrived story of Silent Timber and Lone Wolf, the adventures of a scout and an Indian. *And then they started out.*

When the Depression struck, the Paynes stopped wandering and settled in McCloud, in Northern California. My grandfather, a valuable railroad employee, went to work for the McCloud River Timber Company until the bad times were over. There are still rows of tiny poorly constructed railroad houses in McCloud near Mt. Shasta. They lived in one of them, no one cared which one it was when I tried to locate it. My mother took from McCloud a recipe for toddies: Separate egg whites from the yolks, whip the whites with granulated sugar, mix the yolks with powdered sugar, blend. Then put a few dollops of the egg mixture into a cup along with as much whiskey as desired, add boiling water and stir. Nutmeg optional, a Shasta Toddy is an efficient and tasty way to take in alcohol. My mother said knowingly, "Those Irish, they knew how to drink you know." As if the Paynes were not Irish themselves!

On the porch of their house, abandoned as not worth moving, was a worn-out chair, one of the variations on the Morris chair. This one was called The Royal Chair according to the brass plate on the back, made by the Royal Chair Company. It was oak, Mission style, and reclined by pushing a wooden button embedded in one of the wide arms. Someone had tacked on some cloth to cover the exhausted leather upholstery. My mother and her brother with their gang adopted this relic, naming it the Staunch Chair. Their "gang" was called the Staunches. Their parents did not drive automobiles, so when the Staunches took up Harley Davidsons, there was no alarm. My mother and Ben recalled having a vehicle faster than the town sheriff's, and out-running him to escape speeding tickets. Good healthy fun in an all-American town, in the heart of the Depression there was nothing depressed in this crowd. At least nothing that anyone else could see.

Today I have the Staunch Chair. I cannot recall how it was moved from McCloud or who stored it, but after I was married and needed furniture for a series of cheap apartments in Corvallis where I was going to college, the Staunch Chair was among what I gathered. I cut a piece of plywood to fit across the arms and sat in the chair with that broad stable surface in front of me, studying physics, chemistry, mathematics, literature, philosophy and religion, often with a cup of tea. When I moved East and sold all the furniture for close to nothing, glad to be shedding that part of my life, the Staunch Chair was not for sale. Settled in Idaho finally, I pulled the cloth off the chair, refinished the exposed wood, and found someone to upholster and complete the job. Now the Staunch Chair is again in style with Morris chairs and Mission furniture.

My mother seemed glad that I had the old McCloud gang's chair. "Oh, you ended up with it. Good," my uncle Ben Payne exclaimed with pleasure. If either he or my mother had wanted it back I would have promptly handed it over. It always was their chair! I picture my mother on one of those big motorcycles or camping with Ben and friends by the McCloud River. In those days she had an active life.

My mother had already finished high school, but there were no jobs for anyone, let alone for young, inexperienced people. She had worked in Powers when her father was building the spur line from Powers to Eden Ridge to haul the cuttings from the largest stand of timber ever logged in Oregon. My mother's job was serving loggers in the mess haul. She said that she went to normal school to receive training to be a teacher, the first of the family to receive any education past high school, simply because she couldn't find a job. But even normal school required money. The banks did not make loans on anything so risky as education, but she remembered that a gambler in Powers sometimes made loans. So she looked him up, and he wanted to know the details of what she was going to do and why two years of normal school would make a job possible. He decided to gamble on her. She said that he took close interest in her progress in school; I am sure he was not disappointed. After two years at Ashland, she graduated in 1933 with a Certificate. She knew Agnus Bulmer who started the Ashland Shakespeare Festival and she spoke glowingly of him. After she graduated she needed a job which were still scarce. She knew people all over the Coquille–Myrtle Point– Powers area and found someone with a relative involved with teaching at Coledo, a tiny town built on a shale deposit that was a train stop between Coquille and Coos Bay. There she had a one-half- to three-quarters-time job teaching the sixth-seventh-eighth grades in one room. She got by on that pay. It was still the Depression, and the pay was in warrants because the government had no cash. Banks discounted the warrants by 6% but the gambler took her warrants at face value. Her next position at Coquille was full-time. For two years, she taught the same grades there she had in Coledo.

One of her students in Coquille was a boy named Willi Unsoeld, who became a famous mountaineer and conservationist. "When they are that special, you can just tell," my mother said.

I follow news about mountains and kept track of Willi. His daughter was killed in the central Asian mountains, dying of exposure on the mountain which her father had, in the style of the sixties, named her after. I wanted to meet him, and when he took a position at Evergreen College, I expected that to happen. Unfortunately he died first. When a guide friend in Idaho and I were showing each other knots, I displayed my facility with a one-hand-bowline, a knot useful on ranches with livestock. Most people won't believe the knot I tie is a bowline, as I tie it differently from what is shown in books, and it takes the topology of the knot and some time to convince them.

"I know that one," my friend exclaimed. "I learned it from Willi Unsoeld when he was an instructor in Outward Bound, in the early days."

During the time my mother lived in Coquille, her social life escalated, with drinking and night life. She told me of this only in her attempt to prevent my own marriage. Because she had made a bad marriage and then a divorce, she hoped she could prevent mine. My family is so closed that this was never spoken of except during those tense moments, and I know few details: Who was this person? Did he still live in that small place? Of course this knowledge did not stop me from making one of the major errors of my own life; I made my own uncharted way, using the lessons of ranching and logging but not too often guided by advice from anyone. In this case I should have taken council.

After her divorce, she found a job at Fairview, on Cunningham Creek, teaching at the one-room school. A rancher interviewed her, and said:

"Why should a teacher sign a contract? Why can't we just fire a teacher who doesn't do the job?"

My mother replied that she was happy to work by-the-year, by-the-month, by-the-week, or by-the-day; she said that it was all the same to her. She got the job, and when Coquille tried to hire her back, her Fairview wages were raised for her second year to the highest teacher's wage in Coos County. Each day she drove up to the top of the hill and parked, looking out over the scene. Then she walked down the hill into the world of the children. She told me she healed there on Cunningham Creek. By that time, she had earned a lifetime-teaching-certificate, and she may have been the last living person in Oregon to hold one.

When she met my father in 1940 after her divorce, she was teaching the sixth grade in Myrtle Point. My father was persistent, and my mother was still depressed and desperate after her breakup. Failure and guilt were the bedrock of my grandmother Payne's teachings, and my mother received only complaints and criticisms from her mother. Grandfather Payne was supportive and sympathetic, however. Bessie romantically wrote Ray that they would breakfast at the ranch in morning sunlight. Ray answered back bluntly that she had her directions wrong, that a table in that room could not get morning sunlight. (This is what I was told by my mother, but it is symbolic of what was to come. No sunlight there!) Marrying my father took her twenty twisting miles to Four Mile Creek and placed her into another world.

My father shook out of his lethargy which lasted until he was twenty-nine or thirty. Just starting out, the new couple had next to nothing. He got a loan to purchase the Cox Place, the ranch just upstream from his father's, and he and my mother moved into the tiny house. My father was away on shearing trips soon after they married, and my mother did the ranch chores. The Japanese had attacked Pearl Harbor, and there was much concern about an invasion. In fact the Japanese did send incineration bombs into the Pacific Coast on balloons, but without much success. People worried and watched for the invasion. A little barn built by the homesteader Elizabeth Harper sat down the hill from the house, and it was there that my mother milked the cow, alone with no person other than her baby within a half-mile. She hung my cradle from a hook and milked the cow, while keeping watch on the turn of road toward the Pacific Ocean where the Japanese troops would come. She kept a bag packed with essentials so that she could leave immediately without even returning back up the hill to the house. I never asked where she thought she would go.

My mother and I were close, especially during endless days she and I spent alone on the ranch. I could and did tell her anything. She taught me things, facts about this and that, and she listened to my flights of fancy which included a family, the Boneys, who lived in our trash dump, a family of a mother and many children with no father.

Tying shoes is a big step for a child, and I noticed that sometimes my knots stayed firm and other times they quickly came unravelled. One day I understood how square knots worked (although I had no idea they had a name), and that evening I tried to tell my mother what I had learned. She nodded her head at me but didn't follow what I was attempting to describe. It was the first time in my life that I realized I understood something that another person did not. It was an odd isolating sensation, something important to me that I could not share with my mother, but I remained pleased that I could reliably tie my shoes.

There was another invasion of her house in the early years. During the bitter storms of the darkest winter days, orphan lambs were rescued from the hills and brought inside to the wood burning heating stove. There they were fed diluted-evaporated or boiled-cow's milk. Some would only take a few drops at a time, but the ones that lived went wild at the sight of a bottle, their tiny, delicate hooves slipping on the linoleum floor as they tried to run. Their digestions were expecting ewe's milk, and they quickly developed diarrhea. Damp, warm air pungent with the smell of wet wool and lamb's shit filled the house. My mother hated this intrusion, and when electricity came, we warmed the lambs with electric heaters, first on the back porch, and then as we were wired up, in the home barn.

As the ranch withdrew from her front yard fence and the Coast settled into mid-century, visitors from towns and cities spoke of the wonderful life we led out in the country. For nearly fifty years my mother's total exposure to the outdoors had been an occasional short walk to feed the dogs, that taken only if children and husband were absent. Slowly she began to incorporate "the ranch" into her conversations, and by her eighties was knowingly referring to the lambs, cattle, and hay as if she had had direct experience with their raising. Along with this, she collected figurines of sheep which stood on her shelves. This sanitary herd never got pinkeye or worms, and it never shit on her floor. This affectation and accumulation became more serious as her friends began to die off.

In spite of keeping the farm animals out of sight and mind, my mother got somewhere a Siamese cat that was a great contrast with the farm cats in the barn. It was a beautiful cranky beast with an awful yowl. None of the rest of the family liked it at all. We were more sympathetic with the little dog named Coquette, a toy rat terrier. How she found these tokens of civiilized life I don't know. The cat was killed when my father ran his vehicle over it.

In her younger years, she would have shed my father after a few dates. But with a failed marriage behind her, she could not admit defeat to the world again. So Bessie was stuck out in the country with an awful person, and she fought to control her space, her house. By this time she had a collection of friends in Bandon, The Girls, and she tried to separate herself from the outdoors which my father controlled. As is easily imagined this was not without friction. Frequently my father was busy with the stock or a fence and just did not get to dinner within a couple of hours of the time that my mother had scheduled. The railroad-time-clock my mother grew up with was to her the only correct way to live. My father, growing up in a household where neither of his parents noticed the time-of-day, simply didn't care when he came to dinner unless he was hungry.

"I can cook it, I can bring it to the table, I can even put it on your plate," she said. "But I cannot chew it for you."

This conflict and others were always present, usually just beneath the surface, but often enough they caused my mother to erupt into screaming rages and fits. She yelled and threw dishes and threatened to leave. I had a fantasy that she would leave and that I could live someplace with other children and much shorter workdays. (I heard that some children did not even have to work except for little chores like mowing lawns.) When I learned to read, I added libraries. Just to have books to read and time to read them! But her outbursts always ended in days of tense silence. Migraine headaches appeared regularly, and the house become dark and still. My mother ate handfuls of aspirins and huddled on her bed in quiet afternoon shadows.

Issues of control became more pronounced as I grew up. Now riding in the passenger seat of a car which my father drove aggressively to protect his manhood and dignity, my mother never commented on his brinkmanship driving. But she became stiff and held her breath, while in the back seat we heard her foot thumping the floor, pumping invisible brake and clutch.

The house was the focus of most conflicts. The tiny house which started out with two rooms was extended in those directions that ranch families grow their houses: first more bedrooms, then a living room, and finally a remodeled kitchen, always trying to make the isolated rural house look like it was in Levittown, always failing to become entirely suburban. Just getting workers was a problem, my father preferring not to pay anyone to do anything, and if paying them, wanting to get something he needed out of it such as a new barn. His own abilities for carpentry and detail work were less than acceptable, and he refused to find the time to do work that my mother wanted. My mother was vocal with her complaints, but my father, inarticulate as always, would not say "No, Bessie, I just can't (or won't) do it." Instead he mumbled, perhaps even saying that he would get to it, but getting to it meant when everything else on the ranch was done. My mother, ignoring the ranch world completely, had cause for more screaming spells. And lesser things became large in those tense years. We installed a shower, and after each usage, water dried on the shower walls and spotted them. Unless we each thoroughly wiped the shower walls spotless, my mother lost control again. Was it was a combination of her railroad upbringing with a critical mother and her deep dislike of my father that turned these screws? It could have had a genetic or biochemical basis.

Christmas was a time of great tension. If we were to "have Christmas," my judgmental grandmother Payne would come and disapprove of food and housekeeping. But even when we were spared that, at Christmas the invisible stainless-steel screws tightened invisible wires that hummed at an almost audible frequency. A wrong word from me could send my father stomping off to the barn and my mother going into a tirade. The number and appropriateness of presents comprised one unhappy realm, but for me the Christmas tree was the worst of it. I was sent out to chop down a tree, and when I brought it back to the house, it was not tall enough, not symmetrical enough, or not limbed enough. The problem worsened as the years went by and my mother's anxieties increased, for the number of growing trees on our ranch took a nose dive. We were chopping, burning and logging, generally eliminating trees. So finding any young fir tree was difficult enough, but pleasing my mother was impossible. Once late in the season I actually cut a tree on someone else's land. I had been taught strong respect for property rights, but my mother's unhappiness overrode that. When a tree, however inadequate, was settled upon, decorating it was another ordeal. The symmetric and even placement of tinsel, probably carefully removed from last year's tree and hoarded, never was accomplished to my mother's satisfaction. Broken ornaments, ugly hand-made tree stands, these troubles filled the little house. The ornaments were kept in the original boxes, the flimsy cardboard damp and flexible, with broken ornaments remaining in their allotted compartments year after year.

All this carrying on was private, confined to the people who lived in that little house. We put up a front to the world that said everything in this well-scrubbed hardworking family was just fine. I could sense when my mother went over that invisible line, when something had upset her and there was a click and snap on one of those high frequencies. Later when we were alone, she would explode and fly apart, shattered, trying to even up the score, to gain some purchase on what went wrong. After I went to college, I soon lost my membership in the inner circle and was forever excluded from that fierce intimacy.

10 A Front Yard

My mother wanted more. And more included a lawn in front of her house, with clipped green grass, shrubs and some flowers. Lawn is not the first thing a settler thinks of creating. In my family's case, the yard came to be the extension of my mother's territory out from the house which indisputably was hers. When my parents married and moved into the little house, there was no yard at all. My grandfather Waterman had a fine generous yard that had a large vegetable garden and berry bushes, but also included flowering shrubs, a raised flower bed and some exotic trees. There was a spiky monkey tree impossible to climb which was the nesting place for many hummingbirds. Perhaps my father associated a yard with the laziness he thought his father possessed, but Ray Waterman wanted nothing to do with anything so frivolous as a yard.

My mother went without a yard when at first she tried to help with the ranch. Before long, she withdrew behind the walls of her house, and she tried to control only what went on there, giving up on everything outdoors. Except that her idea of house included a domestic yard. That was profoundly silly to my father: there was grass the stock could eat, so why waste it? It took three or four years to get a small bit of ground fenced in. While the ranch gates and fences were almost never breached, this enclosure was amazingly permeable to livestock. My mother would scream and carry on, and my father would grunt and slowly get the sheep or cows out one more time.

Even after the fence was good enough to keep the animals out and the gate solid enough that my father couldn't leave it open and have it believed that the animals had pushed the latch up, the story did not end. Before he collapsed to fall asleep after a large lunch, he put his horse into the scruffy lawn to eat while he rested. Left long enough, the horse got into the few shrubs or ate the flowers. And of course my mother hated the piles of horse manure that were left.

"Fertilizer," my father muttered, "you gotta have fertilizer."

There is a snapshot of me at three or four years old, standing on a wooden step in front of the side door. I have a pair of my father's boots on, a cap pistol in my overall pocket, and a black western hat on my head. In the background is old Jim tied by his reins to a fence post, the gate fallen to the ground. The grass is typical range species and grows like on the range. It was on the range.

The solution was simple; I grew large enough to cut the lawn grass with a hand mower I pushed around while my father slept, and the horse was tied outside the fence now. I hated work that was not with the animals, but this was easy, just pushing the mower around and throwing rocks into the road when they stuck in the blades. My father never criticized the work I did in the yard. He must have known I didn't like doing it, and he didn't care what kind of job I made of it.

My mother expanded the yard, getting more and better fencing and eventually enough water to keep the plants alive during the dry summer months. Roses, gladiolus, daffodils, mums and other flowers grew, and some flourished. As I reached seven and older, I built fence higher and stronger, so whenever an animal got through it became more of a barrier between the yard and the remainder of the ranch. Finally the fence was constructed of stout boards, so that you could not see through the fence at all. Sitting in her living room, my mother could then look out over her solidly walled off yard and see the ranch at a distance, safely on the other side of the valley. That was as close as she wanted to come to it.

About the time my mother reached sixty, the yard began to change again. The husband of one of The Girls was an expert at growing rhododendron and azaleas. Those plants are native to damp cool climates and grow in profusion on the Oregon Coast. They do not tolerate permanently damp ground and take moisture in through their thick leaves out of the foggy morning air. In a yard, they are very civilized looking, meeting my mother's main requirement along with having beautiful spring flowers. After they bloomed, she picked the dead blossoms from the plants which she believed made them more healthy. Finally she found a cleaner strong enough to remove the sticky residue of the blossoms from her hands. Her yard in ten years came to be entirely composed of these plants, some growing ten feet and higher. They shielded the yard from the adjacent road that ran by its foot. There was no one remaining to cut grass so the ground was covered by plastic and wood chips. When she got my father and brother to cut the plants back, they whacked at them like they were the brush my father cleared out to get the grass to grow on the land in the first place. My father saw to it that there was a large lane cut through the plants so that he could sit in his recliner and spot the Longs when they came and went on his road.

And my mother was happy, surrounded by plants growing in controlled circumstances, with a yard just like they had in towns where people lead regular lives.

11 The Ranch House

Years after my life at Four Mile, I walked into a house on a ranch in eastern Idaho which was owned by a pioneer Mormon family and instantly felt at home. My student who took me to his parent's home was relieved but puzzled that I got on with his parents so well. In the West, ranch houses usually grew from the original homestead house, and they have a particular style and structure as a result. I grew up in one of those houses.

The original homestead house on our ranch was a large one, 24 by 32 feet. I am not sure if Elizabeth Harper had two rooms or one. By the time my parents moved into it in 1941, a porch had been added to the east side, and at that time there were two rooms. The large room contained a kitchen with a wood stove at one end, and the fireplace, an addition earlier in the century, was at the opposite end. This room was later split into two rooms by adding a wall and a door. An addition had been made onto the south side of the house to create a tiny bedroom and a bathroom. There were two outside doors. One was at the wood stove end of the house, and opened onto the porch. The other door went directly outdoors from the center of the house.

There was a spring above the house, with water dripping into a brick lined well, so we had running water from the beginning. There was a windmill but my father disposed of it. As years went by, a spring would dry up, and we would pipe in water from a new ranch. Then the new spring would dry up, and the final solution was piping a spring from the Mitchell Place. The water table was falling because the trees were stripped from the hills, and it was difficult to find a reliable spring. The pioneers had no problems finding water, and I drank belly down from many springs which no longer exist.

My father added a woodshed-garage extending the structure to the south-east again. He didn't throw anything away, and he spent no time keeping things neat. This caused friction between my parents, because my mother wanted everything to look tidy. We brought wood, especially the kindling used to start fires, into the garage to keep it dry. A large section of log was used as a chopping block. So many axe swings had struck this log-end that it had a special contour and rough texture. And this was the place for punishment. Sometimes I was made to choose a piece of firewood and then was bent over that big block and beaten. Mostly it was just a dusty place used to store everything from tools to canned beans. Eventually my father dug out the dirt floor and poured concrete, cleaning it up somewhat.

The wood burning cook stove was a mass of iron and steel. The firebox was on the upper left as you faced the stove, and the flat surface above that took pots and pans. Two circles of the stove top lifted out, and there were special tools that fitted into slots for this purpose. That way the cook could selectively insert wood into the firebox, front or back, and could stir the coals. The top surface of the stove was uniform except for the inset rings and could be used for heating water and keeping things warm. The oven took up the remaining volume, and my mother made excellent use of it. She said later that she always missed her wood stove for baking.

Men's work was so calorie consuming that they ate all they could; diets and weight problems were the sole territory of women. For breakfast we often had biscuits or pancakes (with butter, jelly, and honey), venison steaks or bacon or ham, eggs, and some home-canned fruit. Lunch and dinner included big helpings of pie and cake. Grown men, let alone growing boys, couldn't get enough to eat. As I entered my teen years, I would eat half a pie at dinner and finish a remaining quarter after I turned the cows out before bed. (I could sense my father's intense suppressed anger at me, but I had no idea why my eating capacity caused it. By that time I cared much less about what he thought.)

The odors of baking drew me straight to the kitchen. When my mother made cookies, I helped form them, eating as much dough as possible. Cake dough and frosting I licked from beaters and scraped from bowls. When she made pies, I snacked on sugar-cinnamon crusted apple slices. She took scraps of pie crust dough that she molded into small slabs on which she spread butter, slathered heavy cream, and sprinkled more sugar and cinnamon. Cinnamon, miraculous intoxicating cinnamon, the single exotic spice that somehow made its way into my mother's cupboard! These tidbits were soon baked and the heavy oven door fell down releasing a burst of heat and scents, and unable to wait more than a moment, the roof of my mouth was often burned. She also made yeast bread and rolls. I devoured fragments of raised dough, watching her knead and pound the mass of dough on a floured surface; her forehead damp with perspiration, stray strands of hair escaping, flour dust raising. At Easter she made hot-cross buns, cut on the top into a cross with deep gashes which she filled with simple frosting made of powdered sugar and that thick cream. My mother also made egg noodles, not fine and delicate, but thick doughy chewy noodles I have never encountered anywhere else.

And best of all, my mother taught me to bake. I learned to make drop biscuits, cookies, and a cake — just the right choices to draw me in. My father did not approve but he was powerless in that kitchen. Why did my mother do such a radical thing as to teach me, a boy in the rural West, some rudiments of baking? She explained that when I was out on my own I should be able to care for myself. As usual she gave me no clue what she thought I might be doing when on my own, but cooking my meals was one aspect. At nine-years-old I must have been the best male cook on all of Four Mile Creek, and just as likely, the only one.

My mother washed dishes at the sink, meal after meal, year after year, in the hot kitchen brushing her hair off her sweaty brow with a weary forearm. At certain times she would prop books of poetry on the windowsill before her, and memorize poem after poem, Longfellow and Wordsworth, long rhyme after rhyme. A holdover from when poetry was committed to memory as a sign of culture and class, perhaps she obtained solace or support from it. She never let the rest of us know exactly why she was occupied as she was, but we heard her there in the kitchen muttering mysterious words just under her breath, words not quite intelligible to the our ears.

As a baby, I was placed into the addition that was parallel to the porch, shut off from the kitchen by a hanging sheet. When my brother was born, this would no longer do, and my father and grandfather roughed out a bedroom in the attic. The room was up a steep stairs from the porch, and it had two levels, marking the original homestead house from an old addition. The step up to the second level was about a foot-and-a-half high, and a circular opening was cut into the center of the rise. A gallon can was used as a pattern; tin lined this circular hole. The original idea was to provide heat for the new room, but the opening became known as the peek-hole. My brother and I did peek and sneak at every opportunity. We could listen in secret to our parent's kitchen-table conversations. He and I loved that hole and passed things between upstairs and downstairs through it.

Our trash was dumped into the nearest ravine, off the bank under the willows. This trash heap was called the gunch pile. (Our word gunch, made by some fusion of garbage and junk, caught the essence of our trash. It was tossed out, but anything could be salvaged and reused. We saved tin cans and jars for future needs.) The gunch pile fascinated me when I was small, because there were so many things in one place, even if it all did smell peculiar. I made up a family, Mrs. Bonney and her five children, who lived in the gunch pile and lived off the garbage. There was no father. I had long conversations with Mrs. Bonney and her children which I reported to my mother. She retold those stories to whoever came into her kitchen as if it were news of another family living on our Creek.

The original house foundation was stacks of flat rocks. When the house began to sag, we jacked up the house and poured concrete foundations. Today it does not seem such a complex job, but my father made tense, mysterious work of it. Still the foundation was never complete, and under the house, animals came and went at will. Sometimes skunks got under there and sprayed. The resulting smell was so strong that I woke up with my eyes watering and stinging. The odor lingered, and I was even less popular at school during those episodes. Faint skunky odor had an appeal to me, so much that I was not surprised to hear that skunk glands were sometimes used in making perfume. Still it was a long distance from one of those intense black-and-white creatures to my mother's dresser-top vessels of perfume.

The dryness of summer impressed me, with no rain the hills became a mellow brown tawny color. One summer I decided to keep one spot green, and whenever I could remember, I would urinate on the same spot behind the garage. I never went inside to "go to the bathroom" anyway, so I thought I could create a green area. To my disappointment the green never appeared. It was a mystery to me.

On certain warm summer evenings, swarms of termites erupted into the air around our house. We called them flying ants. I fashioned long, potent paddles from red-cedar shingles with my pocket knife and ran swinging, one from each arm, swinging through the thick twilight air to knock those bugs into eternity with deeply satisfying spats. When the darkness deepened, I dropped one paddle and sank to the earth to spot my remaining prey against the western sky. I never connected flying ants with my grandfather's termite-ridden house. I simply loved running up and down the hills slaying those winged beasts.

One summer night there was an eclipse of the moon. This was before radio reached Four Mile, let alone television, and my family made an event of it. I suspect my grandfather Waterman was behind it as my father was opposed to any wasting of time, and there was a gathering before our house in the bright light of a full moon. Only a few brief clouds were in the sky, and I looked carefully at the moon for the first time in my life. Looking through my father's binoculars, I realized it was a much more interesting place than I had thought previously. I told my grandfather that the moon looked like a tough place to raise stock but at least we wouldn't have much brush to chop.

"Just shut the god damn hell up," my father snarled at me.

The moon had a rugged landscape, and I tried to imagine what it was like with no air. How could a place so different exist? Chairs from the house were set on the thin grass of our front yard, and the adults sat in them chatting while my brother and I lay backs to the ground watching the moon disappear.

My brother made awful sounds as he put himself to sleep, and he irritated me with his whaa-whaa-whaa pillow-pounding chants. I was about ten when he began to use that to tease me and to bother me. I cannot remember what I did, but I had enough of those awful noises. Shortly my grandfather and Harry Gamble went to work converting the remainder of the attic. They were not the world's best carpenters, although they probably worked quite cheaply, my grandfather for free. And I loved the room they made for me. They built a raised dormer window facing south, in addition to a regular window facing west. My mother frequently complained about the south window, and it always leaked when it stormed hard. I did not realize until I was writing this that surely my grandfather put in the south window over her objections. They finished off the room in plywood, floor and walls and ceiling. They installed a light receptacle recessed into the ceiling, along with switches on the wall entering the room and right there on the side of that dormer window. We had just gotten electricity from REA, and I had my own room with an electric light! Perfection! My back was troubling me at this time and I laid a sheet of plywood over the saggy mattress, covering it with a thin pad. This arrangement helped the night pains from my back. I thought the plywood walls showing wood grain were ideal, and reluctantly allowed them to be varnished. My mother wanted civilized paint, but my room wasn't seen by anyone else and she let me have my way. And the views: I could look west and see a sunset if we had one, although usually the Pacific's fogs prevented anything like a sunset. And I could look south and see half of our home ranch, the Walker place, and more. I did not let my mother put up curtains either; it was my room and why anyone wanted curtains covering windows I had no idea. So I spent seven or eight years in that room, with fantastic views and light. I slept right against the house's roof so I could hear winter storms rage and howl at night. The winds went often up to seventy-miles-per-hour, and the house shook in blasts of wind. Of course rain came at all speeds, and a gentle steady drizzle was comforting, things were not getting worse during such rain. Unaccountably this proximity to the weather gave me a deep sense of security and well being, even when the house shook and swayed in the winds. Water dripped in and around that window grandfather and Harry had installed. I just moved buckets around and loved my room.

When I fell ill, puking with the flu or floating on some fever, I retreated to my room (which progressively was farther and farther from the family), and I lay in my bed. Similarly afflicted, my brother situated himself as close as he could get to my mother. Still, isolated as I was, it was blessed relief when my mother appeared, carrying soup or just coming to check my temperature, straighten my sheets and sit on my bed and talk. My father did not involve himself in such matters as our illness. The usual treatment when sick was to wait until it was over, although I have vivid memories of being dosed with castor oil, the most vile tasting stuff. And with a sore throat of having my uvula and the back of my throat painted with a kindling stick wrapped with gauze and soaked with merthiolate, the fumes going up my nose, the fluid draining down my throat, and the bitter taste sticking in my mouth. These were treatments that stayed with you.

Two retail catalogs were my windows on the world and the stuff in it: Montgomery Wards, and Sears and Roebuck. Monkey Ward, and Sears and Sawbuck. First it was toys, wagons and bicycles and cap-guns. At ten I bought a single-shot 12-gauge Stevens shotgun from Sears. In these volumes I learned what women wore under their clothes, and when I became style-conscious I could align the fashions in the catalogs against those in my school. The saddles and bridles were always compelling, and as I accumulated livestock, so was the farm equipment such as an ear-tag crimper. Those giant supply-houses sent out a several-pound annual issue with seasonal updates. They were tickets to dreams.

Electricity arrived when I was in the fourth grade. REA, the Rural Electrification Association, made a tremendous difference to rural life. Being able to see at night was less of it than might be imagined. You could read with the light from a kerosene lamp, and sitting around the kitchen table to read, play games and talk made us a family. But having dependable hot water, an electric cooking stove and a washing machine transformed my mother's life. For me the big change was the radio. There were weekly programs, "Our Miss Brooks" for example, which everyone listened to. Miss Brooks, played by raspy voiced Eve Arden, had that impertinent aggressive intelligence which

I associated with my mother's friends The Girls. "The Shadow" was another favorite of mine.

Who knows what evil lurks in the hearts of men?

Who indeed?

The Shadow knows!

The Westerns played into my fantasies; "The Lone Ranger," "The Cisco Kid," the list ran on. One of the most pleasant afternoons of my life occurred one rainy Sunday. There was no work as my father was away doing something. My mother and I sat in that little living room, toasted by the fireplace, and had rare reception so that we could receive daytime dramas. She sat and sewed; I lay on the floor with some pillows and was transported. I had a little radio of my own eventually, and I heard the birth of rock and roll from Bill Haley onward. (Bill Haley and his Comets: Rock around the Clock!) One night I lay awake listening to the broadcasts about Sputnik that had just been launched, about the science gap our country faced. This made a deep impression on me and likely changed my life. These were intrusions of the outside world that I connected with. The power of the media: Rock On!

Another remarkable technology came soon after electric lights. The telephone was a party line, collecting all of upper Four Mile under one number: FI7-3514 (FI stood for Filmore). The sorting out of who was being called was minor and unending comedy, and of course there were eavesdroppers, for who could resist learning what was going on with the neighbors? Now my mother could more easily contact her family and The Girls. As with electricity, the telephone changed my mother's life the most. Every day she talked with Aloma, each day for the next forty years until Aloma died.

Linoleum was laid onto the back porch, and after years of use it did not wear out. In order to make it presentable, my mother painted it with black, white, red, and yellow paint, put down in patches. I liked it, and now would describe it as a Jackson-Pollock-effect, except none of us had even heard of him. I would frame that floor as art if there remained a piece of it.

In the mid-1950s we built a major addition to the house, almost doubling the floor space, adding one large room to the north-west side. The door between the kitchen and living room was removed, and the set of rooms were joined into one large, open space, striving for the look of a house in the suburbs. For that is what happens to these old houses, the residents want to shed their past and to become contemporary, using acoustical tile for ceilings for example. After I left home, they added a large bedroom onto the south side of the house, with deep-pile carpeting. Old worn furniture is discarded and replaced with choices from some line of early American furniture, a table with gouges thrown away in favor of an expensive model with factory antiquing.

Every year or so, my brother and I were backed up to a door frame and our heights marked into the wood. Horizontal bars with name and date appended.

— Mike Oct 1949
— Charlie Sept 1956

That board alone survived the ruthless renovations, a piece of pine standing as sentimental record.

The ultimate transformation to the ranch house came when it was decided to fix the crazy angles of roof that resulted from the years of additions. The solution was to build an entirely new roof that sat over the house and was patched onto it to make it look even more suburban. And my mother finally had her way with my room. The new roof cut off the southern view. If I had found the courage to lift the curtains she was finally able to install in my old room, I would have seen the gloomy underside of the superstructure. I visited Four Mile, and while I would rather have stayed in Bandon, to please my mother I stayed with her at the ranch and spent nights in that stuffy, dark room which once was filled with air and light.

12 Railroad Man

My grandfather Amos Lunsford Payne was born March 26, 1890 on a homestead in Baker County near the Oregon Trail at the right time to help build the West. The Paynes were Irish with that sparkle in their eyes and the famous gift of gab. Great-grandfather Payne was a railroad worker and he used the homestead as his base. My grandfather was railroading at fourteen, walking track at night with a lantern to check the rails. He kept up school while holding this night job. His father showed him the business, and then a foreman was needed for a track-laying crew.

"My son can do that," his father said.

Amos was sixteen years old, commanding a crew of a dozen men, all of whom were older. Part of his qualification was his ability to read and write: he could keep and submit the time cards for his crew. In my experience, men usually resent their bosses, and I can imagine the strain that having a barely grown child as foreman would create. Our family stories emphasized that his crews liked him very much.

He fell in love with a neighbor girl, Anna Dumas who lived on the adjoining homestead, when she was in the seventh grade. That was shortly before Amos took up running crews for the railroad full time, and before she went to Burns to attend high school. She was away for two years and came back to Baker to teach school. Amos was working out of Huntington then, a little town sitting in another stark canyon, and he courted Anna in every way he knew. I do not exaggerate this; he worshiped her for his entire life. They married in Huntington when they were eighteen. My grandfather loved watermelon but never ate the sweet center; that he always cut out and laid on Anna's plate. True love.

Amos Payne built railroad, grade and track, trestle and bridge, all over the West. It was his work, and it was not a stationary occupation. The family moved one, two, three times a year. "Take care of your mother," he would tell the children before yet another move.

He worked for the Southern Pacific, the Santa Fe, the Great Northern and others. In fact, he even helped to lay out the golf course in Glacier Park for the Great Northern. I doubt that anyone in my family has ever played a stroke of golf; certainly grandfather Payne did not. I heard him describe building one of those high railroad bridges on a curve; the bracing and foundations and spans seem impossibly intricate and involved. In order to do his work he needed to know surveying, drafting and other skills that even his father did not know. So he bought some books, a series in the International Library of Technology, and he studied them. He taught himself mathematics through trigonometry, drafting and so on. I keep those books on a shelf in my office. My grandfather was a self-taught civil engineer.

Amos Payne shared his passion for railroads with Jimmie Rodgers, the singing brakeman. But Jimmie lived the rough and rowdy life of a drinking man who enjoyed women. My grandfather was straight and narrow in his life—I doubt that they would have gotten along. The Paynes were Irish but they always emphasized that they were not black Irish. Except for a brief venture in a drygoods business, Payne & Payne in Bonners Ferry on the Kootenai River, all Amos ever did was railroading. Amos just couldn't stay away from trains.

His loves were Anna, railroading and trout fishing, probably in that order. He fished some fine places, in Montana, Idaho, Oregon and California, in some streams that are now famous and others troubled remnants of what he cast his line into. After I took a job in Idaho and then visited Oregon, I told him that I had fallen in love with Idaho, with its mountains, rivers and trout. My favorite river was the Big Lost, rising in the Pioneer Mountains, running cold and clear down through the mountain valley out into the Snake River plain where it disappears into the rubble of lava. I had driven right to the Big Lost on my first exploration of Idaho, a lucky choice. The rainbow trout of the Big Lost are vital, high jumping fish which it is an honor to catch.

"The Big Lost!" my grandfather exclaimed, "I spent the best week of my life on the Big Lost River. I took the Mackey Spur out to Mackey Idaho and stayed in the Mackey Hotel for the week. I rented a horse and buckboard and each day we — your grandmother, the two girls, and I — we rode out to that river and I fished. I can still remember those trout. They jumped straight up and were hard to stop."

The Mackey Spur went from the Oregon Short Line at Blackfoot, Idaho. It ran along the road I had driven from Pocatello to reach the Big Lost. My haunts were the upper reaches of the Big Lost, but I had fished the river in range of his buckboard too, parking at gravel piles and fighting brush to reach a dangerously swift stream with a slippery bottom. The fish were worth it, but it frightened me. People had been drowned fishing that stretch.

"We almost lost your mother there, in that river," my grandfather went on. "Anna had hung her basket in a bush, and no one was paying attention. The basket fell off into the water and almost washed away. We found it there bobbing up and down at the edge of the current."

Uncle Perry had married my grandfather's sister Ruth, so he was a member of the Payne family. He was a character: he owned the first crystal radio in the family and the first station wagon. (My railroading grandfather Payne never learned to drive a vehicle.) The station wagon was Perry's medium. He put a bed in the back, and while he had money, he and Ruth traveled around sleeping in the car, cooking outside. This was Perry's idea of the ideal life. When the money was gone, he usually borrowed from my frugal grandfather who hated the whole enterprise but couldn't refuse helping a family member. Perry always paid Amos back. On the edge of scandal, Perry's life was a series of minor scrapes like the time in Ashland when he was almost arrested for venison out of season, but somehow Perry escaped serious trouble and stayed out of jail.

My grandfather ran the track building crew that constructed the spur line from Powers out to Eden Ridge, track that was used to bring out the timber from the largest logging operation in Oregon. The family lived in Coquille, and my grandfather lived on the construction site. When the Depression came, logging shut down and with it railroading. My grandfather was out of a job. He wrote a friend with a high position in Great Northern, and that man told him of possible work with the McCloud River Timber Company. They hired my grandfather on the strength of the Great Northern recommendations, and he spent the Depression in McCloud, California.

A man returning late in the night from fighting fire near McCloud was told to go from the train station to his lodgings. Making a wrong turn he entered my grandparent's unlocked house where everyone was asleep. My uncle Ben heard him, and deciding it was not anyone in the family, went through the bedroom of his sisters to reach my grandfather. Amos, Ben and other relatives circled the room, turned on a light and shouted, "Stop! Stop right where you are! Don't make a move!" They were armed with pieces of firewood to club the guy. I heard two endings to the story. One of them had the family listen to him and send for the police who took the poor fellow away. The second ending had a different twist: his story was believed and there was relief on all sides. The fire was built and a pot of coffee brewed and shared by everyone. I like the idea of that pot of coffee.

After the economy picked up, Amos went back to Coquille. Working out on the Eden Ridge line, one afternoon Amos stepped back and fell off the steep embankment and was broken up badly enough to spend days in the hospital and to receive a cash payment for a broken collarbone. When it came time to return to work, Anna said, "No Amos, you stay home. The children are grown and gone, and I am tired of living alone while you are out building track."

"Dad wrote ten letters," my uncle Ben Payne told me, "and he got fifteen job offers. But Mother still said, no, she was going to have her husband at home."

Amos had no idea what to do, life without the railroad was almost unthinkable, and then he recalled a magazine he had read in the hospital that recommended raising chickens. Amos and Anna then moved out to Catching Creek where their oldest daughter Mildred and her cowboy husband George lived. Mildred had George working in a sawmill (which was far from what George considered a fit way to spend his time), so each night George brought home lumber from which Amos and George built two long chicken sheds along Catching Creek. Then chickens were purchased with the collarbone money and the work started. But they were losing money. Finally they decided it was a problem of scale and distance: more chickens closer to town should do the trick. So the Paynes with their son Ben and his new wife moved into a big house on fifteen acres just outside Coquille. The chickens had to be moved too and there was no railroad help this time. Chickens go to sleep at sundown so they traveled to Coquille in crates during the night; it was clumsy work and my grandfather lost patience while his son and son-in-law and future-son-in-law all helped with the great chicken move.

"Relax Amos," they told him as another crate of chickens crashed to the ground, "Relax. We'll make it. It will be over soon."

There were enough buildings at Coquille so George didn't have to steal any more lumber. Uncle Ben told me of working a full eight-hour shift in the plywood plant starting at 3 PM, getting some sleep before he got up to help with the chickens until he had to go to work again. After six months of this they were still losing money, and Ben told his father to give it up and come to work in the plywood plant.

"What? Work in the plant? Why would I ever do that?"

Ben explained steady work at reasonable pay was far better than spending savings on chickens. Amos was skeptical but finally agreed to go see a man at the plant. Ben smoothed the way, and the last of Amos Payne's working days were spent at the plywood plant in Coquille. At the end he was night watchman. I recall his frustration over union strikes that put him out of work. He did calculations to show how many years the men would have to work at higher wages to make up wages lost from the strike time. He stood up at union meetings and presented his data, but he could not prevent the strikes. Probably he hated the inactivity more than the lost income.

During my childhood, the dependable holidays were those three (Thanksgiving, Christmas and Easter) designated to be spent with my mother's family: the grandparents, aunt Mildred and family, and uncle Ben and family. There were two children per family so this was a gang of fourteen people. The wives spent a week cooking their best dishes and trying out the new ones to be sure they would be satisfactory for the big gathering. The hostess spent weeks in preparation, cleaning to be sure my grandmother would not wrinkle her nose at some overlooked dust or untidy mess. But the absolute center of these affairs was my grandfather. He delighted in it all, and radiated his complete profound happiness that he had his entire family in one place. He sat in a centrally located chair and enjoyed being continually crawled over by grandchildren. Fearing disapproval from grandmother Payne, our mothers tried to restrain us, but that was not possible. He told us innumerable stories, many true tales of his life, others fanciful ditties to tease or surprise us. Some of them opened dramatically.

"It was a dark and stormy night. Three hobos huddled by the firelight."

We sat there, on and about him, and listened with our mouths and hearts open. It was a wonderful world.

When television reached Coquille in the 1950s, my grandfather, who was an avid baseball fan, watched every game he could. The tiny flickering screen, the crack of bat against ball, these things seemed foreign to me. But most mysterious was my grandfather's total delight in professional wrestling. It was a puffed-up showy fake and he loved it, enthusiastically talking of the contestants.

"Gorgeous George is in for it now!" he would say with relish of that caped showman. "Gorgeous is in for it!" Imagine the joy he would have taken in a professional wrestler becoming governor of a state and a player in national politics!

After retirement, Amos concentrated on gardening. He grew roses and flowers, but his heart was in the vegetables, rows of corn, potatoes, squash, and tomatoes, all grown from seed. He had a handsome half-acre garden. Neighbors, relatives, friends; he supplied everyone with fresh produce. Working in his garden took the place of having a job. There was little Amos desired more than to become a published writer. He wrote sentimental poetry about family topics, tried his hand at prose, and submitted his entries to writing contests.

One winter my grandfather went down the Coquille River toward Bandon to Riverton where the river is deep and strong and backs up from tides and rains to flood the fertile bottom lands. He joined a few other men who regularly fished for steelhead all day, warming their hands over empty oil drum at a fire made of mill ends called quill, drinking coffee from a thermos. They caught one small fish that day, and Amos told this story several times, always ending with the wistful line, "I don't know about you, but I don't call that good fishing."

When Anna died, something went out of him, and he lost his enjoyment of life. He didn't stop going through his daily routine, but he would not fix his meals, perhaps from a lifetime of having Anna care for him. Aunt Mildred stayed with him for a few weeks, but eventually had to go back to Catching Creek and her family. Uncle Ben stopped by in the mornings to cook his breakfast and at nights to cook his dinner. Otherwise Amos would not eat.

Perhaps out of loneliness, my grandfather and a friend came to our ranch that fall to hunt deer. My grandfather had never shot a deer in his seventy years, but there he was with a hunting buddy, refusing to trouble my mother with their care. They were sleeping in the shearing shed, old shaky men somehow scaling the ladder to the loft where we tossed bundles of wool during shearing season. I came to the Coast on a visit and was bothered by their situation. Not only were they sleeping in less than comfortable quarters, but neither my brother nor my father would help them hunt. To give them some companionship, I offered to take them out.

The Mitchell Place with its two orchards on more or less level ground seemed a good choice. I sent the other man to the upper orchard. As I owned no rifle and had no intention of shooting anything, I took a gun I had never shot in my life, my brother's 308. It had a clip of bullets, and I took no extras. My grandfather had no rifle, and I simply wanted an excuse to spend time with him, to "take him hunting." On getting out of the vehicle, I saw that my grandfather could hardly negotiate level ground, and I changed my already modest planned approach to the orchard. We walked along an old road, talking quietly in the pleasant evening. We passed by the spot where my second shot had brought down my first deer; that seemed a lifetime in the past. This was where the Okies had camped when they logged the Mitchell place after my father bought the land. I did not expect to see a deer but then a small buck walked out ahead of us across a ravine. We both saw the deer, and I could not see how to get out of it. The deer's body was obscured by some willows, and I reasoned to myself that the bullet might go astray. So I aimed at where the shoulder should have been and the deer went down like a light that is switched off. To butcher the deer, I had to borrow my grandfather's dull pocket knife, and then take the knife back to the rusted stove and use it as a whetstone to hone the knife sharp enough to cut the belly. The old men had their deer after all. After this happened, my grandfather at every opportunity told the story ending with his characteristic twist.

"The rest of you make a big deal out of deer hunting. Getting up early, climbing up hills and climbing down hills and making it all out to be a big production. But my grandson Mike and I just go out and take a short evening stroll and then shoot one, a buck, right where you can get the car to it. There is really nothing to deer hunting."

Anna Payne died of cancer in May 1971. Amos Payne died of prostate cancer and a broken heart in November 1971. After my grandfather was gone, there were no more family gatherings; he was the magnet that drew and held everyone together.

13 Taskmaster

My grandmother disapproved mightily of all things not done precisely her way. My aunt Mildred was the sanctioned daughter; my mother did not gain her mother's approval. My self-description at three or four as "messy Bessie's messy kid" was surely a reflection of my mother's self-image as the untidy daughter. Even then I did not like my grandmother, and it was mutual. I was her least favorite grandchild. The only virtue she possessed in my eyes was that my grandfather worshiped her. Why he did so I could not imagine, but he certainly did. Whatever one thought of her it is certain that she was tough as galvanized nails.

Anna Payne was a strong and stubborn woman. She was born in 1889 on the Dumas Homestead in Baker County, Oregon and surely had a difficult childhood. Some of her strict and inflexible ideas about what was correct apparently came from boarding with a doctor's family in Burns while attending school there. Even as a child she had a delicate stomach and could only digest the most bland foods.

Uncle Ira was the youngest of the Dumas children, and Anna was 18 years old when he was born after their father died. And it was he who suffered the most of all from his mother's second husband. Reacting to the harsh treatment, Ira took refuge in religion and became a Methodist minister. He was dark skinned (showing his French blood, my mother said) and married a blond woman Fairy who was a Quaker. The Quaker faith was too strict for Ira and the Methodists too liberal for Fairy, so the compromise was the Nazarene Church where, again to quote my mother, they still got noisy during services. Ira and Fairy became evangelists and they traveled around the West, holding one- to two-week meetings at churches. They were well treated of course. People took them in and gave them the best of everything. My mother told of Fairy delicately pushing up her sleeves, saying, "You know, I never allow my sleeves to go up beyond my elbows." Ira died of cancer in his early forties and Fairy remarried, to another minister who had much more money than my great-uncle Ira. On one of our two family holidays, due to Anna's insistence my family visited Fairy and her husband in their stuffy Victorian mansion in San Francisco. They wanted for us to leave and never to see us again. And that's exactly what happened.

Anna Dumas and my grandfather Amos Payne grew up on adjoining homesteads, and they were a couple from the seventh grade onward. Anna became a school teacher for a time, and then she married my grandfather. Being a railroad wife was no picnic either, and she and my grandfather moved all around the West while he worked for the railroads. Finding a rental in a new town was no easy task with four children.

"Just rent to us for the first month," she told the prospective landlords. "If you are not satisfied, we will move." As she had total control of her children and my grandfather had a good job, she never had to move after that first month.

Working on the railroad had its benefits. Men were available — perhaps not with Southern Pacific's knowledge — for helping my grandmother with many things around the house, even hanging clothes to dry. The family had a Chinese cook once, one of the lonely men without women brought to this country for cheap labor. He

hand painted a tin can with flowers for a tea container. I was given that canister by my mother who saved it. When the inevitable move came, railroad men packed the family possessions into crates which were put into a boxcar.

When my mother was in the hospital having my brother, I was left with my grandparents who lived on the edge of Coquille at the lip of a big ravine near Highway 101 (which no longer goes inland that far). I can recall the noise from the road; cars at all hours of the night amazed me. And there was the discomfort of being confined in such a small space. My grandmother told my mother that after I was put to bed on their couch she came into the living room to hear me repeat to myself in a conversational tone, "If I ever get home again, I'll never leave again. If I ever get home again, I'll never leave again." Anna said I wasn't whining or complaining, I was just telling myself something important and calming.

Anna Payne was the dictator of taste and dignity for the family gatherings. I look on the gatherings with nostalgia, but for my mother they were tests by fire. Would the table cloth be clean enough? Was there dust on the front steps? Would the food be satisfactory? For the delicate digestion of my grandmother apparently dictated the definition of quality food. The daughters and daughter-in-law made the most bland and tasteless food, and if it was insipid enough, it was pronounced excellent. Any freshness or flavor or — god forbid — spice, and the offending food would be quietly and completely rejected. I never understood why I grew up in a family where black pepper was an exotic spice, but many years later learned from my uncle Ben Payne that it was because of Anna's shaky digestion. Not only were the food and the table under inspection, but the whole house was evaluated too. I have a vivid memory of my grandmother, short as she was, reaching up her white-gloved hand to the top of my mother's refrigerator and running her index finger along the edge of the appliance as far back as she could reach. She then inspected her finger, looking for dust and dirt.

14 The Girls

You know I have always called them *the girls*," my mother said, "and I know that is just not done now, but I do not know what else to call them." She was referring to her gang, the collection of women friends whom she had known for fifty years.

She seems to have assembled The Girls instantly after moving to the ranch on Four Mile Creek from the small town of Coquille in 1941. That may not seem like a big change from today's perspective when every house gets talk shows and internet, but subtract electricity, telephone, stores, mail delivery, and then narrow human contact down to one or two people a day, always the same people, and you have the beginning of it. Livestock grazed to the door of the tiny house. Wind blew constantly. There was dirt everywhere. But she already had a life of her own, and in order to keep one, she invented The Girls.

Probably Aloma Gamble, related to the Watermans by some distant connection, was the first capture. This collection came as a natural if perhaps desperate process, not some conscious plan. Aloma herself was an extraordinary woman. She lived in Bandon in a house in which there was one location where one could glimpse where the Coquille River met the ocean. Aloma loved Bandon. She of all The Girls was the most independent in action and thought. Aloma wore slacks and baggy clothes and cut her hair short, the effect being definitely masculine. (Remember this was small-town rural 1941 America.) The girl who did not cook was Aloma, in fact she did not keep house at all: stuff was stacked everywhere without order in the dusty chaos. Her dog

Mamoo was a huge Afghan. (Repeatedly my mother told us how expensive she was.) But Mamoo was never cleaned or groomed, so her hair was matted and clotted and filthy. My father threatened to shear Mamoo but no one messed with Aloma. Mamoo enjoyed moving about as much as her master enjoyed housework. She just lay there in the middle of the floor like the rug for which strangers reasonably mistook her.

"My god, it moves!" one of them screamed.

Mamoo had terrible breath and bit any child smaller than herself who came close, and some who were larger. Aloma did not apologize to anyone about anything.

She had a husband Harry who was, apparent even to me, clearly just a pleasant appendage, a house decoration. Harry had a dapper mustache and dressed well; how he managed that in his environment remains a mystery. No one else wore tweed slacks and open dress shirts with a sweater; he probably did not own a pair of Levis or a work shirt. Harry was cool, again evident even to a child, the kind of guy who would go to Reno to gamble and not play the slots, too boring. He didn't say much but what he said was articulate. Aloma kept him around. And she could afford it or could until she lost her money in an investment in Mexico. Whom else did I know who had an investment, whatever that was? (It never occurred to me that our ranch was an investment—it was the equivalent to our lives, and I could not conceive of existence without it.) Still, after the money was gone, Harry stayed.

Aloma had a sister Fairy who lived in Nevada and owned a mine. Another thin, mouthy, aggressive woman, Fairy came to visit her sister and told stories of Nevada and mining. I am certain that when the children were out of hearing other subjects such as gambling and brothels were mentioned, but I remember the talk of clean dry air, mine shafts, and ore assays. One summer when I was six or seven Fairy gave me a gold nugget, the size of a grown man's thumb tip. As it was rather lumpy and dull colored, I asked more than once if it was really gold. Assured it was the real thing, I kept it in my room for a week or two, and then concealed it in the bank by the gate on the way to my grandfather's house. I forgot my nugget for a few weeks and then could never locate the item again. Lost treasure on Four Mile Creek!

What Harry, what my mother, what some fraction of Bandon not recently on the receiving end, what they all were addicted to was her to the bone, her honest with more than a hint of nasty, her devastating wit. She could see through any amount of deception or makeup to just what was going on and then see the stupidity and irony of it all, and come out with long, rasping laughter. While my mother was much more conforming and proper than Aloma on the surface, she was Aloma's best audience and in fact co-conspirator in the game. They were a pair indeed and after the telephone reached the ranch (1953–1954), they spoke almost daily, sharing much more than they could with their families.

Aloma was the first woman after my mother whom I loved. She liked all children so long as they were not too full of themselves, because children generally tell it straight. Come to think of it, children gave her some of her material. She treated them like people which was fine with me as I had no idea how to behave like a child. There were picnics at Aloma's across the street from her house in a lot she owned with the foundation for an unbuilt house. I hungered for less bland food and had the idea that it was impossible to put too much mustard on a hot dog. We never had such food at home, but one afternoon at a picnic by that windy foundation, I learned that there was such a thing as too much mustard. The tang of mustard and the juicy hot dogs were part of visiting her. In her home, Aloma had a huge encyclopedic volume of practical recipes describing how to make glue, paint, and horse medicine; a sort of guide to home chemistry that described the most unexpected transformations. I had a vast and unsatisfied desire to understand how substances combined to become something entirely different, and this weighty tome sent me reeling. Aloma encouraged this saying, "There are children like that you know." And then not even my father would punish me for this behavior. To be curious was allowed in Aloma's home, even if forbidden at home.

One of my mother's best stories came from an afternoon get together with The Girls at another woman's house. The hostess circled the room serving cookies on her best platter. My mother took one and placed it onto a little plate.

"Oh," the hostess exclaimed, "Take all you want. Take two." This great generosity became a cryptic punch line. "Take two!" Needless to say The Girls did not bring the woman into their group.

Edith van Leuven was another of these grown-up girls. She was a mountain of a woman, 250 pounds or more. Her heart was huge as well and everyone tried to sit near her; she just made a person feel good. She and her husband Willis had three children, two boys and a girl, and the boys were all trouble. Edith did not have discipline in her so far as the children went.

"Oh Johnny," she sighed when one of the terrors scaled some height to break my mother's vase. "Oh, Johnny, Johnny ..."

Edith was an excellent cook and kept house in her way, accumulating nothing breakable. On a rare visit there for dinner, there were mounds of chicken with delicious meat flaking off the bone into gravy. I didn't have the courage to do what the van Leuven boys did, adventures that usually involved some form of violence, but I did manage to keep my brother from being hurt when he was big enough to take part. They thought little kids had arms and legs for the same reason insects did, to be twisted off. Once when I was small they visited the ranch, and the boys tried to frighten me with monsters in the dark. I was familiar with the night and urged them to show me the creatures I had somehow missed. My mother enjoyed telling this story, taking a small revenge on Edith's unruly children.

Willis was one of two men who might actually have been a friend of my father. All social interaction was handled by the women with the exception of work. Willis and my father sheared sheep together, but I think they might actually have liked one another. From his slaughter house Willis carried home a complex odor that permeated their home.

There were other women in the group, but I didn't know them as well. I think that Aloma and my mother ran it, picking and choosing: someone would or would not do. You could just tell. What impressed me as a child, and still does today, is the vivid life these women carried out in an unpleasant environment. Except for Aloma, they all appeared to play by the rules and then did what they wanted in another dimension. My mother's dresser top was a magical feminine reserve: the mirror, the bottles of scent and fingernail polish, and especially the round container of powder which she applied with a wondrously odorous puff. At her dresser she put the ranch with its filth and violence even further out of mind, there she was just one of The Girls. Men did not have these friendships or textures in their lives.

After I left the Coast, I lost direct contact with Aloma, except that my mother kept us each informed about the other, so it didn't seem like I wasn't seeing her or talking with her. Then on a Coast trip in the late 1970s, I saw Aloma. Sitting in her house with a view of the ocean which she so loved, she asked me: "Well Mike, don't you miss the Coast and all this?"

I replied without thinking that I did not miss it at all, and then realized she had meant more than that. I called her a few times then, and we talked as if the years had not passed. Aloma came to my parents' fiftieth-wedding-anniversary party. She was reluctant to come, she hated "that road," she said, upsetting my mother who as always took any criticism personally and hard. But come Aloma did, brought by her daughter-in-law, and she and I sat out outside and talked. Except for seeing my uncle Ben, that was the high point of the day for me. Speaking of the old days, I mentioned that my family, father and mother both, wanted to reshape it into some storybook-pleasant idyll and that I would not go along with it.

"No," Aloma told me. "Not for a minute should you do that."

Later I heard she fell ill and was in the hospital, and I called her then to her obvious pleasure. Then she was put in a home, "we are afraid for the last time," and it looked bad. I flew from San Francisco to see her, and she was great, lively and sarcastic as ever.

"Hello there!" she said when she saw me. "You look even taller."

I was wearing orthotics and was an inch taller. She found the California influx to Bandon a great amusement, those people did such silly things. My mother accompanied me—I would rather have gone alone and been more personal, but the visit was not just for me.... I sat down, and they talked as they always had. My mother said the week before my visit Aloma had been incoherent, but then she just started getting better. Indeed that day she gave everyone who came into view a shot. Like it or not, she always had everyone's number. After my visit, she became steadily worse and died the next week. Every day for the remainder of her own life my mother missed Aloma Gamble.

15 Hauling Stock

An alternative to selling our livestock to a local buyer was trucking the animals to a major market. In the 1950s the nearest big slaughterhouses were in Portland, Oregon and South San Francisco, California. We used the Studebaker truck which soon had rebuilt engines and overhauled transmissions. That truck saw hard duty.

I was impressed with the stock rack my father built for the truck, and it was one carpenter job that he did carefully. The floor or bed was made of thick planks, with metal strapped along the outside edge and slots where the vertical rack could be inserted. The vertical racks were simply six-foot tall movable fences, one for each of the four sides of the truck's bed. They had feet which slid into the bed's receiving slots. Then the racks were bolted together where they met at the corners of the bed. At the back of the truck, two tall pieces of the end rack would push up, and if pulled out before dropped back down, could be removed to let livestock in or out of the truck. Another feature was a second floor, made by laying planks across the floor halfway up the rack onto boards bolted to the inside of the rack. This made the interior into a two-floor apartment, and sheep could be driven onto either floor. As always sheep made for more messy work than cattle.

This literally set the stage for hauling sheep. About fifty lambs went on each floor. They were loaded at various times of the day, depending on the length of the drive and on the prevailing theory about how to preserve weight of the lambs on the long haul. We often loaded in the dark, shouting and shoving the lambs into the truck. The bottom level was the hardest to load, because we could not get at the sheep to move them over for the remaining animals. We pushed, shouted and used a device called a cattle prod. The cattle prod was a long chrome-plated tube full of flashlight batteries with two electrodes on the business end. The only flaw in having this shock the complacent sheep into moving promptly along was the insulating wool that covered them. Still a good hard push before pressing the button, and the lamb might be slightly stimulated. Eventually the sheep were loaded, and my father would drive off into the night.

The first big city I ever saw was San Francisco from a stock truck. I am not sure how old I was, perhaps six or seven, and I had not asked to go. But there I was, climbing up into the truck amidst the bawling of the lambs, trying to settle myself into a level spot on the seat which was covered with boxes of food and clothing. The floor was packed with jugs of drinking water. We were off.

The driving time to San Francisco was at least a day with a car, and with the truck it was substantially more. We stopped for gas when both the main tank and the secondary tank were empty. We also stopped to check the sheep and to fight them up onto their feet. If they lay down, it was trouble because the other tightly packed animals would injure or suffocate the resting animals. And they must have been exhausted, standing up on those swaying decks which became more and more slippery with urine and manure as the hours passed. The lower deck was always a nightmare, again because we could not get in there to directly handle the sheep. On some of these trips, animals were actually lost, smothered or trampled to death.

Mostly I remember the endless road. The modern highways had not yet been built, and the worst of the road was near the beginning of our long drive. The road was familiar to me as far as Port Orford and I had even been once to Gold Beach. Then we came to Pistol River and started up that mountain. It was steep, and the road was crooked. Here the truck was tested to its limits, and here the sheep started going down. I was not too sure that we would make it at this point of my first trip. The unknown stretched out there in the darkness, and it appeared to be inhospitable judging by Pistol River Mountain. Finally we came down the other side to daylight and Brookings, Oregon. The costal plain widens here, and there are more estuaries. The Chetco River runs from deep in the mountains. I always looked at the rivers, straining in my seat to gaze at the Chetco River, and later the Smith River, the Klamath River with its stone bears flanking the bridge, the winding Eel River. I wondered about the fishing, what trout and salmon swam their waters. I was right about the streams we crossed in the next few hours; some remain fine salmon and steelhead rivers. Then a milestone indeed: we passed from Oregon into a foreign place, California. I was excited just by the idea of it. California. I had now been in two states.

I passed my father sandwiches, apples, cake, cookies, and cups of water. My mother packed thick homemade peanut-butter cookies which reeked of peanuts. We did not talk much. My father's idea was that anything I said was stupid, showing my inferiority. I was just irritating to him. So I took the approach of keeping as quiet as I could and just passing him whatever he asked for. Actually this was a luxury because there was almost nothing to do, so there was little I could do wrong. I can imagine that it was difficult to stay awake a day and a half, driving all the while.

Deep in the food box was concealed a treasure wrapped in heavy wax paper. Rhubarb pie. My grandfather's homestead rhubarb patch grew heavy stalks, green with lavender streaks. Baked in that thick scorched-cream glossy crust, the rhubarb pie was a sculpture, cobbled layers held there by a gelatinous fruit-juice, flour, and sugar mortar. I opened my mouth wide and bit off as much as I could stuff in; pastry, juicy sweet-tart, fibrous at first, smooth as custard after a bit of chewing. Rhubarb pie and an adventure, things couldn't get much better.

Inspired by the approach to Spanish California, my father told me a truth about Mexicans which puzzled me.

"Them Mexicans," he said, "they don't move much. They just get in the shade of a telephone pole. And move along. They stay in that shadow. All day long. In the shadow." Well, what could you make of that? I am now sure he meant it to show the inferiority of Mexicans, but I didn't get that at all. I tried to picture what was happening with those Mexicans, whoever Mexicans actually were. There couldn't be any other shade, except for a telephone pole. I imagined such a stark landscape, and placed in it a person and a scattering of telephone poles. Here the redwoods were flashing by outside the truck, and I was trying to imagine a desert with a person narrow enough to fit into the shade of a telephone pole.

The Trees of Mystery are advertised by a sign that depicts an Indian sitting slumped forward on his horse, holding a spear. I could not fathom this either, but I decided that in a new country you couldn't understand everything. And we went through the redwoods, past the mysterious tourist attractions, on to the slaughterhouse. Somewhere on another mountain, there was a stop my father always made. At one time a dog always came after him at this stop, but then he had used the cattle prod on the dog. I forget the details, but he liked to tell the story of shocking that dog. The trip went on and on. We drove and stopped to shove sheep around, and then we drove on. Getting gas was a great event, because I could run around a little, unless my father saw me. The road noise was in my ears now, whether we were driving or not, and there was a layer of twenty-four-hour road-dirt and grease covering me. The sheep and the road made a peculiar smell, different from sheep in the pasture or barns at home. I could doze a little, so I suffered much less than my father; I was just cramped and crazy from being cooped up in that tiny space. And the engine roared and the transmission whined and road went on.

Then after a day and a half, we made it. The fog was blowing in billows from the cold sea, and we ground onto the Golden Gate Bridge. I remember it as night, but it may just have been dark from the fog rolling across the road, blowing by those huge bundles of cable which swept up into the grey darkness. I was so excited I couldn't believe it. I was on another planet. If space creatures had appeared on the hood, I would have leaned out and shouted to them. Anything was possible if a place such as this existed. And what was on the other side? What was San Francisco going to look like if you went over a bridge like this just to get there?

My father was not skilled at doing new things, things not routine on Four Mile Creek. And he was not one to ask anyone's advice or directions. This was not his first trip, and perhaps he went with someone else the first time. Because he knew how to traverse the city, the City, and continue on to South San Francisco and the stockyards. I glimpsed this strange world flashing by me, flashing even though we were actually crawling, this world of lights and mysterious stores and strange people. It was my first big city, and I fell permanently in love with the City, a condition I tempered but never really changed in fifty years. I still believe it to be a miracle.

We did finally arrive at the stockyards and unload the lambs. My father went to the office where he could ask about lamb prices. The question of whether it had been worth the effort of trucking the sheep was answered right there, in cents-per-pound. I had no idea about that and did not care. Then we went to a really sleazy hotel. Even I could tell this was at the bottom of any barrel. I remember my father's elaborate precautions with the locks at the door, and him propping a chair against the door handle. I didn't sleep at all in that room; instead I listened to the night, which had weird noises to a child used to sleeping on Four Mile. Gradually the road-roar in my ears subsided, and I could hear people coming and going and strange traffic sounds in the background. My exhausted father snored away beside me.

The trip back was much easier. There were no sheep to work with, and the truck ran better unloaded. We stopped at a motel, and my father parked the truck down the highway, out of sight. The woman asked him about his car, where had he parked it? I suppose she could smell us, and he mumbled something. I would not want that stinking truck parked by my room at night.

16 Raising Sheep

A herd of three-hundred sheep is packed into a tight corral, a gate swings open, naked just-sheared animals rush the opening. They jam the gap to freedom, their necks being far less wide than their shoulders. Then they make a jerking increasing flow, the dust raises and the speed gears up. We are gate side, counting the flock. Tallying one-by-one will not keep up; an average person counts by twos. My family did threes, seeing the racing, bouncing, plunging herd in triples. I heard of someone who counted in fours, but his eye was wider than ours.

The principal crop on our ranch was sheep. Most of the income came from selling lambs, and wool was sold too. My father said he could raise eight sheep on the ground that would support one cow. It was my belief that, although the income from eight sheep was greater than the income from one cow, the increased work far outweighed the increased income. This was not an unbiased opinion! The herd grew with the ranches, and by the time I started high school, we sheared over one-thousand sheep each year. Next I will describe some of the work that came with sheep.

The cycle starts in the fall of the year. All the animals have been sheared, and the lambs sold and shipped. Ewe lambs to replace the old ewes that would die or be sold next summer went into a pasture by themselves. The previous year's ewe lambs, now yearlings, were also pastured separately, and for years we did not breed these animals when they were yearlings. Instead they grew for another season to gain size and weight. This resulted in a really nice herd of breeding ewes, which were from

two- to five-years old. Beyond five-years old, and the sheep's teeth are worn down so badly that they have a hard time eating enough grass. We culled the herd by checking the mouth of every animal. (I had a private joke of false teeth for the old sheep so they could live longer on the range.) Sheep were in different pastures according to breed, so that we could let different breeds of rams fertilize determined numbers of ewes. That was necessary because the herd was mostly Romney, a good breed for both meat and wool, and there had to be enough Romney lambs to insure an adequate number of replacement ewe lambs. The remainder of the ewes were bred to a breed like Suffolk that produced a heavy lamb for sale. This sorting required knowing sheep well and having thought out what the objectives were. It also required fenced pastures, not open range.

In the fall of the year we herded the sheep, moving them from one place to another, and we let the rams into the pastures at the proper times. Even this has more to it than might be guessed. The ewes had to be fertile, and different herds needed to lamb at different times, so we could care for them. And there was a lottery aspect too: if you bred for early births and it was a tough winter, you lost your lambs or they were stunted. If you bred for late births, an easy winter would put your lambs behind in development. In the fall, you made your decisions and turned the rams out. Handling the rams was always interesting, because they weighed three-hundred pounds and more and sometimes didn't do what you wanted. When the rams were out, the only work was to ride the range and see that the rams hadn't broken into another pasture, that two of them didn't fight and injure themselves, and that some predator had not killed and eaten some of the herd. That was about it. We took the rams away from the ewes at the end of the breeding season, and they went back to their luxury bachelor lives on bottom-land pasture.

Sheep are dumb animals it is said, but that is an excuse of people who do not understand them. When you drive sheep and hurry them a little too much, they become winded. Then they just stop or go downhill to the lowest point of the pasture and remain there. Not much can be done then except to wait until they get their breath, something which is not quickly accomplished. A better way to herd sheep is to ride along on your horse and just nudge them in the right direction, letting them eat a little grass along the way. It is helpful to know when they are tired or frightened. Animals sometimes decide to test you to see if they can get away. They will break from the herd, and you must let them know that you see them by stopping and looking right at them. They will hesitate and then you move slightly in the direction you plan to take if they continue, all the while looking directly at them. This usually does the job of putting them back into the herd. These small dramas occur frequently, sometimes several at once, and they make herding livestock an absorbing task. In most situations when I am close enough I talk to animals, telling them what I think is happening, what I hope they will do and what I am about to do. This information generally has a calming effect on all involved. Steadiness, strength and empathy are all required to herd stock.

A sheep-dog is born with a herding instinct. Our puppies tried to herd the chickens. They are born wanting to move other animals into a group. In contrast, the usual predator picks out one animal in a herd and chases it. Our border collies loved to work. They were kept tied up and had almost no human contact unless they were working. In fact few of our dogs had names. We named horses and that was it except for Goggles the cow. I could feed the dogs their dinner but was not allowed to pet them. When approached they frantically twisted their bodies in anticipation of freedom; when unchained they streaked over the nearby hills, flashing by us to see if we were heading out to the range yet. They understood my father's commands far better than his children did. I watched his frantic arm motions and listened to his incoherent shouts to the dogs to see if I could break the code.

One unfortunate characteristic of sheep is that they can lie down and then be unable to get up again. This can happen on level ground, but a slight depression greatly increases the chances. The fatter they become, the more likely it is that this will occur. If I came onto one soon after it "got down," it was a simple matter to get it mobile again. Down a few days, the sheep found it hard to walk or even to balance on their feet. They can easily die from this. If they are down long enough, the animal will begin to decay where the flesh meets the earth. Then it is necessary to shear the wool off and treat the decayed flesh. Maggots crawling in living flesh; you can smell that 20 feet away. Sheep lost weight during the winter, and sheep getting down was then much less a problem than starvation.

Often we moved sheep and cows from one pasture to another. We rode out, and my father gave directions. I could never tell what he wanted me to do; his directions were all related to local details, offered out of order, and were entirely unintelligible. I listened and carefully tried to maneuver as directed, always ending up at the end of his rage. "Never send a kid to do a man's job," he said. "Never send a dumb kid to do a man's job." I was willing never to be sent but that was not an option.

One fall day we rode out on the Indian Allotment, and he gave directions that were even more tangled than usual. "Turn at the tree," he repeated. It did no good to ask which tree or which direction to turn. I rode away not having any idea what to do. Then I stopped my horse on a little hill and looked out over some of the range. "Look," I told myself, "you will screw up and not do what he wants. But these are just sheep, and he went in that direction and here I am. If I do thus-and-such, I will get the sheep where they have to end up." So I just aimed at the end goal, and amazing to me, I didn't get cussed at. From then on, I only listened to my father long enough to get a glimpse of what we were trying to accomplish. I paid no attention to how he wanted anything done. If he saw me work, he usually became angry, but if he didn't see how I did something, I usually escaped. If I had continued to try to follow his directions, I might have spent my life in those hills looking for one crooked bush or another to turn left at.

By November, the heavy rains started. By January and the beginning of lambing season, the weather was intense. Storms stacked up over the Pacific like the folds of an accordion; they came in one after another with an awful rhythm. The rain blew in from the south and southwest in heavy layers at an angle of thirty degrees from horizontal. Cold rain slammed into your face and there was no escaping it.

Every day we rode out to look at the sheep and to feed them pellets or nibs. I filled a couple of sacks, tied one to the back of the saddle, hooked the other over the saddle horn, and rode into the weather. We had ineffective rain gear, and I often wore a cold-weather parka that my great-uncle Leo had brought back from Alaska which took longer to soak through than the other clothes. Out on the ridges and hills, the sheep came in from their short feed and ate the nibs off the ground where I threw them. By that time of year, the grass was eaten to the earth. Here one could vary the location of the feedings so that the mud didn't get as bad as at the cattle barns in winter. I always liked feeding animals but this work had a dark damp desperation to it, and it seemed that spring would never come.

The ewes found shelter to give birth when the weather was about to turn bad. Otherwise they stayed out on open exposed slopes. They had much better weather forecasting equipment than we did; we tapped the mercury-filled barometer on the mantel at home, but it seldom gave us useful clues about coming storms. When a scud of altocumulus clouds formed, my observant grandfather Waterman who called it a buttermilk sky would predict rain. It was a safe bet.

Most births went well. The ewe ate the afterbirth, the lamb struggled up to suck for the first time, and it was a happy family. Twins were not uncommon because our sheep were large and in good condition. Sometimes a ewe could not complete the birth, and the lamb's head was sticking out of the ewe. It was then necessary to pull the lamb, a messy business. This was especially the case when a lamb did not come out correct-end-first, and it had to be forced back into the ewe, turned around, and pulled out again. These were bloody operations, and sometimes sheep died. If a lamb was born dead, we tied the dead lamb to the saddle and herded the ewe into a barn. Sometimes another ewe died or lost her lamb in the hills, and we had extra lambs. If not, a twin was taken from its mother. In any case, an orphan lamb was put inside the skin of the dead lamb, which had been skinned so that the legs were not split by the knife. The little guy looked sad, going around in this grisly costume, but it allowed the new lamb to smell like the ewe's own lamb. In this way, we could get the ewe to adopt a lamb. There were times when we had a half-dozen lambs in our house by the heating stove, being fed with a bottle and waiting for surrogate mothers.

Lambs without mothers were called bummers. Meanwhile the rains hammered the hills, the buildings, everything out there living or dead. I liked the animals; I hated the weather.

After lambing came tagging. Wool had been growing all fall and winter, and now in March the ewes had accumulated manure on the wool around their rears. The lumps of dried sheep manure were called tags; trimming the wool on their rear ends was called tagging. Some of the sheep had dried lumps of manure that actually rattled when they ran. Others had juicy runny tags. Picture this: it is a wet cold March day, and there are two-hundred sheep in the corrals, milling around in three or four inches of soupy mud. You bring them forward, a small pen at a time, and then at the shearing floor, upend each of them, sit them on the floor and shear the tags off them. Everyone gets wet, the person doing the tagging and the person handling the sheep. Trimming the bits of good wool from the tags is fitted in between the other jobs. After all, that wool too can be sold. This was one of the jobs with the sheep that I could happily have missed.

Marking lambs was another long task that came in March or April. Each lamb had to be earmarked. We used a right crop for the ewe lambs, just cutting the outer quarter of the ear off with a knife, and a left under-bit for the males, clipping a notch out of the lower side of the left ear. This allowed us to quickly see on the range what sex a sheep was. The tails were cut off, clamping down on the tail at the appropriate point with a multiply hinged stainless-steel device with trade name Burdizzos (pronounced ba-dez-ers), and after the tail was crushed, it was cut off with a knife. The released tail started welling blood, and we smeared bone-oil over it. Bone-oil was essentially pine tar, and it stopped the bleeding or at least slowed it down. Males were castrated too with a few clamps of the detailing device.

This was long, bloody, hard work. Usually I held the lambs while my father operated on them. If we let them get too large, they were difficult to hold, and the operations really knocked them for a loop. The younger the better, with the exception that the inevitable cold rain could blow in and really hurt the lamb's recovery.

One year we marked about three hundred lambs on a weekend, and then the weather turned cold. By the next weekend, almost all of the lambs had infected tails and were really sick. My father bought some thick clear goo that was supposed to help them, and we spent two days breaking open the infected scabs that had formed over their tails, then smearing this new stuff on the now bleeding sores. That bleak cold weekend went on and on, and I thought we would never finish torturing those animals.

Other diseases came along. Pink-eye got into a herd and spread rapidly. We took each sheep and squirted medicine into its eyes. This took days and had to be repeated if they did not recover. Worming the sheep was much the same. Early on, worming meant shoving a pill down the throat of a sheep in a long tube and then ejecting it. The head had to be held high so that the sheep would actually swallow the worm medicine. Later on we mixed a liquid and squirted it deep into the sheep's throat. Some animals came down with lung-worms. My father had a bottle of ether which he held under a sheep's nose while it threshed about trying to escape. The treatment was potentially lethal to the animal, and to kill the most worms my father would try to come as close as he could to killing the animal. Worse than pink-eye or worms was hoof-rot. A sheep's hoof has an outer shell and an inner part with blood vessels and tissue. It's like a finger nail. Hoof-rot was a fungus that ate away the tissue and crippled the sheep. To treat this, each sheep had to be set on its end, and for every foot, the outer hoof trimmed away with all possible rot, down to the bleeding quick. After trimming, we ran the sheep through a chute with a vat containing a solution of copper sulfate or blue vitriol. I have a crescent-shaped scar on one finger where I whacked a chunk of flesh off while operating on a sheep's hoof.

Shearing sheep took a couple of weeks and was satisfying work in better weather. Each morning we went out in the dark and brought a couple of hundred sheep into the shearing- barn corrals. It required planning to have the sheep flow along day after day. There was a rotation of animals from pasture to pasture while we sheared for most of the daylight hours. I did a lot of the corral work, bringing the pens of sheep forward to be sheared. Dust was always part of handling the sheep when it was not raining. I spent days moving sheep through a series of corrals, dust rising and swirling, dust that was essence of urine, manure, decay—distilled decades of sheep: birth and disease and death. It all clotted in my nose as it was impossible to stay upwind. The bare weathered wood of the corral fences became polished by the oily fleeces of the sheep. At the last stage before shearing, the sheep were behind a burlap curtain made of wool sacks. Here the floor was a rough concrete polished with a deep glowing finish of grease, manure and urine, slick as could be; we all slipped around there, men and sheep alike. Someone reached behind the curtain and pulled a sheep, weighing perhaps two-hundred pounds, by its hind leg out from behind the curtain, then grabbed its neck and up-ended her into the shearer's legs. Held correctly, the sheep just stayed there, its back leaned against the shearer's legs. Then he took the first strokes, shearing her belly. Then he lay her down on her side, and sheared up her left side. A critical point was when the shearer tilted the sheep back up and sheared down the right side, because a careless shearer can break the continuous fleece and lower the value of the wool. This was a notion of my father's which does not hold up; the wool was going to be spun into threads and the integrity of the fibers was the only point of importance. The thought occurred to me then but I kept it to myself. Only when showing at fairs do such matters enter in.

There is lanolin in wool, and the surface of the shearing area and the surface of the shearer's pants became shiny with pungent grease. After the sheep was sheared, someone quickly pulled the fleece away with a wide broom and then folded the wool into a bundle, tying it so that the round fleece displayed the beautiful clean wool that was next to the living flesh of the sheep two minutes before. That fresh wool from mature sheep has the white-gold color of clouds lit by a just set sun. The fleece of a lamb doesn't hold together so it was dumped into a dynamite box with the wool twine looped through the notches cut into the middle of each side of the box. My grandfather Waterman, too old to do much heavy work, was wool-tier.

There was a cadence and symmetry and beauty to this work, and it wasn't over yet. The fleece was tossed up into an adjacent loft where a burlap wool sack eight-feet-long hung from a circular hole in the floor. A few fleece were thrown down into this hole, and you let yourself down and began to tromp wool, as we called it. It was a process of binding the fleeces against one another in the bag, and bringing new bundles into the bag, tromping them down, and in that way, working up to a full tightly packed bag, using your feet to wedge it between the other wool and the burlap wool sack. Bringing the wool by your face makes you smell the grease and the sheep and feel the warmth of the animals and the day. Then you work the bundle firmly down into the bag. When the bag was full, the bottom was blocked up, and then the top freed from its binding ring and sewn up, leaving the ends for handles. The ears at the bottom of the sack have tufts of wool sewn inside. These ears were used to handle the heavy bag, and move it out of the way of the next bag. That was the end of the job so far as that wool goes, until the bags were hauled away to sell.

Lambs were separated from their mothers and then separated into those to sell now, those to sell later after they gained more weight, and the ewe lambs to keep on the ranch. The anguished heart-broken cries of the lambs and their mothers filled the air. Buyers take lambs that are seventy to ninety pounds in weight and put them into feed lots to fatten before slaughter. These range lambs are the raw material for others who I believe make much more money for their efforts than does the rancher. But money is not the main motivation for ranch life, no matter what a rancher will tell you.

Shearing or other work with the sheep went on for days. On the last day, we finally came to the last corral of animals, and then the last shearing-pen full. Then we came to the final sheep, and then every year my grandfather Waterman who tied the wool said the same thing.

"Well, there the son-of-a-bitch is. That's the one I been waitin' for." Then he would take a long pause. "What I want to know is just why-the-hell didn't we start out with this one."

17 Chopping Brush

My father was still going away on shearing trips. I was nine and had my own horse. I would have been happy to spend each day riding around the ranch. Leaving me idle was not a consideration, but it was difficult to find a long enough list of jobs to keep me busy. My father found a solution. He put me to chopping brush. My assignment was directly across the small valley from the ranch house, and he could with a glance to check my work when he returned.

Brush grew back as soon as the timber was cut down. First the alders sprang up and grew rapidly and thickly to heights of twenty-five and thirty feet. If left alone, firs would eventually grow up through the alders and the shade from the firs would kill the alders. This has a nice symmetry as alders fix nitrogen in the soil, preparing it for conifers. Ranchers did not find this interesting; their only concern was in keeping the alders from growing in the first place, or failing that, to stop them as soon as possible. Regular burning helped control the brush. If that failed, they called on a man with an axe. Or in some cases, a kid with an axe.

Alders had grown up at the base of a hill in some old logging slash, and the grove of alders extended down the hill toward the creek next to an old logging road. The land had slid in the heavy winter rains, and along the road the alders grew in the slide-drainage area. I was supposed to cut this jungle down with an axe. It was an overwhelming task.

I went up to the alders at the base of the hill. The ground was more firm there in the flooding rains and I had better footing. I took a single-bit axe and pounded at the trees. The axe was dull, and bounced straight back from the tree. I then tried the smallest trees; the axe became dull when I regularly missed the little trees and struck the earth. Eventually a tree was severed from its roots, leaving a ragged stump with slivers of wood pointing away from the trunk in various directions. I worked eight-to-ten hours a day and accomplished little. At the end of the week, my father returned and complained about my laziness. Indeed I was lazy but had worked hard without much to show for it.

"Look at the stock instead of sleeping on the job," he told me. "And swing that axe more this week."

So now I was supposed to ride the range and rescue livestock as well as cut much more brush. It was nice being free of my father during the week, but this was a little more than I could handle. The second week went the same way, and I hurried my horse over the ridges looking at the sheep and cattle early in the morning and late at night. The complaints were more severe the second week.

By the third round I was depressed. I came to a group of large alders and wondered how I would ever get them cut down. I tackled one. It was not that I was unfamiliar with an axe. I had cut wood at a chopping block for a few years and had a pretty good swing for that. But standing in these trees, I would miss the tree trunk, sometimes overshooting it and really whacking the trunk with the handle of my axe. My hands stung from that. Then when I got something of an undercut into the downhill side of the trunk, I optimistically expected the tree to fall when I hit it a lick or two on the back side. When that did not do it, I chopped all around the tree, creating a beaver effect which did not prove effective. I was in the process of trying to push one of my beaver-chewed trees over, when up the road came my grandfather Waterman.

He was wearing old pants with more patches than his usual pair, and he had his straight-handled double-bit axe. None of the original finish remained and it gleamed like silver. The handle had some worn tape around it. Also he brought a file and a round whetstone, and even better, some water and a snack. He looked at the results of my sorry attempt to cut the tree down, and said:

"Sit down and take a little rest."

And that's what we did. We talked about something else. I drank water and he rolled and smoked a cigarette.

"The first thing is to be sure your axe is sharp enough to cut with. Yours needs some work."

Then he showed me how to file the axe, even out in the brush like we were. We laid the axe on an old log, and took some time just looking down the hill while sitting on the log. He told me about various axes and their blades, including those that have one straight or level side and the other curved or bevelled side that is filed to it. They are for working straight surfaces into timber, as when you are trying to make boards from logs. The pioneers needed those tools, and he knew I would have little use for them in my modern day of sawed boards. I have a hand axe with a blade straight on one side that belonged to him. We filed away the nicks I had put in the blade of my axe by hitting dirt and rocks. There is a nice feel from a file stroke on a good axe blade that takes away a measured amount of the blade, readying it for more work. A burr hangs over the edge from the last filing, and he showed me how to polish that off with a whetstone. You spit on the round whetstone, a good satisfying spit, and then just work the whetstone into the blade from the edge with a turning motion. The round palm-sized whetstone is held with your fingertips, taking care that the fingertips do not extend so far that they are sliced off.

Then he told me just to watch, and he cut two trees down. It looked easy. The undercut was made by swinging alternately angled up and down, and the chips flew impressively out from the tree. The pungent, sharp smell of the fresh alder chips filled the air. The sap had no resin and quickly seeped onto the newly cut surfaces. The swings made sharp squishing sounds as a chip slapped against the tree it had just been severed from. Then, when there was an adequate undercut, he swung the axe down on the back side, making a narrow groove angled down that would, if continued, hit the undercut a little forward of its deepest point. But things did not get that far. The tree leaned over and fell down decisively, with creaks and an appropriate whoosh. I was encouraged just to see it done. Then he coached me through another couple of trees, making me aware of various ways I could hurt myself. He emphasized the danger of hooking a tree limb behind me and then hitting myself in the head or neck or leg on the forward swing. He spent almost as much time clearing out around the tree as he did cutting the tree down. Then we set to work, and we cut alders the next couple of hours. He went home, and I knew not to mention to my father that I had received help. Also I knew with certainty that my grandfather would not say a word about it either.

From then on I had a pleasant summer, the happiest weeks of my childhood. After I milked the cow, I cut brush from four- to six-hours per day, laying it down like my grandfather had shown me. Then I got on my horse Berry, untied the dog, and we had the day and the ranch to ourselves. I could even touch the dog with my father away. My mother did not register anything outside her house and yard, so I was safe if my father asked her how much I was working. And he stopped complaining about the work I got done now, although it was in half the time at much less effort. I developed a knack of swinging the axe from my hip which gave my swing a lot of power. A couple of times I saw why my grandfather had warned me about hurting myself.

I cut all the trees higher on the hill and began to chop alders down in the gully. This was a terrible idea because the entire hill was beginning to slide toward the creek in the winter rain. The alders gave the tenuous slopes a little stability. At about this point my father, who probably thought I'd never get that far, began to find other things for me to do. The gully remained brushy.

18 Stretching Fence

The fall of the year brought a decreased urgency to ranch work. The lambs, calves and wool were sold and trucked away. The sheep and cattle were in good condition and putting on weight in preparation for the coming winter. Most of my mother's canning was done, and the kitchen was a cooler and quieter place. Apples were coming on, and deer season was right around the corner. The days shortened, and perhaps we had a few frosts. It was a nice time of year.

The major work we did in the fall was fence building. Every year my father, my grandfather and I built from a half-mile to a mile of woven-wire fence. It had to be tight enough to keep sheep from getting through it; it had to be tall enough to keep the cattle from walking over it; it had to last thirty years.

The fence posts were made by splitting red-cedar logs. We started with a big red-cedar log, from one of those giants that stood dead at the edges of our ranch. They were always dead snags. The only living red-cedar trees were small and young. I never understood why there were none between the stark, dead snags and the young trees a few inches in diameter. The dead snags do not burn up in forest fires because of something in the wood that retards fire. Sometimes we split posts where we fell the tree, right at the stump. Other times the log was pulled by a bulldozer to a more convenient location.

If the log was not newly cut, there was a mild cedar smell. The length of a log to be split into posts depended on the height of the fence; usually our posts were eight-feet long. To get started, sledges and wedges were required. A big log requires a big wedge. Our most interesting wedges were made by inserting a small-diameter shaped piece of white-cedar into a hollow wedge. Then an iron ring was slid an inch or two down the round end of the white-cedar. When pounding this long wedge into a log, the end being struck by the sledge would fracture and be prevented by the iron ring from splitting. The battered wood at the end of the wedge curled down over the iron ring. These long hybrid wedges were ideal to get a big log split, transferring the pressure deep into the log. The first wedge was started at the center of the log, vertically aligned. Then after it went into the log, with thuds if the wedge had a wooden end, another wedge was started in the crack as far as it extended. Then another wedge was inserted symmetrically from the first. And now the center wedge could be hammered further into the log. Metal wedges were driven in with pealing rings that bit at my ears. Now it remained to successively drive the wedges deeper and deeper into the log. The sounds had a cadence and variety to them, and they punctuated the silence of the calm scene. Finally the log split, opening with a cracking and then a dramatic final crash as the two halves fell apart, rolled on their backs and then came to equilibrium. The first impression after this happened was the wave of intense cedar smell, an ocean of it rushing into the silence. The smell was overpowering, similar to that of cedar chests but drier and more astringent. The smell dispersed but never left. It just stayed there lapping at our legs and splashing up to our noses. The old snags were weathered to gray on the surfaces and black in the cracks. They split open to reveal their color and name. If it was a smaller log, some strands of red-cedar probably remained, the ends joining the opposite halves. A sharp double-bit axe was used to trim these strands away.

Now the process was repeated, making quarters out of halves, and so on until the pieces were ready to be made into posts. Just imagine the posts marked onto the log's end, with concentric circles the depth of a post apart. The splits now were on the concentric circles and finishing the rings into posts was deliciously easy. There was a little axe work to do on each post, and then they were stacked in a large pile or onto a wagon. That was splitting posts.

Short pieces of log can be split into roofing shingles in a similar manner. The little rounds are called shake bolts. I regret that I never helped to split shakes. We bought sawed shakes for a house repair, and I compared their smooth sawed surfaces covered with tiny irritating slivers to hand-split shakes that had been split along the growth rings.

Big red-cedar logs were used by the Indians to make boats. Apparently our local Indians did not build large sea going boats, but Indians of the coast of British Columbia and Alaska did. I had a book, given to me by Mildred and George, called the Holling C. Holling's Book of Indians, which had beautiful graphics of those canoes and the Indian's sea-going adventures. Those Indians hunted whales on the open sea with their large red-cedar vessels.

Building fence took fence posts, woven wire, barbed wire, and an imaginary line across the hilly landscape. Two endpoints were necessary. Then, while sighting from one point to the other, one of us guided a person at a high point to the exact position of the line. After enough of these points were located, we started building the fence. The sighting process was repeated to find the points to dig the postholes, about twelve feet apart. If we were lucky, the ground was without rocks or roots, and the posthole digger could be used to steadily dig the hole. That is an odd process. The digger has parallel rounded half-shovel blades which are jammed down into the ground and pinched together to pull the dirt up. It becomes a balancing act to get the last of a two-foot hole cleanly dug out. But normally the rocks or roots had to be broken out with a heavy iron bar possessing a sturdy sharp end. Crunching rock is fun if the rock isn't too impervious to the blows. After a series of holes are dug, posts are dropped into them. Now, in spite of the best planning, the holes are not in a exact straight line. It is the time to rectify that by planning how the wire will come: on the uphill side of that post, the downhill side of the next. Then the posts are set. Small rocks are hammered down to the bottom of the hole, then some dirt tamped in, building up to a post that is set firmly into the earth, standing true to the vertical. A single-bit axe has a curved handle, and a double-bit axe has a straight handle. I can still take a double-bitted axe, hold it up with the thumb and forefinger of one hand, and check a post or tree for vertical plumb.

Next the woven wire was rolled out, threading the posts as planned, and one end nailed to the anchor post. A pair of 2 x 4's were nailed to the other end of the wire, and the wire was stretched tight. Stretching it was accomplished in a number of ways. The pulling was done first by horses, later on by the tractor or a mechanical winch called a come-along. Then the other end of the stretch of fencing was nailed down. In between, you had to be sure you could get the wire down in the low spots and fully up in the high spots. This usually took a good deal of cursing. Nailing the fence to the cedar posts with the heavy staples was nice work, the staples biting into the cedar. Cedar is soft enough that it was usually possible to push the staple ends into the wood by hand, while holding the wire firm with the other hand. Then, after a struggle to get the hammer, the staple can be pounded into the post. The taut wire invisibly vibrated, making an electrical tingle in an ungloved hand, a high-pitched buzzing sound in the cold air. Stretching the single strand of barbed wire at the top of the fence was not difficult, although it was easy to get scratched by the barbs. This strand was to keep the cattle from walking over the fence. Things were always less tense with my grandfather around. He had a longer view of the urgency of getting in another two-hundred feet of fence, and he also had a smooth work style. We put in beautiful fence, straight and tight and geometrical.

There were braces to be placed at critical locations, at gates and other spots where the posts received a lot of stress. Once Jack Donaldson came to see us about something when we were building fence on the Abbott Place. He pitched in to help. He and I were bracing a gate, and the brace required us to do it in two pieces, with a post in between. Jack said we should be able to know the angle from first principles, although he didn't put it that way. I was taking plane geometry and said that I knew how. I figured the parallel lines and was confident that I had it. We marked and cut the board, feeling certain it was right. *Then it did not fit.* I was shocked and set out to understand where I went wrong. The theory was correct, of course Euclid knew what he was doing, but a fence post is not a perfectly straight line nor is it set perfectly vertical. I then decided to just place the board against the world as it existed there on that ridge, and to mark the board in accordance with the post. My braces looked great after that.

The gates came in several varieties. Big heavy wooden gates swung by hinges from massive cedar posts and could stop a grown steer at full speed. Other less substantial versions drooped from their own weight and had to be drug across the earth to open and shut making a furrow in the road and grass. But most plentiful were the woven-wire gates, a stick of cedar or vine maple at each end to be attached with loops of the ever-present baling wire to the posts at either side of the opening in the fence. It required various contortions and levering to shove one end of the gate-stick into the bottom loop from the post and then finally get a tight wire loop over the top to secure the gate.

We were always mending fence, and after thirty years of wet winters, the cedar posts were rotted badly enough at the ground level to become shaky. Then we pulled the deeply-eroded staples out of the post, embraced the post, pulling it out of the ground. Then we reversed and reinserted it, nailing the fence back using as many of the old staples as possible. If hugging the post did not work, a board was nailed to it, and the post was lifted out using the board against the ground as a lever.

Fencing was work that fit in and around other activities. Our family was going to town late the summer of 1956, and we stopped to stretch some wire at the Lower Place. My mother and brother waited in the car while I helped my father. We had begun to use steel posts instead of cedar, and my father put the steel posts where people could see them. So there were steel posts mixed in with a few wooden posts, and we were finishing the fencing job by stretching the barbed wire. My father was using the come-along, and I tested the wire a couple of times, finding it loose. This has to be done in awareness of the other person. A car pulled up. I was testing the wire with my glove off so that I could feel the tension, that rattlesnake buzz in my hand, like water about to boil on a hot wood stove, and my father cranked the come-along another notch. Before I could pull my hand away the wire broke with a snap, twang, and then swish as it coiled up, pulling rusty wire through my partially closed hand. I had always been horrified at men's hands with a finger or two missing. For some reason I found that more frightening than the prospect of a more serious accident. I looked in horror at the mess that my right hand had become. It was like losing a finger; before the blood welled out I could see the tendons of two fingers and was unsure if they were cut through.

My father was already talking with the neighbors in the car that stopped. I went over and told him I was hurt. He paid no attention. I think I was already going into shock. I went to the car and showed my mother who said to go get my father. I went to him again, and he ignored me, a little more irritated now. I flexed my fingers to see if I had cut the tendons clear through. I knew enough about anatomy from butchering animals to know some of my potential problems. The fingers moved at least. I went between the car and my father three times before the neighbors got bored and drove away. I was afraid and in shock. We drove to Bandon where there was a little hospital. They were at least as frightened as I was by my hand and sent us away. We went on to Coquille, me gripping my wrist with my left hand. I could now see that I had another long gash in the flesh of the palm. In Coquille Dr. Lucas who knew our family well and had delivered me took care of my hand. He injected pain killer in the fleshy places but couldn't in the area that looked like hamburger. I was in increasing pain when he began sewing up my hand. I didn't fall apart and got through an agonizing time while he put in thirty-seven stitches. The doctor was unsure about whether I would regain full use of my hand. We visited my grandmother and grandfather Payne for a while and then went home. I went straight to bed and cried myself to sleep. It was a relief to be back in my plywood room again.

It was not until I was forty that I understood this story. Until then I thought it was about my father and me, which was true enough, but there was my mother unwilling, unable to crash through the indoor-outdoor barrier, even for a bleeding son. And my brother at ten patiently sitting on the sidelines.

One benefit came from that accident (in addition to the longest holiday I had had from milking and feeding the cows). I started at little Langlois High School that fall, and there was a freshman initiation. Bob Stankavich saw that I was a painfully shy, awkward child, and when we were gathered in the gym for our humiliations, he assigned me the task of turning cartwheels the length of the gym floor. Damn, I thought to myself as I held my bandaged hands up for all to see, I got out of that easy! After a few months my hand healed wonderfully, and while there remains a faint tangle of white scars, I use my fingers as well as I ever did.

Cedar became scarce, and the time to build good fence was prohibitive. My father tried out a power posthole digger. It was basically a power saw attached to an auger instead of a cutting bar. The principle was correct, and it is possible to find them at some rental agencies now. The difficulty was the Four Mile soil. The auger would be going into the earth and then hit a rock, jerking the saw against the legs that were bracing the tool. There were pairs of handles on opposite sides, so two men would go flying. I was about to graduate from high school, and I enjoyed this work for two reasons. First putting a hole into the ground with this machine was fast when it worked, and I liked bracing for that twisting kick. Second was that, with the promise of fast holes, my father suddenly did not care a bit how the holes lined up, something he had always been almost fanatical about. The power saw was never strong enough to be dependable for this work. A more effective solution came after I left Four Mile. My father bought a small bulldozer, and he chained a post to the heavy blade and let the weight of the blade drive the post into the ground. His fences went in looking like a drunk had done the job, the posts in at various angles to the ground and staggering across the landscape in a deliciously non-linear fashion.

19 Family Holidays

In the Coos County Fair my father rode Jim, a big roan horse with a large white blaze down his Roman-curved nose. That only lasted for a few years, but we often went to the fair for one day each year. At four or five, I was entered in the greased-pig contest. I could not keep up with the pack of older boys and can still summon up the terror I felt when the pig, escaping his pursuers, came straight at me across the dusty rodeo arena. Pigs were not part of my experience until that little hog, the thick layer of grease now covered by a crust of dirt, knocked me sprawling into the thick, powdered earth. The crowd applauded this small comic piece, and I was relieved then to stay far from the beast.

Beginning in the 1960s, my mother worked at the Fair, handling the display and judging of the baking contests. She was written up in the local paper once, and the reporter interviewed my father too. Rather than confess ignorance, my father gave advice on making pies, something he knew nothing about. (The reporter did correct his grammar which here I have left in its native form.)

"We like 'em cooked," he said. He followed that insight even farther down the track. "We don't like them white pies," he added. This from a man who seemed not taste the food he ate! I have come to use "white pie" to reference anything or anyone without genuine content or strength of character. "We do not like them white pies."

Other than the Fair, our holidays numbered three: Thanksgiving, Christmas and Easter. Christmas involved the most ritual and tension. Early the morning before

Christmas, my brother and I each took a bulging stocking from the mantle. They were stuffed with filberts, walnuts, candy canes, and a few small toys. And the one orange I would eat that year, a mysterious fragrant orange with a textured, almost oily surface which gave way to my blunt fingers to reveal a sectioned globe of juicy fruit. I tore it apart and ate it as slowly as I could, section by section, trying to taste all the fibers and juice. During work that day I remembered the orange and found its smell on my hands and its rind under my nails. Tomorrow was a day off.

New Years would have been included in the holiday list, but it was too close to Christmas, too much of a good thing. How holidays were organized before the telephone came to Four Mile and to Catching Creek I have no memories. My mother visited her parents with some regularity, so that probably explains it. My grandparents Payne were at the center of those delicious days. For my grandfather, these must have been among his happiest times; he gloried in having his children and their children all there, in one house on a special day with all the food and talk and warmth. For my grandmother, holidays were duty, but even she must have been happy in her fashion. She was judge of the quality and condition of the house and of the children and spouses. Grandmother Payne with her white gloves and pinched face; grandfather Payne with his soft dress slacks and wide smile. They were king and queen for a day, three days a year. This went on for at least twenty years, and few people ever achieve the wealth that my frugal grandparents possessed on those days.

Each of the three families at the Payne family gatherings had two children. Ben and Betty's children were Steve and Patty; George and Mildred's children were Chuck and Ben (little Ben); Ray and Bessie of course had Mike and Charlie. Chuck was three years older than I. Steve, Charlie, and Ben were all close to the same age, and Patty a little younger. A flock of post-war children. We only saw each other at the three yearly family get-togethers, so none of us were really close with the kids from other families. The days we cousins did spend together were intense and layered.

There was an entirely different aspect to holidays at our house, where my mother spent weeks in preparation. She agonized over having things clean and proper for the day. Going to another house was more fun for me. When we went to Catching Creek, we got up early in the dark, quickly milked the cow and fed the stock, and then dressed in our good clothes. For me, this meant a small torture of stiff blue jeans and a new plaid shirt. The drive to Catching Creek where Mildred and George lived took an hour and a half, and I stared at the farms and houses out of the car's window as we drove along. Past Myrtle Point, we travelled up a narrow valley with its bottom land parsed into small fields, frosty if it were December, filled with poorly fed cattle and grazed down to the earth. Finally we came to the King's tall unpainted house and went inside with presents and the carefully packed food, to loud greetings and cautious hugs between the women, gruff hellos from the men. Close as they were, this was a don't-touch-me family. Then we sat down, and endless conversations started. The women attempted to control the children before the big meal, no easy job with young farm boys, but these women had been trained by my grandmother in control, and they made a job of it, keeping us in hand while in the house at least.

Not that I minded that. Soon my grandfather could be distracted from his more serious conversations with the men, and he had almost nothing except his daughters that were common interests with Ray and George, George who seldom uttered a word anyway. What he wanted were his grandchildren, and he fascinated us, tailoring fishing stories for me and ghost stories for the smaller ones. He liked stories that stop, end, done with story.

"But what happened to you?" someone then asked.

"Me? What do you mean, me? But of course, I was killed," he answered.

"Killed dead." "But Granddad," one of us shouted, "you don't talk dead!"

He told of his work all over the West, and with delight, of his crews. One story was about a crew of Greeks, recent immigrants who spoke some English and were sitting by the tracks during a break speaking to each other in their native language. My grandfather caught the name of a boss, a guy who was mean and treated his men badly. The crews were going to be reassigned soon, and my grandfather guessed what they were talking so intensely about. "Don't worry," he told them at the end of the break. They looked blankly at him, wondering what he meant. "I will see that you don't have to work for so-and-so," naming their worry out loud.

The Greeks were astonished and spread the word that Amos Payne could understand Greek. Well, he couldn't understand Greek, but he understood men. Imagine the impression and influence this man had on a boy who had never heard one word of a foreign language and who had twice been the entire distance of one-hundred-and-fifty miles to the Willamette Valley.

If it were Christmas, late in the morning before dinner we sat packed into a small living room, and opened gifts. Beginning this ritual was the appearance of Santa Claus, played by one of the uncles. Santa dropped off a big burlap sack (which on prosperous years was an eight-foot wool bag) full of presents, gruffly shouting, "Ho, ho, ho!" This was exciting for all the children, because each family bought every member of every other family a gift. Around us were snacks, carrots and nuts in little bowls. There were peanuts, walnuts, almonds, filberts, and dark Brazil nuts (which were called nigger toes). The room and windows were decorated for Christmas, and a fir smell came from the carefully decorated Christmas tree. And odors from the baking in the kitchen floated out, from a turkey, a ham and sweet potatoes, food I only tasted on these occasions. It was a delight, even if the new, stiff, unwashed pants had chaffed my legs. Then the opening of presents went, one present at a time, youngest to oldest, around and around the room, youngest to oldest, again and again, the small children becoming dizzy with what they had, with what they would get, and sometimes becoming so absorbed in some present that hit a particular fancy, that they had to be shouted at to be brought back to earth to tear open the next fantasy. My grandfather beamed at all this, having almost as much joy as did we, watching us go wild within those strict limits our mothers tried to maintain.

When things calmed a bit, it was time to eat. Most of the smaller children were reluctant to leave their new toys, but each person sat where he or she was assigned. There was a kid's table, set up somewhere in the small house, and that was easier than failing to be proper for grandmother Payne. At the main table, the hostess had gone as far to the limit as her budget, resources and imagination allowed. The bland-food ethic of this family operated here too, but that didn't mean the overcooked green beans couldn't be mixed with corn or even have some nuts added. God save anyone who might have cooked an onion, that sort of behavior was just not tolerated. The table was set with the silver that each of these modest households amazingly had, covered by white-lace tablecloths which like the silver only appeared on these occasions, and was in the end absolutely crammed with platters and bowls of turkey, ham, gravy, home-baked bread and rolls in various shapes, sweet potatoes plain and sweet potatoes baked with marshmallows, white potatoes done in two or three ways, peas, corn, green beans, and pitchers of milk and water. To go over the top, the hostess might have added a roast of beef with its own gravy, just to be sure there was enough. I have no idea how this was accomplished in the tiny kitchen, but there it all was, odorous, steaming, heaping mountains of plenty. The food went around and around, with loud directions to take more, to eat your fill, and with laughter and groans from the adults. My grandfather always told everyone that they had not eaten enough, and he urged third and fourth helpings on anyone who could be pushed to it. Then there was clearing off, the women bustling about, and coffee offered to the adults. Now the stops were out. The doctrine of bland did not cover sweets, and the women strove to shine at constructing desserts. The eggs and cream that they had to work with made them dangerous at this business. Stand back and take a deep breath, you are about do some heavy eating. There were layer cakes, with varieties of frosting and whipped cream and chopped nuts joining the layers, chocolate cake, angel-food cake, white cake with frosting finished off in waves like the sea, and pies too, apple, berry, cherry, pumpkin, chess, and chocolate pies, all of this to be served with or covered by whipped cream and homemade ice cream. When I was a teenager, I could eat a tremendous amount; growing rapidly and being so active, it was hard to keep me fed. My grandfather Payne loved to urge me and my cousin Chuck to larger and larger pieces of cake and pie. Grandfather sat there with cake knife in hand.

"Shall I cut it here?" he asked. Then he motioned with the cake knife to indicate larger and larger portions. "Or here? How about here?" His joke was that when he cut the first piece, the remaining cake was really what he had "cut" and was meant for one of his grandchildren. He reveled in this; he sat at the head of the table and watched us eat. I doubt that there existed a happier man.

Conversations at the table never involved politics or religion. In fact there was almost no talk that did not relate to the food, how much of it there was, how good it was, how full the speaker was. National and international events did not exist as a subject at any time, although I might hear my uncle Ben mutter something about Europe—but never at the table. Anything that might require a genuine opinion was suppressed. Instead from the men it was "Pass this, give me some more of that please." The women branched out with "The turkey is really good this year, isn't it? Nice and moist." "Yes it is, Mildred, you did a great job." And the men, offered this guide to noncritical evaluation, would mumble "Right, good job Mildred." They could not have come up even with that on their own. My grandfather Payne, unlike any man I knew then, could actually say something. "Hey little Ben, you going to fall in the creek again this year?" After the smiles and moans that brought from the women, he'd add, "Maybe you've grown wings and you can fly right over the water this time." The other men were mute in the presence of such flights of fancy.

After the stupendous meal, the women went to work cleaning up and doing up all the dishes. This must have been a huge job, and in those days, a man in the kitchen would have been a scandal. The men staggered off to a couch or chair and even fell asleep sometimes. Pretty dull business for the cousins, and we were off, our mothers shouting to us to behave and for-goodness-sake stay clean this year.

We went outdoors if it wasn't raining and sometimes if it was; we just couldn't contain ourselves. If there was sun, it was that thin afternoon sunlight illuminating a landscape which we knew a little, but nothing like at home where every rock and stick and bump was familiar. For years, invariably I got seriously muddy or fell into Catching

Creek from a shaky beaver dam. I knew it upset my mother, but I couldn't stop myself, racing about looking at everything. The Kings had some old barns, and we could explore those, rain or shine, so there was always something new to do. My cousin Chuck had a devious streak, and his pleasure was in getting the younger children into trouble of some kind, or to humiliate them in some way. He would get someone to try to ride a horse known to buck, saying it was their most gentle ride. The worst trouble he got me into was the rabbit episode. Wandering around the countryside we came to a small yard where the absent owners raised rabbits. Chuck, seeing I was fascinated by the rabbits, told me that I should take one, that these people would never miss one, and that I could say I had caught it in the hills. I was six or so and went for it. I wanted a rabbit badly and had visions of having it as a pet. The story fooled no one, and I was made to return the rabbit and apologize to the owners. I became too wary of Chuck to be taken in, but he could get the other kids to lock each other in closets and to climb trees they could not get down from, that sort of trick made Chuck happy. I never liked him at any time.

I did have a revenge of sorts on him. A dog had been dumped on our lower road, and as he looked like a stock dog, my father did not shoot him as he normally would a stray dog. He turned out to be an awful sheep dog. He picked out one sheep from a herd and chased it, infuriating my father and causing a mess each time we tried him out, sending animals in all directions. He possessed no herding instinct. Still the dog looked really great.

"Maybe he's a cow dog," my father said.

I set out to see. Each morning and night, I brought the milk cow in out of a fifteen-acre pasture to the barn. One evening I took the dog with me and sicced him on the cow. He was overjoyed but so dumb that he let the cow kick him in the head. Well, maybe he needs experience, I thought. The next night, bang! Kicked in the head again. I began to have serious doubts about handsome animal. Eventually I could get him to bring the cow in, but he lacked the instinct that stock dogs have and was worthless on a ranch. I liked this good natured animal even if he did have mud for brains, and I didn't want to shoot him, the solution that my father would take when he thought about it. Then I had an idea of what to do; I would get Chuck to take him to Catching Creek. Brilliant, I thought, the dog will have a good life up there, and I can trick Chuck. For a couple of months I worked him hard. On a good day, I could gesture and say, "Get the cow" and off he went, and if the cow was in the right place, she appeared to be driven to the barn. And maybe he would stay far enough from her back feet that he wouldn't be kicked in the head again. I cannot over emphasize this dog's low IQ. We had a lot of dogs, and this guy was by far the least intelligent. To make him even more attractive, I trained him to wait for his dinner, sitting with his tail rapidly thumping the dirt while I filled his pail with milk. Not only that, he was not to move until I said, "Eat, now!" Then he lunged at the pail. This dinner trick also took me two months to achieve, and like the one of not getting kicked by the cow, it was pretty thin. The big day arrived and the Kings came to our house.

"We have a new dog, a nice one," I casually mentioned to Chuck. Then later I asked him to come with me while I milked the cow.

"You know," I said on the way to the barn, " this is a nice little dog, but he's really a cow dog and you know we have mostly sheep. I don't know what to do with him. Seems a shame ..."

The day went well, the dog got the cow, at least it looked like he did, and he didn't get kicked. When I said, "Eat, now!" I could feel my cousin take the bait as the dog devoured his milk. A dog so well behaved that had stock instincts was worth money. Much later that evening, Chuck allowed as how he could do us a favor and take the dog. I pretended to think it over, and this stray had a new home on Catching Creek.

Later in the day, everyone gathered at the table and ate more. Finally dishes, leftovers, and children were loaded into the car, and we went home. I found those drives back to our ranch, when I curled up in the back seat of the post-war Lincoln with the roar of the highway and occasional flashes of light from the cars we met, deeply satisfying and comforting. It was a rare sense of security, a knowledge that everything was right with the world and that my place in it was safe. The hum of the tires, the deep darkness around us, the sweeping turns, another holiday not quite over.

20 Mildred and Her Cowboy

My mother's older sister Mildred was not troubled by self-doubts. She pleased her own mother, one of the most rigorous tasks I can imagine. She loomed there ahead of my mother, setting the table precisely and on time. The stories of her correctness were legend in the Payne family. When the family traveled on the train to my grandfather's newest job, the children ordered waffles as a treat served in the Pullman car. My mother and her brothers ate theirs swiftly while the older Mildred buttered each and every square individually and then carefully put syrup into each square. The whole business must have been a cold slab when she finally ate it with a superior air. Grandmother Payne encouraged this behavior and gave my mother trouble for being sloppy and undisciplined.

There was no hint that Mildred participated in the McCloud motorcycle gang or in anything else that sounded like fun. Her satisfaction seemed to be in being correct in behavior and attitude.

My aunt Mildred married late, perhaps because she was one of the most bossy people that one is likely to come across. She was a school teacher in the Myrtle Point area, inland from the Coast and from the town where her parents lived. She met her cowboy, probably at a dance, and George was substantially older than she, nearly twenty years older. This was unusual, and given her prissiness and desire to be perfectly conforming, Mildred must have been damn desperate to marry the guy.

George the cowboy was thin as a hand-split red-cedar fence rail, and rode a horse as if he were part of it, with absolute grace and rhythm. He was just a ranch hand when he and Mildred married, living in a rough shack out on the cattle range. George made coffee by throwing a hand-full of ground coffee into boiling water, and he sweetened it with condensed milk poured from a can with two holes he punched with his jack-knife. George and Mildred went to Western dances, and especially liked Maddox Brothers and Rose who in the 40s and 50s played Bob Wills' flavored music in California's Central Valley and regularly swung through outlying regions such as Myrtle Point. Rose Maddox was one of those, along with Patsy Montana and Kitty Wells, who opened up country music for strong women, so it is no surprise that Mildred would like her music. "Rose drank too much," Mildred said with disapproval, and then her face brightened. "But oh my goodness could she sing!"

Mildred soon put George to work. They accumulated a ranch choked with greasewood and poison oak on which they ran cattle. Sheep were I believed too much fussy work, although more money could be made than with cattle. I envied my cousins for having such an easy life, as they didn't seem to work much on their ranch. Looking back on their unpainted house and isolated life, and thinking of my spirited but uncompromising aunt, I no longer find much to envy.

Just after World War II there was a family gathering at Mildred's with photos of the women and then the men. It was at the prime of their lives. From left to right appear my mother, Mildred, grandmother Payne and Ben's wife Betty.

I wonder what George thought of Mildred, if he even knew what hit him. He did let her run their entire life. What was notable about him is that he seldom spoke. Now the easy hypothesis is that he couldn't get a word in sideways. This idea has some merit, but even away from his wife for long periods, he just did not talk much. Occasionally he slipped an observation, maybe a one- or two-word comment, into the space of a conversation, and people acted as if it contained great wit. I now think people were just happy to learn George could speak and wanted to encourage it. And as a kid I did not receive any direct words from him until I was old enough to have a trap line. Then at a family gathering at our ranch, I was in the woodshed fussing with my traps, and George came out and asked me what I was catching and how I worked the traps. Amazing, I thought, maybe I really am growing up if George actually speaks to me.

Mildred and George had two sons, Chuck, the mean one, and Ben, a sweet boy who was good-natured and game for anything. Tragedy struck when Ben got polio, and his side was paralyzed, just a year or two before the Salk vaccine was developed. No Langlois child had polio but I could tell by my mother's silence when the subject came up that she worried about it. Years later, learning that most children were immune from polio by viruses picked up in the dirt and that polio was most often a disease of children in sterile environments, I wondered about that. My aunt Mildred kept her house spotless, and her children did not work outdoors. But they were out there in the country and lived in that drafty old house.

It remains a mystery to me, but it made Ben more special. He was determined to do what everyone else did, with his arm in a brace, and he studied hard at school. "Ben will have to make a living with his head," the adults said. None of them knew what that meant, but Ben certainly didn't have many alternatives. He couldn't going to be a ranch hand, and the logging woods or lumber mills were out.

George died of cancer in the 1970s at the age of 92, and as he died, he became thinner and thinner, vanishing before our eyes. Laetrile and probably a little religion was applied to no avail, and knowing Mildred, not too much expense. She had a painting made of him, a big portrait in oils of this slender high-cheek-boned cowboy in a big hat, showing the blood of his Indian ancestors. (It had been conveniently forgotten that George was part Indian. I learned of a relative named Running Fox.) He was beautiful and probably always had been, although I didn't quite know it until then.

After George died, my aunt Mildred took some classes to keep busy. She tried one that taught women how to be good wives, to greet their husband at the door in a nightgown and just make him happy he is a man and his wife is not a feminist. She didn't have a husband on whom to practice what she learned, but that probably was beside the point for her. One of the main directives was not to nag the husband.

"Now that is just too much," she said. "If I hadn't nagged George we wouldn't ever have had anything." She surely was right about that.

In her later years Mildred became warm toward me as did I toward her, and once she brought up my "success." (Success meant that I had left the Coast and had not yet returned in defeat. I even lived out of state.)

"Just how did it happen," she asked, "you coming from the Creek and going so far?"

I realized that she was puzzled as to why her correct behavior and the proper rearing of her children had not resulted in the better product. How had my obviously inferior mother accomplished this? It was a mystery to Mildred but never for a moment diminished her confidence and superior airs. By this time I had come to greatly admire this aged woman so full of energy and vitality. Once she told me a story of my father's driving, of him refusing to admit he had gone the wrong direction. Suddenly she shifted to the early days of my parent's marriage, "Ray was so cold and mean. I used to feel sorry for your mother because of how he treated her."

In the mid 1980s I mailed her an article that appeared in a LA alternative newspaper about Rose Maddox (who had long since broken off from the Brothers), and told her of seeing the tough old lady sing at a small club in Los Angeles.

"She's still got it, and one of her grandsons plays in her band," I told Mildred, and then I had to reassure her that Rose was no longer drinking.

I saw Mildred in Myrtle Point after she gave the ranch to her son Chuck and moved off Catching Creek into town. The Kings had earlier sold their biggest stand of timber and gave the proceeds to Ben for his education and future. Mildred had a full life and kept busy. We walked to her afternoon task of watching over a logging museum in a round house full of an eccentric's collection. The building had been constructed for Chautauquas earlier in the century and had been everything from dance hall to revivalist church. I liked the idea of it as a country-and-western dance hall. I could see the stand for the little band, guitar and fiddle, and imagined drinking bourbon while watching the dancers circle the floor. Suddenly I had an image of Mildred and George dancing the Texas two-step and for the first time in my life it occurred to me that they might actually have deeply loved each other. (When I lived on the Coast I simply assumed that most marriages were feats of mean-spirited bitter endurance.) Mildred and her old cowboy: cheers for them!

That round building with all its history and ghosts was now just a tiny museum in a tiny town far from a main road. I knew most of logging equipment from my own experience, and asked about a object or two I did not recognize and could not figure out. Mildred knew nothing about any of it and was not in the least interested. She just was doing her duty, signing the few visitors in and out. It's how she lived her life; she found out what the rules were and then followed them. That's all there was to it for Mildred. The idea that there were reasons people might have that brought them to her museum and that she might think about how to respond to visitors was not part of her job description.

Myrtle Point had a Senior Citizens Center where Mildred served lunch and dinner; at eighty-five she did not consider herself ready to sit down and be served. That would not be right.

"Why, they give me my meal free. Isn't that just something?"

21 Soldier Ben

Uncle Ben, my mother's brother, was a warm presence at the Payne family gatherings. He was concerned about his children, obviously loved his wife, and was easy with conversation. In other words, he was the opposite of the two men his sisters married. He worked in the plywood plant in Coquille then, and lived on a fifteen-acre farm just out of town with an orchard of filberts, which is what hazelnuts are called in Oregon. He didn't work the farm or even harvest the nuts to sell, but just lived out there, sometimes keeping a pig and some chickens.

He had been born in cold country up near Canada; premature, he fit into a shoebox which on the advice of a doctor was kept in the oven where it would be warm at night. The idea of a small fire to heat the stove for a baby instead of biscuits, a carefully wrapped tiny baby in a shoebox, seems quaint and reckless, but it worked and Ben survived. He remained puny until he was nine-years-old when he had a burst of growth.

And Ben went to high school in McCloud where his father landed at the beginning of the depression. They had the motorcycle gang they called the Staunches, named after the abandoned Morris chair found on the front porch of the house my grandfather rented. Ben was working in a mill when grandfather Payne went back to Powers to finish building his last railroad track. The mill job ended, and Ben went on the road, riding down the highway on his Harley. He needed some money when he came to a small town which had been flooded with roads washed out. They were hiring all the men they could find to shovel mud. He went on the job that night, shoveling mud until 4 AM, then back at 8 AM for another day of it. This lasted three days.

"I like the way you handle a shovel," the foremen told him. "We're letting everyone go. Show up here at 8 o'clock tomorrow." Ben appeared to find he had a job on a crew, building bridges for the California Highway Department.

One of workers on the bridge crew had a sister and told Ben he should meet her because she was going out with a jerk.

"I rode up on my Harley," he told me, "pulled up in front and flipped my wrist, revving the Harley, you know, just like they do today. Then the prettiest little girl I had ever seen came out of the house."

"Hey!" Ben called out. "Want to take a ride on my motorcycle?"

"No, I don't," she answered and went back in the house. Ben went back in a week, tried it again. "Well," she said. "Maybe. OK."

"I never let her off my motorcycle, " Ben told me.

Betty introduced him to trout fishing, something that amazes me as his father was an original trout fisherman. "Dad was just too busy" is how Ben explained that.

The summer of 1994 I visited Ben Payne in Weaverville. I asked him about the war, and he told me that he never talked about World War II. Then I spent the evening listening to him describe his war experiences. At one point, he took me to the back of his trailer, and there over the washing machine was a framed display of Ben's war honors which his wife had made for him while she was dying of cancer and preparing him for life without her. She left him written instructions for running the washing machine and for balancing the check book. Theirs was a real love story. Hanging there on the wall were certificates, the purple heart, the bronze star, other medals and ribbons. Years later I looked him up in the official records and they are missing—who knows what they were all for and what he went through to be awarded them. His wife had also made a scrap book, and we went through it.

"I have only shown this to two other people," he said.

The book was full of cartoons, letters, and press releases, beginning with bootcamp. Basic training sounded like hell. The Olympics were on television, acrobats flipping and turning.

"Have you ever done that?" he asked.

I replied that at no time in my life could I ever have done anything resembling what we were seeing on TV.

"Well, when we trained to become paratroopers, we had to do a lot of acrobatics because who knew how you would land."

After they were trained, he had an interesting opportunity. The usual scenario for sending the paratroopers into battle was to fly behind the lines, drop the men, then repeat this several times, while the opposition would figure it out and know where to shoot. If the men could be sent in on gliders, then they could all be dropped at one time. Problem: Would the chutes open when a paratrooper jumped from a glider? Any volunteers?

"Sure, I'll do it," Ben told them. He went first, and the chute did open. "It was fun," he said emphatically several times. "That sure was fun."

As it turns out, paratroopers at that time could say "No, I won't do that." In the entire army, the only guys who would jump from a glider were the men in Ben's platoon, the men he had talked into it. The whole scheme then folded, and paratroopers went into battle the old way. "I was supposed to get a ribbon or something for that but didn't. You know, we thought we were the top, that no one was our equal." He shook his head in wonder. "Hell, we hadn't even been shot at yet!"

The military reasonably thought that the Panama Canal was vulnerable, and Ben was stationed there for one-and-one-half years. "I liked Panama a lot," he said. The photographs from the canal had a heart-breaking innocence to them, of healthy happy young men who didn't know that they were about to enter Hell.

Then he went to Europe and parachuted into southern France near Nice on one of those after D-Day invasions (August 15, 1944). He had a photograph, widely released to the news, of the drop. Across the horizon is a line of stubby planes, and under that are the parachutes, round with sunlight on one side, shadow the other. They spread over most of the picture below the planes, against the background of the hills of the South of France. The parachutes have not yet fallen so far as to obscure the light, crisp fields at the valley's bottom. It is a awesome photograph, and I said so.

"Well, they planned to drop us at night, but I think they waited until daylight so that they could take this picture."

Puffs of cannon fire appear among the chutes of the paratroopers. How many men died to produce the photograph I admired? He told me a mortar shell blew up a G.I. carrying TNT.

"They ID'ed him by his name tag; everything else was gone. Lots of guys worried about their balls. I always thought I'd get it in the shoulder."

Ben fought in France, and then he walked and fought across all of Italy. "I went over thirty days without washing at all; it is interesting what you can do when it is necessary."

The pictures were now of soldiers in snow. "Gosh, it was cold," Ben said several times. "It sure was cold." The men did not have conversations in the trenches as one might think, he told me, they just quietly waited.

Finally he was wounded in Begium during the Battle of the Bulge. There were only ten or twelve men from the one-hundred-and-fifty in his original drop unit who were still alive in Belgium. Most of those were killed in the Bulge. The unit was discontinued at this time as there were not enough men remaining. Ben told me that in the hospital they left him with a spray bottle, to spray his leg to keep the smell down. He wrote home to his family from his hospital bed and the letter was published in the Coquille Valley Sentinel. His letter haunts me. I have read it many times, and I wonder about the brave good-hearted men who fought and died in yet another war to end all wars. And those who were hardly more than children. Small-town newspapers all over America must have printed letters from wounded and damaged men. Someone should collect them into a volume, but I do not have the courage to read more of them. Letters from men like my kind gentle uncle. For that matter, corresponding letters must exist in Germany, letters from the ordinary men who fought the war, thrust into unimaginable circumstances. There could be two bookending volumes, one from each side of the line. "Now, I have not killed anyone in civilian life," Ben said to me when he was in his eighties.

Early in the evening Ben told me that he took prisoners only early in the war, never again after he saw the results of German tortures. Late in the night, thinking about the end of the war, the end of his war, he told me that the Germans then were fielding very unprepared troops. Once as he was coming along a timbered ridge, he encountered a troop of Germans who "just weren't paying enough attention." He shot one, and there was another, so old that Ben could not believe his eyes.

"What the hell are you doing here?" he asked. A boy came along. "Can I have my grandfather? Bitte, bitte." he pleaded. Ben said he looked from one to the other, paused a long time, and then said:

"OK, just get him the Hell out of here!"

After he was home there was a family gathering at aunt Mildred's with a photo of the men: Ben still wearing his uniform, uncle George, my father Ray and grandfather Payne.

Soon after this, Ben and his father went camping and fishing up the Chetco River, far up the river below the lookout at Quail Prairie. They caught some fine trout, but they went because they needed to go away and be together after the hard times of the war.

"Betty and your grandmother, they understood."

Then he went to work at the plywood mill in Coquille and bought the little farm.

"I bought that farm for my family. Betty didn't have to have any close neighbors, and my kids could grow up free out there, so that they could run up and down the hills. You know, like you grew up."

I didn't tell him that I was far from free as a child, and in fact had deeply envied Patty and Steve for their lives as his children. His deeper motivation for buying the farm probably didn't really make sense, he said. But when he was fighting in Europe, in France, all across Italy and finally in Belgium, he saw that people in the country seemed to have it better in rough times, that country people just lived better during war.

"The country is a better place to be than cities, the world being what it is."

Ben bought a new car every three years, big fat elegant Buicks are what I remember, new cars he drove to the family gatherings in that steady calm never-exceed-the-speed-limit way he had. My father negotiated endlessly with car salesmen when we finally replaced a car. "I Jewed them way down," he proudly muttered. I could not imagine Ben Payne doing anything like that.

By the late 1960s, he was running plywood mills for Georgia Pacific. Georgia Pacific had certain mills that were losing money hand-over-fist. Ben would take over a plywood plant and make it profitable again. I visited him at one of those mills, where my long hair and beard created suspicions at the entry gate. Ben welcomed me, and as he was showing me around, people working the plywood production lines called out to him over the loud noise of the mill, "Hello, Ben." "Hi there! How are you?" he shouted back.

Later we returned to his office, which hung on the edge of the big building above the busy factory. It felt as if it had been tacked up there as an afterthought.

"You know, this is an easy job," he told me. "I come in, and everyone thinks I am going to do something drastic. Well, I get to know them — you know, I've done every job in the plant — and they find out I am just a regular person. Then I ask them what is wrong with the plant and they tell me what is wrong and then I just fix it."

He made enough money in eight years to retire on the Trinity River when he was fifty-five years old. While he said he was in idle retirement, he had a shed full of saw sharpening equipment which for some time was kept busy with huge blades from sawmills. Then as sawmills went out of existence he sharpened hand saws and knives. Not everyone can sharpen saws, he told me. On a visit to see him we walked to a restaurant where everyone knew him, and he promised to deliver their knives "sharper than new" in two days.

I wish I had visited Ben Payne when steelhead still ran the Trinity River in the mountains of northern California, when Ben was living at Big Bar and would catch a steelhead on the short daily trip to get his mail. I imagine him showing me the holds of those fish, telling me where to cast, smiling delightedly when a steelhead hits and strips off my line in a high-pitched reel-screaming run. Instead I came later, after the big dam had killed the wild-fish migrations, after the love of his life Betty had died, when Ben was spending his last years living in a double-wide in Weaverville.

22 Little Charlie

My brother Charlie Henry Waterman born on October 7, 1946 was a great disappointment to me. His name was a disappointment to my mother who, exhausted from giving birth, was unable to prevent my father from filling out the birth certificate with the name he wanted, that of his own grandfather. Resentful at first, my mother quickly became accustomed to the sound of Charlie Henry. My own desires for a companion were more slowly and less satisfactorily fulfilled.

Charlie was fair, with blond hair and skin easily sun-burned even under our cloudy skies. In our house of bland food, he was picky, willing to eat nothing at all rather than to try something new. He hated vegetables and despised peas in particular. Foods like garlic, onion, and artichokes were as foreign to us as China and never appeared on our table. Except in summer the vegetables were usually tasteless, but Charlie Henry refused them anyhow. When he was two, my parents hit on the concept of forcing him to eat one pea per-year of his age. That worked until he was five or six when, I believe, he could see that this was not going to stop, and that he would continue to get more and more peas on his plate, on and on until his plate would be only a mountain of peas. So he abruptly set the dial back to zero peas. There were tears and carrying on, but even my father, who wanted absolute control over his children, was unable to get this frail child to eat one pea. Charlie was served special meals. The rest of us ate one meal, and Charlie had another. His plain food appeared on his plate in discrete, separate clumps, with open space surrounding each clump. These food wars continued into his school years, and I admit that I hated the cafeteria lunches. My brother refused to eat anything that the school served, and soon my mother was packing a box lunch for him, every day of grades 1 through 12. He had his way, with food as with many other things.

About the time Charlie was born, space in the attic was made into a room so that he and I would be out of the lower house. There was a tight, steep stairway up to the room, and eventually both Charlie and I occupied it. As a baby, Charlie developed a habit of putting himself to sleep by emitting a steady sound.

"Whaaaa ..."

He lay on his stomach and pounded his head on the pillow or mattress, continuing the vocal while his mouth was muffled by the pillow.

"Whaaaa—whaa—whaa ..."

The pitch would vary as would the length of time the mouth was covered and uncovered.

A musicologist or psychologist might have made something of this behavior, but he and I were in that room each night, and year after year he continued to pound himself to sleep, driving me crazy. Years afterwards he married, and frequently I was almost overcome by the need to ask his wife if he still whaa-whaa-whaa-ed himself to sleep each night.

My brother had a different early life from my own. Our family saw something about my brother, saw how fragile and vulnerable he was, and he was therefore protected. In the typical fashion of my family, it was unspoken at the time and denied later. While there was as much ranch work as ever that desperately needed done, my brother played with his toys all day and was not given jobs to do. Long after the age I was put to chopping brush all day, and the amount and quality of my work judged harshly at day's end, my brother was making elaborate roads in the dirt for his toy cars and trucks. If he was taken along for work, he stood by while my father and I did the job.

Charlie was put on a horse that my father and I were leading along the road. My brother, who couldn't have been more than five or six, promptly fell off the tall horse. In his John Wayne style, my father put my screaming and crying brother back on, when he promptly fell off again. It was a long way to the ground, and this kept repeating, with Charlie's hysterical cries. I could not think of any way to distract my father and also realized that I could not remember when I learned to ride, to stay up there without fear. Finally my father gave up, and my brother was allowed to walk, sobbing the rest of the way to the house.

When Charlie was six, my father and I were working with the tractor at the creek below the house late one damp fall afternoon. Charlie came down to watch us work, and when it came time to return to the barn, I walked up the hill. Sometimes I rode perched on the tow bar or held onto the back of the tractor when going up hill, but this hill was steep, wet and slick. I refused to go near the tractor when it was going up a sharp incline. Charlie was riding on the tractor with my father, something he frequently did. My father was fearless on the steep slopes with that unstable vehicle. When he tried to drive the John Deere up the muddy track, the vehicle slipped downhill and sideways, almost overturning. My brother fell down between the metal mudguard the large back tire on the right and downhill side. I watched him slip into that wheel-well, thinking he was about to be crushed and killed. Somehow the vehicle stopped sliding and tipping, and Charlie stumbled out muddy but uninjured.

For a long while Charlie did not learn my name and instead called me Bap. My mother was an excellent teacher, and Charlie learned to count to ten without error for the first time the fall he started first grade, when he was almost seven-years old. (It was always said that he was five years younger than I while it was a bit over four years.) He was the youngest in a small family, and we all cared for him, each in their own way. Usually we referred to him as Little Charlie. As for myself, I wanted to shield him from my father, so I did what I could to save him from bearing the brunt of the work and the punishment. When we were left to watch a half-mile of fire line with the dense smoke drifting by, I sent Charlie home as soon as my father was out of sight.

I loved to gather the sheets of mica that existed in some rocky places around the ranch. The flexible texture of the material satisfied something deep within me; even though worthless it was treasure to me. When I was ten, I found a thick-layered deposit on a ledge of a large rock by Frog Creek below the barn. The ledge ran ten to fifteen feet above the rocky and brushy creek bed. I was crawling on the ledge to pry off some mica, and my brother kept trying to come too. I was successful keeping him back until I was far out and frightened, and did not notice Charlie start along the ledge, from which he promptly fell. I was terrified, and repeatedly shouted down to silent willows. So I ran around on the road and down the hill to find him, fearing that he had been killed. Instead there he was, in the heat of the afternoon coming up the bank, a little boy so fair that the sun had bleached his hair almost white with brilliant red blood spreading in rivulets down across his face and dripping off onto his striped t-shirt and the short summer grass and plantnum which was dried to almost the same tawny yellow-white color as his hair. The grasshoppers made their whirring escape while he trudged blindly uphill. I doubt that he could see much, but at the sound of my voice, he picked up some rocks and flung them at me as hard as he could, fury combining with fear and shock. That intense little boy, that bright blood, my relief that he was still alive, for me it still shimmers there in the hot afternoon sun. Realizing I could do nothing for him but be a target for more rocks, I ran straight up the hill and fetched my mother. I am still amazed he was not injured more seriously from that fall. His forehead carried a small dent and almost invisible scar for the rest of his life.

Once he was to meet me at some location on the ranch, and he did not show up. I became worried, and knowing that he had been going to the Mitchell Place, I ran to the upper orchard, then the lower orchard. There was no sign of him. Finally at dusk I found him walking home, and I instantly switched from concern to fury. I laid into him as if I were my father, using identical swear words, phrasing and movements. In the thick of this furious display which my brother accepted as if I were my father, I realized what I was doing and the tirade abruptly halted. At that moment it was absolutely clear to me that if I was not extremely careful, I would grow up to be my father, doing all the things that I hated about him. It was a sobering, totally terrifying thought.

We bought a Jersey cow, pretty and with a calf, and I milked her. She was amazingly spooky, and the least sound caused her to kick the bucket over. I made a campaign to quiet her down, and at one of those times, Charlie sneaked up and threw a rock into the barn that landed by the cow. I lost the milk and was angry with him, thinking for the first time that I had milked for years by his age and why didn't he have to do something other than cause trouble. I was fourteen or fifteen, and he was ten or eleven. The summer I turned sixteen, I had a summer job with the Forest Service, two months at the Coos Bay station. The relevance to Charlie was that he had to milk the cow; at almost twelve, he was finally given a real and steady chore. When I returned, he was a lot nicer to me, and we got along better then.

My dislike of my father was so great, and his sense of being a parent was so vague, that in my habit of protecting my brother from my father, I taught Charlie how to do things which I had learned by trial and error. My father's teaching skills were limited to grunts, disapproval and anger. I taught Charlie to drive the tractor, a John Deere with a front end so light that it was almost impossible to let the clutch out without the front wheels leaving the ground. I taught him how to shoot a gun, showing him how it worked and how to aim it and how to hit what he aimed at. Also he learned what I knew about tools, but he had fine instincts for tools and machinery. And I helped him buy his first car, an old 1939 Chevrolet four-door sedan, a beautiful old machine which we paid $50 for. It had sat on blocks during World War II and had only recently been started up again. I had to purchase the car with Charlie so that my parents would allow it. Charlie was almost fourteen then, and he loved that car. I think the closest I ever felt to him was when he drove me along the ridge of the Indian Allotment, me riding in back on that prewar-plush upholstery and him sitting proudly up front, driving along a trail through the grass. The dry mature pasture of summer brushing against the car's underbelly, mature heads of rye grass and plantnum clicking against the metal.

I built up a herd of one-hundred sheep and six or seven cattle. I kept them the first year I was at college, sharing the profit with my brother who took care of them. Then I realized I was never returning to Four Mile and sold them to Charlie. He also had a small herd of sheep that had been given to him over the years. He built on that, increasing the herd and keeping record books which were superior to the ones I had puzzled out in high school. He thanked me once for not charging him interest. It never occurred to me. I never received my record books back from Charlie; he threw them away. I was already outside the ranch and Four Mile and had lost my rights there, even Charlie knew that.

In school Charlie would solve his mathematics problems and turn in neat papers (in contrast to my messy smudged work). When he made an error of any kind, no matter how trivial, he would throw away the effort and begin anew. His teacher Billy Kolibaba tried to convince him to erase or even to cross out mistakes, but he refused to do that.

My mother had her heart set on a college education for both of her children, and she wanted Charlie to follow my footsteps to Oregon State College. I felt that instead of Oregon State, the Oregon Technical Institute was perfect for him. In fact Charlie would have preferred OTI but went to Oregon State. I helped Charlie by having him live in my house his first year at school, as I was married then. My guess was that the dorm life would have proved difficult for him. He had a difficulty with subjects like English Composition, and I helped him with his essays. He passed two terms then, and on the fifth year of his four-year program, he got a passing grade in the third term of English.

By the time he left college, the Vietnam war was in full throttle. Charlie was no draft-card-burning liberal child of the 1960s. Instead he was a born conservative, never then thinking of being critical of his government. A great many people including me were to be sent over there and killed. As did many others, Charlie joined the National Guard. (I took deferment after deferment.) He went to boot camp in the South, and visited me in Michigan where I was a graduate student. Boot camp solidified his shared prejudices with my parents about Blacks. He came to Michigan on his break so he could go to Detroit and buy a new Corvette, a dream of his. Well, they don't make Corvettes in Detroit, and he didn't order one, all the time saying that if he went home without spending that $5000 dollars, his parents would not allow it.

"Nonsense," I said. "It's your money and you be the one who spends it."

He went home, and he did not ever buy a Corvette. That was the last time, 1967, he visited me anywhere I lived. It was not for lack of invitations.

Instead of buying his dream car he went to work for our father. After a year or two, he bought the Walker Place, about 550 acres, from Ray, and the plan was for Charlie to have the entire ranch transferred to him. Charlie complained to me that he was paying more for the land than what my father had in 1959. That seems OK to me, I said, what could he get for it today? Charlie did not answer.

In the early 1970's, a close friend took a trip to the ranch and reported back amazed. "Your father told me that you hate the ranch," he said. "I told him that was just not true. No one could talk like you do about the ranch and not love it. And you are not going to believe this: your brother is getting the ranch. You are going to be left out." This was no surprise to me, although such things were never discussed. And of course the prediction was 100% accurate. All I ever wanted was to find my own life, and by that time it was clear I had. But events took a different turn which was not reversed for years: the spring of 1975 my brother became furious with our father.

"Get off my land," Charlie told Ray. "And don't never come back!"

They did not speak for six months, our father shocked with the realization that if you sell land you no longer own it. I heard of this from our mother; as usual I had to sense something wrong and then to pry it out. I was in transition, having returned to Idaho to pack for a permanent move to New Mexico. I took time from packing and settling my affairs to drive across two states and get my father and brother to speak again to each other. We had a barbecue, and they could not find excuses not to see me and consequently each other.

This split caused my brother to go to work for Production Credit Association, a company making loans to farmers and fishermen during the land inflation of the 1970s. The Walker Place was a nice place to live, but the property was too small to support a family. A few years later the value of land crashed, and my brother's conservative approach to loans, surely learned from our father's cautious practices, made him look like a hero. He was rapidly promoted to a higher office where his abrupt style caused him to leave the company. By that time wounds had healed, and he came back to Four Mile to run the ranch.

"I just don't know what Charlie would have done if we hadn't given him a job," my mother told me after that.

"He would have looked around like anyone else and would have gone where he could get work," I replied. "What do you think he would have done?" But there she was, still protecting Charlie. I did not mention that I had left Los Alamos Labs and did not have a job after a visiting position ended in two months.

Once in later years my aunt Mildred and I went off on being oldest children. I told of Charlie's increased appreciation of me after my summer with the Forest Service, when he finally had to milk the cow. My mother who was listening to us was shocked.

"But he was just a little boy!" He was twice the age when I had regularly milked the cows, but Charlie was just a little boy who had a childhood.

My brother had two children, Franklin and Amy. Franklin had his father's innate skills with tools, and he was an excellent mechanic. He had no intellectual interests, preferring hunting and fishing to reading. I called him on his sixteenth birthday; he was not home but out in his pickup spotlighting skunks in the road and shooting them with his birthday present. AK-47s were about to become illegal, so his parents bought him one. A Russian-designed Chinese-manufactured AK-47, the weapon of the enemy in Vietnam, was that evening laying out an arc of bullets on a Four Mile road with that flat slap-slap-ping as they struck dust and grass and gravel. I never heard how many skunks died that evening. Franklin went to technical school at Bend in eastern Oregon, and stayed there for a few years. He didn't like working for his grandfather or ranching. He returned to the Coast to run a garage in Bandon.

Charlie's younger child Amy did almost no ranch work, and consequently thought the ranch was *the* perfect place to be. She had elevated intellectual ambitions, although I could not understand what subject she was pursuing. But her goal was clearly stated: she wanted to become a college professor and pass what she knew on to her students. This seemed far from my grandparents Waterman who optimistically creaked across Oregon in that wagon. She said she wanted to change the world, and I said that biotechnology or computer science were the two subjects that had the most potential for that. This was not what she wished to pursue. Finally I said, "Well Amy, I had an advantage when I went to college. I knew I was dumb." She shot back: "But uncle Mike, I am from here and I know I am smart!" Amy refused to go to one of the state universities and instead attended an expensive private school with a much lower academic rank.

My brother, distinguishing himself from our father, loved his children deeply, and unlike most people his age, thought the new generation far superior to earlier ones.

Once I made the observation that my father had no friends of his own, that his entire social life was arranged by my mother. When I told my brother this, he became silent and remote. Later I realized that his life was identical, that except for one or two college friends who lived conveniently far away, he seemed to have no friends or social life except as arranged by his wife.

For years I called Charlie on his birthday. He never returned the calls, on my birthday or otherwise. Still I continued to do this. Then one year, some environmental issue arose in the conversation, and although I did not voice the strength of my opinion, I did say that there were arguments on both sides. He became angry, with suppressed but evident anger.

I waited until I was in Oregon and picked a time when we were alone. He was filling a stock trough with water. I told him that I could tell he had been upset, and that while I did not think I had done anything wrong, I hoped he would tell me if I had, as he was important to me.

"I was so surprised that you would be in favor of these environmental regulations," he started off by telling me. "You are *from here*."

Then his monologue went in another direction, concentrating on how under appreciated he was, and on how the government regulations hampered and restricted him.

"There is no one telling you what you can and cannot do, is there!"

I told him he could not imagine the regulations of universities and government grants, but that made no impression. We were at his barn, inside of which his son was overhauling an engine and rebuilding a jeep, overlooking the Pacific Ocean. His land surrounded us for a radius of at least one-half mile, and his house built of wood logged from all corners of the ranch stood nearby with wide views and a native-rock fireplace, high above the protected building sites that the homesteaders used. It was difficult to sympathize with him, but I kept my mouth shut and let him recount his persecutions.

The old idea of being the king of your own property comes into this. Regulations for safe use of pesticides were absurd, according to Charlie.

"If I go out there to spray, I am the one who gets the most exposure. What business of the government is it?"

I didn't suggest that the folks downstream might have stake in it too, the subject was too volatile. When some water rights legislation was passed, Charlie feared that eventually the legal right to water the livestock might be taken from him. "I just hope I can go on raising stock on this ranch," he told me. I have heard this rancher's refrain from Alberta to Idaho to New Zealand. So much of the world has changed, continues to change, and all Charlie wanted to do was to be able to go on raising cattle and sheep exactly as his father had.

"The talk around Bandon is that your brother has become mean and that now he is just as bad as your father," Aloma Gamble told me with concern. "I cannot believe that it is so." When I told her that I was not surprised, she shook her head. "He was such a sweet boy." There was a long silence. "Such a sweet sweet boy."

23 Town Trips

Visitors from town were rare, there being little reason for anyone not living on Four Mile to go there. One of those who came drove his car up the little hill to our house, and parked his car awkwardly straddling a flag bush on the slope. He set the hand brake, and then carefully locked the car doors before approaching my father who was loading fence posts into a trailer. The man's questions were answered by deep, brief grunts, and the loading went on uninterrupted. Eventually the visitor gave up in disgust, returned to his car, unlocked it and drove away. My father told of this for years.

"That bastard," his account concluded. "Locked his car right up. Right there in front of me. Son-of-a-bitch thought I was gonna steal somethin'."

I am sure that the guy drove down the crooked dusty road thinking that my father was a rude and uncivil man, and that neither of them understood what happened that cloudy afternoon.

For years we got our mail at the Four Mile Store, just three-quarters of a mile toward Bandon from where the upper Four Mile Road hit Highway 101. This was a combination store, gas station and Post Office. Decades before 7-11 spawned the convenience store, the Four Mile Store filled the same role. Both U.S. mail and gossip was available seven days a week.

I best liked going in with my grandfather, up over the worn stoop with its wood steps chewed away by years of logger's calked boots, into the dark store. We got the mail, and then my grandfather would hang out, there is no other way to put it, talking and idling away the afternoon. He would smoke and maybe get a soda pop. It was from him that I learned to savor the variety of flavors. Grape soda, cream soda, root beer were learned from my grandfather: try this, drink it slowly, breath in some air so you can taste it, like this ... Leaning against that red cooler with the silver top which I hinged up and then slid the cold, icy pop bottle along its groove and up out through the tight opening, and finally pried the bottle top off with that satisfying whoosh. There was nothing else so luxurious in my life.

We bought almost no groceries at the store as it was more expensive being so remote. There was an array of candy, always coveted by me but seldom purchased, and snacks and small groceries. The tourist business picked up in the summer, and stop they did, usually frightened by the curves and log trucks, sweating and ill-at-ease. I wondered at the things they bought, wondered if they ate like that on their whole trip and what they ate in their own homes.

I doubt that anyone made much money running the Four Mile Store. After the mail was delivered to rural mail boxes instead of picked up at the store and they lost the Post Office franchise, the Four Mile Store was doomed. In the late sixties, someone had a crazy dream to make an amusement park there. They put up signs advertising a Game Park, then built high fences to block the view unless you paid to go inside. Traffic has increased and blasts along year-round today, cars full of tourists desperate to find something to do that makes their trip different from staying home, and the penned-up game-animal park has prospered beyond anyone's greatest expectation. I think now that it is a payoff to those generations who bought a cheap roadside business in hopes of hitting it big, and especially to all the previous owners of the Four Mile Store. I have no idea what my grandfather Waterman would make of it, but in a dream I drive him there to show him how things have changed.

"Want to go inside?" I ask him, and we go in and look it over, two men in denim you would be surprised to see at Disneyland.

Trips to town were infrequent too, and when they occurred, they were usually to get something for the livestock or for the repair of failed machinery.

"We're goin' to town Mom," my father would mutter to my mother if he was near enough to the house to let her know.

She never came along and never asked about the trip; it was the man's domain and she had given up her claim to that territory. Sometimes there was a ranch task for me while my father was gone, and I was left to it, that being fairly pleasant. It meant a few hours of uncriticized activity, shoveling or chopping or nailing. I could work hard for thirty minutes and then slack off, sometimes even escaping to the timber or creek if I happened to be assigned to jobs in the best locations, other times just getting behind a hill out of the wind or rain to daydream. It was important to be at the job when my father returned, probably receiving a little more more criticism than if I had done a really bang-up job which would have been inadequate in any case.

Other times I was told, "Get in." Probably there was a job to do on the way to or from town, that being the motive to take me, but sometimes he just didn't want to leave me alone not working. Down the road we went in that old Studebaker truck running whichever rebuilt engine it had that year.

Our road crossed the North Fork of Four Mile Creek just upstream from a beautiful meadow at the joining of the streams. Steep heavily forested land enclosed this tight damp chilly place. Just across the road was the home of Mrs. Whitman, a remarkable woman who outlived several husbands. Her two daughters Inez and Leona married two full-blooded Indian brothers Elmer and George. Leona and Elmer lived a hundred yards upstream from Mrs. Whitman in a tiny house that had once been a schoolhouse, and Inez and George had a small ranch a mile upstream on the North Fork where the valley began to open up. Elmer and George were social men, ready to stop their pickups or work to talk. Mrs. Whitman was unlike anyone I knew, she could talk about nothing for hours. Selling magazines for my school, I spent over two hours with her without coming close to making a sale. Only darkness saved me, and I left with a faint implication that she might spend money if I came back for more talk. She leased her dew-jeweled meadow, the most handsome property on Four Mile Creek, to Fisk a gyppo mill-owner, and after the mill was going, she married a young mill-hand who was at least forty years her junior.

"You know what he's after," people on Four Mile said. "You know damn well what he's after. But he's got his self a surprise a comin'!"

He tried to stop work but Mrs. Whitman kept him going to the mill. We called her Mrs. Whitman no matter whom she was married to. She received his pay directly from Fisk and handed out a bit for an allowance. After a year he realized he was not going to inherit anything soon and disappeared. The mill went bust after a few years, the millpond eventually drying up to be overgrown by alders and willows. Over twenty years later my brother filled in the pond and cleaned up the scrap. Mrs. Whitman was delighted as she paid Charlie $400 less than the deposit Fisk forfeited by not returning the land to its original condition, never mind the destruction of the fertile field which had gleamed with morning dew. "I came out ahead," she said. "I made money on that deal." My brother had in the same year not only concluded conversations with Mrs. Whitman, he had actually extracted money from her; obviously he had talents I did not possess. Mrs. Whitman lived to be 100, triumphant over the variety of social and economic conditions of her century, talking the ear off anyone she could corner or trap right up to her last few days.

On the Four Mile road meeting someone meant stopping to talk, stopping immediately in the road blocking the traffic, which almost never came along. The men sat a few moments, silent in their still vehicles, and unless it was raining or they were in a hurry, they slowly got out. One might sprawl across the hood of a pickup with Stetson tipped back, elbows just holding his body up from the engine's heat, while the other leaned back against a car fender, chewing a long joint-stemmed stalk of Johnson grass, eventually creating a cud large enough to spit in a big wad back over his shoulder toward the ditch. The conversation could be interesting, especially during hunting season or the salmon runs when deer, fish, and the gathering of them could spring into the conversation at any time. Mostly though it was dull stuff to a boy, and I tuned in and out. A favorite topic was tracing who did what in the dim past. Was there an outhouse behind the Billings' house when Jackson owned it or was that just during the old homestead? Remember Merchant's uncle who came out to visit and broke his ankle in the gully next to the barn? Current events consisted of leaking roofs, visits to neighbors and to town, and the endless story of animals and crops and condition of land and property, sub-textual tallies of who was doing better and worse with their ranch. Nothing escaped attention, certainly not big trips that might be made to remote places. Remote being fifty miles or more. On the rare occasions that someone travelled over the Coast Range to the Willamette Valley to buy or sell animals, the trip of about one-hundred-and-fifty miles was news.

"Did you hear about Deos?"

"Yep, guess they went Outside. Bought some damn expensive ram. A Romney."

"They don't do well here in the air, over here when they ain't used to it."

That sent me in a spin, thinking of my own two of trips Outside to the Valley and what the weather and roads and houses were like, wondering what it was like to live there among all those people. Finally the conference would end, and we'd go on down the road.

Spud McCloud was stubby man who forced those he met to stop whenever he could block the road with his wreck of a pickup. He was ragged and dirty with a wild curly head of hair and the only beard on Four Mile. His hair was a light-orange color while his face seemed permanently to be pink. The McClouds had a ranch on the headwaters of the North Fork, a hilly place that once it was logged off had never been burned so that it was jumbled with logging trash, fireweed, alders, and eroded traces of logging roads. Their sheep received the same care as the their land: none. The stock ran free with fat tails and enormous loads of rattling dried pellets of manure on their rear ends. You could hear them, even when they were invisible in the brush. Those sheep were nearly wild animals, almost impossible to bring in except with a rifle. And Spud himself was barely in control, angry at everything he encountered. He would carry on in his Scotts burr complaining about the condition of the road, an imagined theft of sheep by one of his neighbors, and any trace of government authority of which he became aware. Spud hated taxes most of all. One day when my father was serving on the school board, Spud caught us working sheep in the Lower Place corrals. He and my father stood by a pile of old lumber, and Spud carried on a long monologue during which he became more and more outraged. Toward the end of his tirade when he was almost shouting, he picked up a small board and for punctuation he struck the lumber pile with it. Soon he was taking his fury out on the lumber, and first the bark and then pieces of board began flying. I wondered what he would do when the stick had totally shattered, and edged away. When Spud worked the stick down to a splintered stub, he seemed to wake up, surprised to find himself standing there with a piece of wood in his hand. There was a long silence as they stood there, my father twice Spud's size, and then Spud went back to his rusty mud splattered pickup, his muttering increasing as he stomped away.

Reaching the highway we turned right for Bandon and left for Langlois. Usually it was Langlois, a few miles closer, possessing most of what we needed or at least most of what we could expect to find. Just on the outskirts was a feed store, Barklow's Feed and Seed later on during my childhood, that was a place to get certain tools and especially feed, such as grain for the horses and milk cows. If there wasn't something to use me for, sometimes I was forced to stay in the truck and wait. At least I could not screw up when I was in the truck. The down side was that my father might engage in an endless conversation for one or even two and more hours, and there I was trapped in a small space. Once ordered to stay, I could not just decide to come in, that would have been a loss of control.

My father desperately wanted to be accepted and admired, and he tried to fit himself into the talk. Unfortunately he understood less and less of what was said for every foot of distance he placed between himself and his ranch. He tried to be tough, and he came out mean. He tried to be all knowing, and he produced some gems.

"That's a car. Yeah, that's a car, that's for sure," he offered in response to a new design from Detroit. "Yep that's a car."

He was as cryptic to those men as he was to me, but he spent hours trying to belong. I believe this is why he joined the Masons. When the subject of Blacks came up, I heard my father say "I saw them, too. There in Frisco. I was drivin' through and all them were out. Just standin' on the street. I had the woman right there. In the car." This was 100% of my father's life experience with Blacks, seeing them in San Francisco as he drove by.

Inside, the feed store was clean and had the smell of oats, barley and especially of molasses and alfalfa, sweet and decaying at the same time. I didn't often eat the molasses pellets we threw to the sheep on the range during the wet cold winters, but when I did chew one the sharp, musty flavor matched its odor perfectly. Loading the stuff we bought was usually easy, a few fifty- to one-hundred-pound sacks of feed. Sometimes we bought block salt for the animals on the range, small one-pound bricks and big 25-pound blocks drilled with a hole so they would slide onto a pipe driven into the earth and be held off the ground. I liked to take a lick of the salt when no one was looking; the grains were large and sharp enough to cut my tongue. When we got the winter supply of pellets — nibs — it was a lot harder, an hour and more spent carrying and swinging sacks from platform to floor to truck bed. And then there were the truck loads of alfalfa bound with baling wire that we tossed into piles in the barn after feeding the hay. Without balin' wire I cannot imagine we how could have run a livestock ranch. Still this was work in the presence of others, and I noticed that my father was less harsh while other people were around. Anything I did that caused people to notice me, even it was taken positively by those people, was the basis of his strong anger later, so I tried to remain as invisible as possible.

Usually there was more conversation at the store, distinct from that along the creek. Here a different set of people were talked about, including the school administration and coaches and teachers. I am not sure why, most of these people really did not care much about the education we were getting. Probably they saw the taxes for the schools (and roads) as some of the government imposition that they could affect. And the teachers and administrators were outsiders so they were both of interest and suspect. Any differences in clothes, language or attitude was a conviction, as good as if it was from a judge and jury for stealing. By far the conversation which now interests me the most — certainly not then — is that concerning prices of wool, lambs, and cattle. They had indirect information about these prices as they occasionally saw a newspaper;

mostly the prices discussed were those offered to various ranchers by traveling dealers. There were options of a restricted kind: you could sell early before the livestock were ready, gambling on the commodity price going down. No one played the market except through the livestock dealers, and never did someone even suggest there was a larger context or another way to do the selling. These men with limited world views and extremely scant information about national and international events were gambling in almost complete darkness.

"What do ya know? McKenzie givin' sixteen and a quarter [cents per pound] fer feeders to that old man on Pend's place. Huh. Price 'll go up, ya'll see."

Next along the way was the Aldrop Garage. Here the odor was different, of old oil and kerosene and diesel and gas. Parts were strewn everywhere, and people were briskly moving about. Here I was always let out of the truck. My father was a mediocre mechanic, something I didn't know then. My attempt in all these environments was to slip by unnoticed, if the effort that involved could be considered a slide. There was some great stuff laying around the garage: big rusting gears sitting in pools of old oil seeping into the ground, car doors ripped from their frames leaning against knots of logging cables, fragments of huge saws blades from mills waiting to be used for something else. The pulse and urgency of the place came from loggers more than farmers or ranchers. Their trucks or log loaders or mill equipment broke down and had to be fixed, as soon as possible. These guys were good mechanics, so when they needed a garage, it was a collaboration and not a giving over of an impossible task to a greasy priest of tools. The background was the sound and odor and flashing light from arc welders. My vivid memories of this joint have tall pumps for gas and diesel out front with everyone filling up: the loggers in a rush to get back to the woods, the farmers who have a big tank of cheaper gas at home mounted over a ring of petrol-killed grass but are buying a little gas for the pickup just because they are a little low, and tourists from California who are shell shocked at the endless curves — "Don't you have any straight roads in this state?" — and are getting fuel so they will die with gas in their tank at least. I was fascinated by the tourists. They appeared to have descended from another planet and had nothing in common with anyone I knew, and this was one of the few places I could see them up close. I think they were as interested in us as I was in them, but not much crossed the cultural barrier. Here too the wait for our business could stretch into oblivion. It was a toss up: if the cutter-blade frame on the hay mower was cracked, it might be a long wait to get it fixed but that just postponed the inevitable work that piled up behind the uncut hay. Aldrops was a interesting place with more dimensions that the creek road or feed store.

The third place we often went was to Luke Henry's Hardware Store. It was a square two-story building which seemed tall, made of weathered, unpainted boards. The porch sloped out and down toward the highway, and inside it was a dimly lighted and generally disorganized place. Here I hated to be left in the truck. Inside there was stuff and stuff and more stuff piled into rows between what must have been intended as isles but what seemed to me like trails, so many things heaped there that I could always find something that I had not discovered before and wonder just what it was and how it was used. Back on one side was a fishing counter, my love fishing featured with cheap poles, handfuls of hooks, some bobbers and line and reels and other fishing gear. I never was allowed to spend a cent on fishing, but I received hours of pleasure looking at that display. Then when I was back at home I could daydream about what it might be intended for. It did not stop there: cooking equipment was piled beside another isle where you could pick out a present for your mother when you couldn't get to a bigger town for a birthday or Christmas, hinges and bolts and cotter pins and nails, barrels of nails and staples which were measured out in the tin scoops that they were gathered into, then knives and axes and hammers and sledges and wedges in another area. It went on and about in this cramped space. I think the Henrys might have lived on the second floor, but I'm not sure. The store was confined to the ground floor and seemed endless like one of those mathematical tricks you see that show how boundless infinity can be concealed in a bounded space, only I knew nothing of those ideas then; there was the excitement of the novel and the unknown which was perhaps unknowable. I do not believe my father knew I liked Luke Henry's more than the other places.

Conversation here was of another variety. People came in to buy rope or chain or fence staples and stayed to talk to bald Luke who probably knew more about the inhabitants of Langlois (with less than one-hundred people) and the surrounding regions than anyone. He had an even quality, a steadiness, not worried about his own place in things and not trying to be responsible for the rest of the world either. Certainly he was an interesting person: who else could have assembled that magnificent pile? He had a complex connection with the world outside, and I think he was born on the Coast but was less insular than the others. The people in Luke Henry's would talk about anything, including politics.

"That Wayne Morse, he's somethin' ain't he? The son-a-bitch sure has some ideas but ya know they hear of old Oregon when he gives em hell!"

U.S. Senator Wayne Morse was dean of the University of Oregon's law school before he became a politician. He was liberal and had few beliefs in common with these men, but they respected his honesty and integrity and his giving them all hell in the name of the state of Oregon.

There was a room toward the back of the store which had almost no light, but I was drawn to it where I stared at the deer antlers nailed to the wall, a half-dozen antlers sawed off the heads of Coast blacktails. This was as close as myth came into my life, close enough to touch: these wild and almost intangible creatures brought to earth and into our lives. Otherwise they were just glimpsed on the edge of the timber or in an old man's stories. One afternoon there were a few men in this dark room talking with all their long pauses, and Luke told a story.

"There was a feller come by once from California with a big car and California plates and shiny paint. [In our country, the salty Coast air put an end to shiny soon after purchase.] He wanted gas, we had gas then out front by the highway, and then he got interested inside the place. He had a woman out there in the car, a young one and he weren't no new chicken his-self, I tell ya. He kept her out there or she wouldn't come in, I don't know which. But she damn well never set foot outside the car. He pays me and then asks me can he look around, did you ever hear of that? A few of us was talking back here and he comes in and just lights up when he sees them horns. What's the stories behind them horns? he asked. No stories, I said, Them's just horns. Well, how much you asking for the horns, he asks me, and I tell him, Ain't for sale. No, he says, now how much, and takes some money out of his pocket. Pretty quick he is at $50 and then $75 — hell he could have bought the damn land them deer lived on for that kind of money. I tells him no again and pretty quick he comes to the nub: I will give you $100 and you keep the horns, just tell me their stories. I told you, I said, There ain't no stories. Well, the bastard left $100 just sitting on the counter and his address. I said, I won't take it, and he said he would wait for me to mail the stories to him in California and if I didn't mail them he'd come back. You know he was a writer fella, got money for writing up stories, he wanted to know about these so he could write 'em up. Yeah, some kind of writer from Frisco or the Bay there. I sure didn't send anything and he didn't get back here."

As it was hunting season, Luke then told the tale of killing one of the fine bucks that had his horns nailed to that wall. I always wondered if Luke kept the $100. Later when I went to college and took American literature, I imagined Jack London sitting out there in the car with his young companion, wondering just how he had screwed up and missed out. This scrubby Oregon Coast certainly was a far cry from the bars of Alaska where you could have a drink and talk to people.

Some years after that the old building caught fire late one night and burned down. A crew of people rallied to fight the fire, but the building was so dry that the weathered wood burned like a tall stack of kindling. People tried to rescue some of the goods and were confused as to what to carry out. Things were not arranged by value, that's for sure. But the people kept dashing back inside, bringing amazing goods out to the bright flickering light, things like axes, knives and kettles that had not been manufactured for fifty years and more. And then it was over, just a pile of glowing coals and ashes.

This story of the old hardware store burning came to me from my mother along with an image of the uncovering of old goods. Then years later I was driving through Langlois, and noticed a building close to where my memory locates Luke's old store. Apparently the store that burned was not Luke's. The fire could have been in Bandon, and my mother so disconnected from world beyond her doors that she thought it happened in Langlois. I did not ask her or attempt to settle the matter; it seemed best to let it be. Memories and ashes.

24 Road War

My father's battle with John Henry Long who lived up the muddy dirt road from our house began before I was born. Their quarrel took form in the road, and I will come back to that. The Long ranch figured into our family stories from the beginning. When my grandparents first moved to the Oregon Coast, they lived in a shack on a lonely butte east of the Indian Allotment above what was then the Cope Place, and daily my grandfather hiked down to work in the dairy. My father was born in the Cope house, and his twin June died there at birth. A locally famous round barn was built there where the cows ate their hay standing in a semicircle below the hay loft. Grandfather helped build this barn; everyone helped in major building projects.

The Longs ended up with the Cope place, and Mrs. Long had three sons. One son, Marlin, and his new wife were living there at the time my parents married, and Troy was born at about the time I was. The few visits I had from a child my own age were made by Troy. Those events are documented by snapshots in which Troy's mother appears as a wan poorly nourished child herself. Marlin left not long after Troy was born, and another Long son, John Henry, just back from World War II, took over. Soon he courted and married Marie who was fifteen and lived on lower Four Mile. I heard an ugly story about that. On his wedding night, John stumbled into a bar and drank several quick whiskeys.

"Boys," he said, "I just married the Anderson girl and she is in a room up at the hotel. I give it to her as much as I can but she just won't quit. If any of you want to help me out, I'll show you the way."

I do not believe this story and my father never repeated it, but it shows that not everyone liked John Henry Long. For that matter, not everyone liked my father. Neither of them were what you could call warm or sociable.

The road on our fork of Four Mile Creek was never paved, although in the late 1960s the main Four Mile road was covered with blacktop. The road from the highway was maintained by Coos County up to the last turn in the road before our house. The original arrangements were measured out in units between bends in the road. For convenience, the road equipment turned around at our house, and therefore county maintenance of the road stretched to our house. The homesteads that were originally beyond our house had by this time been taken over by my father or John Henry, and there was eventually only one family living there, the John Henry Longs. The Longs had one-half mile of road to drive beyond our house before they entered their ranch. That one-half mile was the focus of great hostility. I think the crux of matter was who controlled the road, my father who owned the land or John Henry who had legal right of access and must drive on the road to get to his land. I do not know who had the legal obligation to keep the road in repair, but there was no peace on this matter.

When John first asked to grade the road, my father told him to go ahead. But John also ditched as well as graded, and the ditch placed a gap between the road and fields my father wanted to drive into. So the ditches were then filled at the fields by my father, then re-ditched by John, and these men grimly shoveled dirt, mud and rocks in and out of the ditches, over and over, without ever directly discussing what they were doing and why. My father said he told John, "You fix it," meaning the road, but the conflict never ended. If the road was graded and it rained, the grade and road was damaged by the steady rain. Never mind that rain was unavoidable except in the brief summer months; this was John's fault. If mudholes were filled with gravel, the gravel was composed of rocks too small (or too large) to do the job according to the one who had not done the filling. And so it went, on and on and on.

In a few years, the post World War II housing boom created a market for lumber, and ranchers had been cutting and burning timber to get at the land to grow grass. Now they could sell the trees, and small logging outfits, known as gyppos, moved into the area to cut and haul the logs to sawmills. My mother hated the log trucks that spun dust into clouds which settled onto her furniture and floors. After a year or two of campaigning, she pressed my father into trucking our logs down a special road made yearly into the creek-bed. There were no so called environmental laws then. My father did not allow John to use our road for his logs. So John's logs went over his ridge and down the main fork of Four Mile, at great inconvenience and significant expense. And John was just as stubborn as my father. When he decided to sell his logs, he fell the trees himself. He bought a small bulldozer and pulled the logs to a landing where he loaded his logs onto his own truck. Most men who logged alone died alone. My father waited to hear that John Henry had been killed or injured. That never happened.

And both men strove to one-up the other. John had five daughters, all younger than I. After each was born my father would tell him, for example, that in many cases the third child was a girl but then the fourth was a boy. This was telling as sons were needed for the endless labor, and daughters, it was believed, could only help with the much less-essential housework. My father considered this one of his funniest jokes, each new daughter became a laugh line. And, my father told us, sons can carry on the family name. I don't know if John was jealous of my father, but I do know my father thought so and felt superior because of his ability to father sons. Without sons, John ranched alone, hiring no one to help.

John Henry ran his range to the limit, and my father was proud of our longer feed and better conditioned stock. You could see it at the long boundary fences, taller grass on our side next to the chewed-to-the-ground Long range. Probably John Henry made more money than we did on the same acreage, but during tough weather, his animals suffered. "His stock shore is poor this year," said my father referring to their skin-and-bones condition. My father was more concerned with the appearance of his land and stock than with the bottom line, although he never would have admitted it.

They each threatened lawsuits but were too cheap to actually go to court. John looked into getting the rest of the road onto county maintenance but failed. Still, they consulted lawyers more than once over turnouts, log trucks and who knows what. They each had friends or spies in the courthouse who told the other what was up. It was like getting dogs together in hopes they would fight.

Finally it came full circle. My father was driving on the disputed road and met a Long son-in-law on a sharp turn. Neither would budge, while either party could have easily backed up and let the other by. A grandchild was sent up the road for John Henry, but as my brother Charlie told it, they didn't know that he was working nearby. The exact significance of this escapes me, but he emphasized the point. Finally my brother came up to the vehicles and demanded to know why the man did not give way. He answered, saying that my father Ray could move ahead.

"Why don't you back up?" said my brother loudly. "What are you trying to teach these children?"

"I am teaching them to stand up for themselves!" the young man answered, raising a clenched fist.

My brother came back with a line which sums it up for me.

"Well, you oughta be ashamed of yourself!"

25 Burning Off

I was fourteen and we were planning to burn logging slash on the Wilson Place. My father had saved on fire trail against the Walker Place which was being logged at that time. The man from the Forest Service was walking the fire line on the south side of the Wilson Place with me and was quite winded. Catching his breath, he noticed that I walked up the slope easily. I told him I ran at night and pointed across the valley to where I ran the roads in my work shoes. He looked at the distance and rugged terrain and just shook his head. Probably he was too tired to look carefully at my father's thin fire trail on the other side and he approved the fire permit.

We set it off the next morning. My father left my brother and me to watch the south side of the fire, and he went to the west side against Walker's. I worried about my brother in the fire and sent him home as soon as my father was out of sight. The fire was burning pretty well already in the morning but then it got going. I ran my horse up and down the steep slope putting the fire out as it burned up to the trail. I ran for pleasure, but burning was serious and you saved yourself for real work. Over against Walker's, the fire was going strong, sending huge billows of smoke, doing some good as my father would say, but it had obviously gotten out and was burning on Walker's. This gave me even more motive with my side of the line. If it got away and the only bulldozer in the country was already being used on Walker's, there would be a lot of damage that we would be liable for. I did fine until about 1 PM when the fire jumped the trail and got into an old snag about twenty feet high. I worked that afternoon with an axe and shovel and wet sack as hard as I ever have. As the snag burned, embers fell and blew off of it to start new fires. I would get the fire trailed and contained and that rotten snag would spot-fire once again. Several times I was sure it was gone and that thousands of acres would be burned. But somehow I held it, clearing off a lot of ground on the steep slope downwind from that snag. When things looked better, I ran my horse as fast as she would go to the spring for more muddy water for my sack bucket. I didn't go home until almost midnight and wondered about my father and the glowing roaring Walker hillside. Every so often another tree would explode in flames and flash the sky. With the help of a bulldozer, he had stopped the fire at the ridge, with some timber lost on Walker's. My father never said anything to me about the fire I stopped that afternoon; we never spoke about it. Still I knew that in the smoke and heat I had saved us from a disaster.

Fire was a tool to clear the land and to keep the brush and trees from growing back on the cleared land. Left to itself for a few years, the hilly ground is soon covered with alders, and after a few more years, conifers begin to grow up through the alders. A cycle from burned slopes to mature climax firs is about one-hundred years, so in an amount of time equal to that of European settlement, Four Mile could look as if no humans had been there. After a few centuries more, old-growth firs and red-cedar giants would return to walk the land.

The Indians, my grandfather Waterman told me, set fires on a regular basis. This kept some clear, open areas, and the big timber seldom burned because there was not much left to burn under the trees. This strategy depended on regular fires. Otherwise there was too much forest litter and the whole country would burn up. Clearings were essential for growing browse for animals like deer, elk, and even rabbits. Under the canopy of the big firs and cedars, there was little undergrowth, and consequently there was no food to support those animals. My father said the small natural prairie on the Indian Allotment was the result of this strategy.

So we burned whenever we could, creating a livestock ranch by slashing and burning. Fortunately the soil chemistry of the North American continent makes this a viable strategy: after burning, the soil remains fertile. In South America, slash and burn yields one or two crops, and the land is ruined. Essential nutrients are lost forever, and the land cannot revert to the former jungle. Our never ending battle with the brush was a sign of our good fortune, although I never saw it that way when at the job of clearing land.

On September 26, 1936, fire exploded in the countryside in and around Bandon. The usually cool humid weather vanished; instead it was so dry and hot that people were uncomfortable just sitting. People living on the Coast find eighty-degrees unbearably hot, so they thought they were in hell. When fire started breaking out, everyone went to work, at first fighting fire and then trying to escape fire. The Bandon Fire almost completely destroyed the town.

On Four Mile, no houses were lost thanks to cooperation between neighbors. My father told of fighting off the fire at my grandfather's house when news came that fire was threatening a house on the main fork. Immediately they rushed over and saved that house. They spent a day and a night racing up and down the roads. Some outbuildings were lost, but that was a small price. There was no hope of stopping the flames; they just fought fire at the houses and let the rest of the country including the livestock burn up.

Later George Deos came to get my grandmother. "Mabel, can you come over? Anna needs some company." After the world had burned up, his wife was upset and needed some comfort. "I never thought he was that kind of man," said my mother who knew these people later.

After World War II, most major land clearing was by logging. The post-war possibility of selling the trees that stood between the landowner and his dreams of grass must have seemed a miracle. Logging was all clear-cut, leaving the country devastated. Big bulldozers built roads everywhere and pulled out the salable portions of the timber. Stumps were as dense as the trees had been, and limbs, treetops, and rotten logs covered the land. It was not a pretty sight but was only the first step for the ranchers. Their next move was to wait until the litter was dry enough to burn well. That was in the fall, hopefully after a dry July and August. Then they took a box of matches, figured the winds and where they might stop the fire, and then touched it off. These were big fires as there was a lot of fuel. Often they set the fire on the windward side, where they could control it and created a fire line as they went. Then the fire had to burn into the wind to reach more fuel. That could work and often did, but of course winds change or the fire just might not burn against the wind.

A wildfire can burn timber, especially when it is so hot that the fire crowns, burning from treetop to treetop, driven on by a strong wind and blowing sparks. Most dangerous was the rare east wind, blowing in from overheated inland regions, bringing in heat and low humidity from Outside. I saw a crown fire at night burning on the north side of the main fork of Four Mile by the Deos Place. It destroyed salable timber. I remember shivering in that hot smokey night, feeling lucky that it was going away from our ranch. You cannot fight those big fires as they go. Instead you must get ahead of them on a ridge, and cut everything down that will burn, working down the slope toward the fire, trying to rob the fire of its fuel and to stop the rivers of sparks that carry the fire along. Still it will probably jump the ridge, and you stand a chance of being killed as the wave of flames goes by and uses all the oxygen. Life and property depend on knowing what to do. Smaller fires work on the same principles and were never treated casually. They could explode and cause more damage than good.

In the early days, we had no machines to help with fighting fire. There were all the natural fire lines: roads and creeks and green pastures. To construct the rest of the fire line, we used shovels, adzes, axes, and crosscut saws. And of course a burlap gunny sack with a pail of water. One person can stop a grass fire by swatting it with the wet sack, hitting the blaze with a swinging motion, and this can go on just as long as you have water in that five-gallon bucket. So it is a balance between using enough water on your sack so that the fire stays out after you hit it, and not using so much water that you run out before the fire is stopped. I liked the wet sack work best of all fire fighting, with its rhythm and the chance of success. Even so, the smoke could be overwhelming and roll over you so that not only was it hard to breathe, but you could lose orientation. Then you could not tell what was happening, one of the dangerous situations when you could lose control of the fire just because you failed to see that you needed to run to another spot and put it out there. In those days, fire lines were made by setting as much backfire as possible, then working like crazy to keep the fire contained.

Fires were set with those big strike-anywhere wooden kitchen matches that in these days of legislated protection are much less common; Diamond Brand, Ohio Blue Tips. I rode along a stock trail across the Indian Allotment, going downhill with the reins tied together and looped over the saddle horn. In my left hand I held the match box, opened partway and tilted down so the matches fell down into the opening as I used them. With my right hand, I pulled a match head along the striking surface with a sweeping motion and then let the match fly down into the grass and weeds. If my rhythm was on, the match sputtered as it was falling and then burst into flame when it hit the ground, and a fire would spring up. I liked that, the riding, the swing of my arm, the aiming of the little match sticks. Next morning there was the dead-out charcoal smell of burned grass, heavier ashes marking where limbs had been laying on the ground. Our snot and spit came with streaks and spots of soot for a day or two after fighting fire.

One fall we were burning the slope above the Wilson Place falls, below the road to the Mitchell Place. This was a low-key day, just burning out some briars and old logging slash. Suddenly the fire was roaring up the slope, rushing to the Lincoln that my father bought after the war. (Whenever ranchers had the money, they bought big cars like Cadillacs and Lincolns. There was head room for their Stetsons, and the big trunks could hold a roll of fencing wire, a calf, a lamb, or a bale of hay.) Losing this car was no small thing. I was about nine and hesitated to jump into the car and roll it down the slope. I wanted to but lacked the courage. Instead I ran around the car, through intense heat and smoke and found my father who was unaware of what was happening. He was able to get into the car and to roll it out of the flames that were shooting up past it. The paint on the downhill side was blistered and hung off the car in shreds. If this happened to me today, I would stand back and watch the Lincoln burst into flames.

Along with logging came a wonderful tool for burning, the bulldozer. These machines could scrape a makeshift road around the fire, making more and better fire line in an hour than a person could dig in a week. They cost too much money to rent, so at first my father used them only when absolutely necessary. There was a tradeoff there, saving money on fire trail against spending much more when containing an escaped fire. Then the Forest Service got into the picture, some of the first government regulations that were to infuriate the independent ranchers. The Forest Service had to issue a permit to burn, and they were so afraid of having a fire escape that they were wary of issuing a permit when something might actually burn. That was the conflict: the ranchers wanted land cleared, and the Forest Service did not want any escaped fires. So my father did battle with them, sometimes claiming he had fire trail where he didn't, counting on their laziness to prevent them from finding him out and on his ability with fire to contain the blaze. And as they did not issue permits when it was dry and hot enough to burn well, he would get a permit in anticipation of hot weather and try to keep enough smoke going so that he could touch it off later when it would really burn. The Forest Service guys caught on to all this, but they just couldn't put as much energy into it as did my father, and he often got effective fires. A good burn, he called it.

The Forest Service made an essential mistake. They followed their bureaucratic directives of preventing forest fires, and consequently much logging slash remained unburned, becoming more of a fire hazard every year. The ranchers muttered "Bandon fire, there'll be another Bandon fire." They had a point. There were some disastrous fires, thankfully nothing on the order of 1936, and then the sixties ecology movement, "natural is good," came into fashion. The new directive was to clean up that logging slash as soon as possible. The Forest Service was even more strict with the ranchers, but the ranchers had been right all along.

When I was sixteen, I was allowed to work for two months at the Coos Bay Forest Service with a crew of high-school kids. We lived at the fire station high above the Coos Bay sloughs and I learned what mosquitoes were. It was a lot of fun, and the work much easier than on the ranch. In fact I hardly considered it work; instead it was a two-month vacation for which I received higher wages than I thought possible. We practiced building fire-trail in some brushy land north of Coos Bay, fifteen or twenty of us in a line, applying axes, pulaskis (a combination axe-adze, an effective tool), and shovels. The emphasis was on deep trail, and on putting every coal out when a fire was contained. I was given the axe once, and then the foreman didn't give me that job again. I was already expert and certainly couldn't learn much about using an axe from those people. It was a different approach than at the ranch, where if a fire wasn't escaping onto the neighbors, we were winning. We fought a few small fires, making the enclosed fire into a mud puddle thereby insuring it wouldn't get going again. The work was boring, but it was nice to have company. I had a good time in Coos Bay. There was some time off, and I went to a few dances and learned to drink coffee with milk and sugar at small cafes. The one movie I recall was "Jailhouse Rock" with Elvis Presley. Elvis in full color on a huge screen singing rock and roll. Heaven.

The most interesting event that summer in Coos Bay came when we answered a call to go to one of the roads that went from the Coos Bay Slough into logging country. Fire was burning up a steep slope and it had just started. The boss in poor physical condition didn't get far up the incline and sent some of us on. I soon found myself with two other kids; the others took the easy way out, resting and pretending to scratch out a fire line on that nearly vertical slope. Meanwhile the fire was running faster uphill. I realized if it was not soon stopped at the top, we had lost it. I just couldn't get in front of it. There was a roaring and racket as the fire jumped up the slope. The other two boys were gasping for air, and I left them to keep the fire from burning horizontally along the slope. I raced the fire, going with all my strength, and then came to an old logging road that had been punched across the slope. I was able to stop the fire at that road, and while it was Four Mile fire fighting style running back and forth to stop the fire crossing the road, I kept that small fire from burning a lot of country. About a half-hour later, a couple of boys made it up to the road, and in another hour, more people came up. I heard two higher level Forest Service men talking quietly about how lucky they had been to stop it there. I never have told this experience to anyone; it only occurred to me years later that I might have explained to them what I had done and that it was not just luck. I learned from my father to keep my head down and not to expect praise. I had also learned how to fight a fire.

At home on the ranch, after the fires had died and the earth had cooled, we seeded the burned areas to grass. We had a device for broadcasting grass seed, a sack holding a gallon or so of seed which fit over your shoulder and the bottom hit just below your ribs. The bottom of the sack was a thin board, and there was a adjustment for the amount of seed that fell onto the aluminum fan just below. A crank turned the fan, and the seed was then broadcast out, away from and ahead of you. With the right rhythm, you could stride up and down through a burn and spray an even distribution of grass seed in a ten- to fourteen-foot strip. I got sooty and dirty, and liked the work, the seeds falling evenly into the ash. The seeds made a fine whirring sound flying through the air, striking the ashes with a sputter. It was difficult to keep your orientation so that the entire burn was seeded. Then, with luck, there would be a light fall or early winter rain. Then the seeds would sprout, covering the charred grey-black hills with a delicate short green velvet, holding the earth in place for a luxuriant spring growth. If we didn't get the seed sprouted even more of the earth would then be sluiced off by the heavy winter rain storms. In the late fifties, the large seedings were done from an airplane, and we just had to check and seed the spots that were missed.

The Stonewall Wilson homestead that my father once hoped to get cheaply just sat there for years and then it was logged in the 1950s by Moore Mill. Those tall firs standing naked against my grandfather's cleared pasture land were part of my vision of frontier—past those trees might have been wilderness, if I squinted just right. Then that landscape disappeared in fact, if not from my dreams. The resulting logging slash was not going to be burned by the timber company and who knew what would happen to the land? One afternoon it caught fire.

"It is amazing," my mother said, "how it caught fire in a little line with puffs of smoke that seemed to move across the bottom of the hill."

I already guessed that my father had set the fire by the way it burned, and could hardly keep from laughing at how naive my mother was about this. A big Forest Service crew stopped the fire at substantial expense to the government, but my father did a good job of setting it and the entire logging slash was burned. He paid to have it seeded to grass by an airplane, and the stand of luxuriant grass surprised the officials from the timber company. They were as puzzled by this mysterious growth as my mother had been by the fire itself. Naturally my father couldn't keep his livestock off such good feed.

26 High Waters

The first year after we got electricity, it rained over one-hundred-and-fifty inches. Rain came and came and came, slabs of it tilted slightly from the horizontal. It blew right into your face when you stepped outside, and getting to the barn to milk was awful. The mud and manure and muddy water was at the top of my boots, and I tried to find firm footing through the muck. Everything was afloat. The horses and cows sank deeply into the mud, causing more craters which filled with dark liquid. The cow's bag drug through the filth that she sank into and had to be thoroughly washed before milking. I neglected to shovel out the barn for days; if you opened one of those southern windows and heaved a shovel full of manure out into the heavy winds, much of it came back in your face.

It was inevitable. If the trees are stripped from the land, something will happen. Floods came to Four Mile. The rains did come down in those days, over one-hundred-inches a year, winter after winter. The trees were gone, the trees that my grandfather Waterman taught me held the water back for a regular flow. Instead water gushed off the hills into muddy gullies, then rushed into swollen streams. Forget about the fish! What about the roads and bridges and houses? Anyone who built a house by a scenic stream was flooded out. The exception was my grandfather. Although dark muddy water swung through the oxbow around his house, he never seemed concerned. I think he did not worry about much in life, he alone on Four Mile truly had it made. When the storms blew a tree down, he would say that the wind had never blown so hard in the history of the world. "That's the first time that tree ever blew over," he said to prove his statement. My grandfather was at peace with days of rising waters; the rest of us watched and worried.

On the Lower Place the winter's water expanded, covering the fields and sometimes the roads. High tide reflected the flood water upstream to stop what traffic there was on Highway 101. Farther up-creek the floods were translated into muscular flows that were over my boots even at the most broad crossings. I waded out into Four Mile Creek, scuffing my boots on the gravel bottom to retain footing. Flood water was often the color and consistency of chocolate milk, and that winter it was as if sacks of ground dark brown chalk had been dumped in. The earth was heading out to sea.

The entire land mass was floating, and the least pressure sent another hillside slipping down into the creeks. It is possible to see the slippage of large masses of earth by looking at the surface of the earth. There it is: a line of fallen ground tracing across the hillside. And the trees have been missing a long time now. After I left Four Mile, there was a period with fifty-five and sixty inches of rainfall per year. Still when I returned for visits, I saw new lines, like those patterns: "cut here." More heavy rains, and more land runs down to the sea. Trees had been allowed to grow on the two slopes adjacent to my parents' house, but not on the hills above the house itself. Perhaps that would have appeared to have been giving in to the trees that were beaten back to create the ranch. My mother said that the ultimate slide destroying their house would have to hold off a little longer, referring to her age and the remaining time she needed to live on Four Mile.

The school bus came up my fork of Four Mile Creek toward the end of its route. Often I was the last kid left, but sometimes the children from lower Four Mile and Laurel Grove were on when I was dropped off. On one of those rainy trips up my creek, a tree top remaining from the logging on the hill above came crashing into the bus, smashing through a window. The bus driver heard the loud crash and slammed on the brakes, sliding to a stop on the muddy road. The branches scrapped one of the children, ripping her shirt and leaving her shoulder bleeding. The tree top was pushed out of the window, the girl calmed, and the bus route completed. So far as I know, that was that. I was glad to escape being hurt and vowed never to sit on the side of the bus next to a hillside.

There were blue-clay deposits on our ranch. When dry, blue-clay is leaden stuff, solid as poorly mixed concrete that has set. It is almost impossible to shovel unless first worked over with a pick. But add the water that pours down in an Oregon winter, and this material transforms to become a blue-green pliable substance. Its slickness and ability to absorb truck loads of gravel made it the bane of road builders. But I had a different motive and loved blue clay. I mined it out of road banks and used it to dam Frog Creek. This small gully was dry in the summer but ran a healthy stream in the winter which after rains became a torrent. I made dams with channels to handle the overflow, dams with wooden sticks which I removed to create fountains shooting out the front. My unattained goal was to build a dam that didn't leak where the clay met the muddy soil of Frog Creek. Finally I found a place where the creek ran through a clay deposit, and I could make almost leak-proof dams. The next rainstorm quickly removed my construction.

When the rains came I felt guilty about rejoicing that I escaped work because of rain. My father would have held me responsible for the rain. The sheep were in more trouble because of rains during the lambing season, and our kitchen filled with orphan lambs. At night unaccountably I felt secure and safe listening to the howling wind slam the rain onto the roof next to my bed. The house shuddered as I lay warm under a heavy quilt, Sometimes there were such fierce storms that trees crisscrossed the roads and stopped the school bus.

My parents, Charlie and I were in Bandon returning home. The rain continued, and the landslides finally all happened at the same time. Even my headstrong father wondered if it was safe to cross the bridge to the south fork of Four Mile. The swollen stream was hitting the deck of the bridge which was vibrating against the forces of the black waters. We got the car across the bridge to our road but were soon blocked by a large mud-slide. We started to walk home in the darkness, heavy rain blowing in. My parents, especially my mother, sank into the mud more than my brother and I who went ahead. There were seventeen landslides into our road in one mile. My mother, not at all an outdoor person, lost control and began her routine of screaming at my father. Here he could not mumble and go to the barn; he stood there silently waiting for her to finish. I took Charlie by the hand through the mud. We were lightweight and if we moved rapidly we usually didn't sink too far. We went above the slides I thought we couldn't get across safely, in darkness trying not to fall into the new gaping holes in the hills. Finally we made it home. It was a surprise that the newly installed REA electricity had not been taken out by a falling tree. Charlie and I had the lights on, and my mother always remembered the relief she felt when she and my father rounded a bend and saw lights through the driving rain. They had three slides remaining to get through, but the idea of a lighted house gave her the stamina to make the final stretch.

27 Herding Cattle

Soon after my father purchased his first ranch, he bought a small herd of purebred Hereford cattle. They were beautiful, red with white faces and white ruffs along the back of their necks. Real beef cattle, they were a different animal altogether from the sheep. For one thing, they never laid down in the middle of a pasture and then refused to get up again. They just grazed on the range and didn't cause me much trouble. I liked the way they looked, and I liked the fact that they were a lot less work than sheep.

The herd expanded with the ranch but was never a large fraction of our livestock. Each spring we herded them into corrals and marked the new calves. That meant that all of the calves were ear-marked, notches cut into their ears with a knife against a red-cedar shingle. At least one person held the calf down while this went on. After it was available, we applied dehorning paste to the bumps on their heads where horns would grow. Stock with horns are hard to work, and they can injure other cattle when in corrals. Dehorning paste is a vile caustic substance which burns the horns and kills their growth. This was applied with a little stick, and it was usual to get some smeared onto your skin or clothes. The small calves kicked and bawled when we caught and wrestled them down to be marked. It was better to separate the cows from the calves so the cows wouldn't charge us when we operated on their calves, and sometimes we did that. Castrating the male calves was done by smashing the cords to the testicles with the same multi-levered Burdizzo clamping tool we used for cutting off the lamb tails. We only branded the cattle to be permanently kept on the ranch, using a small fire to heat the branding iron which made a stench of burning hair and hide when applied to an animal. All in all, this was another noisy, smelly, bloody affair, where getting kicked and drug through cow manure was usual. And of course, the drama of driving the cattle into the corrals and handling bigger animals made it more fun.

We were in Salem on the way to the Portland stock-yards with a truck-load of steers. A car was honking and a man yelling at us, but my father ignored him until the car pulled alongside in the lane for on-coming traffic.

"Stop," he shouted through his passenger window. "You lost a cow!"

That did it. We halted to find that a loading gate at the back of the truck was missing. A steer had jammed a leg through a slot in the gate and pulled the gate up. The gate had fallen out a few blocks back and one steer had jumped off. I stood in the opening between the remaining steers and their freedom. A cop showed up by the time the gate was brought to the truck. A good-sized crowd gathered in the residential area, and there were more people than cattle now. After lengthy discussion, the truck was moved a couple of blocks and maneuvered so that the truck's bed was only a little higher than the lawn we backed up to. Then we and the cop and a bunch of eager city people harried the steer up and down the streets. They didn't have much instinct for herding cattle, and the steer detoured through a couple of backyards, knocking down barbecues and lawn chairs. I had a hopeless feeling that we would never get the steer back in the truck, but I also found the situation pretty interesting. Amazingly the steer didn't spook too badly. My father shouted gruff and incoherent commands to people who were happily doing what they could to take part. One woman complained loudly about the manure that had been deposited on her lawn. The cop was good-natured about the Salem Cattle Drive, which ended when the steer was pressed back into the truck by a wall of suburban bodies with my father pushing the hind end and twisting the tail as hard as he could. We tied the loading gates firmly to the stock-rack and resumed our journey.

A traditional cowboy song that I learned in school caught in my ear with its clippety-clop rhythm:

> *Whoopee ki yi ya, get along little dogies,*
> *It's your misfortune, ain't none of my own.*
> *Whoopee ki yi ya, get along little dogies,*
> *You know Montana will be your new home.*

The Watermans yelled "Whoa-whoop! Whoa, whoa, whooa-whoop!" at their stock, but I got the idea. However cattle usually went to slaughter and not to pasture in Montana, and I thought that the singer was just being kind to his stock, not openly revealing their destiny to them. Once after we unloaded a truckload of animals in Portland, I took a tour of Swift's packing and slaughter house, a huge cold sanitary factory that took in live animals and spit out neat stacks of hamburger and steaks. I thought it was an awful place and resented raising animals for such an impersonal end. At the conclusion of the tour we were rewarded with a cold wiener. The trick is to get on the right side of "It's your misfortune, ain't none of my own."

By the time I was in high school, we began to eat some meat other than venison. Three-year-old steers, raised on grass and fattened on clover were trucked to my father's shearing partner Willis's slaughter house with its nearby reeking mountain of offal. The resulting steaks and roasts were delicious although they could not be described as tender. Decades after leaving Four Mile Creek I wondered if my memories of that flavorful meat were just sentimental constructs, if our cattle had tasted as dull as what I ate cities all over the U.S. Then in Vinca del Mar, on the edge of Valpariso Chile, I went into an Argentine steakhouse and was served a chunk of grilled meat that confirmed those vivid childhood memories: that was how meat tasted when it came from an animal that had walked about the world living well on grass and clover.

In the winter we fed the cattle, often from the schoolhouse barn where my father had attended grade school. By then it had the sides torn off, and open sheds built out from the sides so the cows could come in and receive the hay we forked out over the sides each day. I thought it strange and wonderful to own the school you had attended and to use it as a barn. That sounded like fun, but my father didn't remark on this at all. The sheds were to keep everything nice and dry, but that was underestimating the power of an Oregon winter. The earth under those open shelters became so muddy that the cattle sank in up to their bellies, just able to negotiate their way in to get some hay. This left the area dense with deep pits of dark water. I wore my rubber boots, but it was not uncommon to sink down into the mud and manure and urine so far that the muck ran down my legs. There was a light-footed trick of stepping quickly from crater edge to crater edge. Reaching the building, I scrambled up the ladder to the loft of the schoolhouse barn and forked hay out to the bellowing cattle.

During the 1962 Columbus Day storm when the wind meter at Cape Blanco broke at 120 miles-per-hour, the wind took that barn my grandfather had moved over to the South Fork of Four Mile Creek so that his son didn't have to travel so far to school, it took that barn and scattered its fine grooved boards and all of it that remained up that hill and far across the fields.

I bought a few cattle and enjoyed owning them, although one was born crazy. Anything out of the ordinary set her off. Her tail would stand almost straight up, and she crashed right into whatever was in her path, timber or cliffs or fences. It is almost impossible to handle an animal that will do anything, however dangerous or harmful, simply to stay free. Nothing could stop my cow.

"She come down that hill goin' hell for breakfast," my grandfather Waterman said years before of a crazy steer that crashed through a thicket of alders. "If we be quick about it, we won't have to chop brush any more. Or plow either."

Instead I decided to sell my cow, but just getting her into the truck was difficult. I kept watch, and whenever she was with other cattle, I tried to get the whole herd into our stoutest corrals and so capture my cow. Finally I succeeded and then loaded her into the stock truck on sale day. My father warned me that she would be purchased for hamburger, and would not bring the price a breeding heifer would. I hoped she would calm down and that he was wrong, because she was a beautiful animal. But she busted into that sale arena with a wild look in her eyes and foam on her mouth. The ring-master ducked for cover and hamburger she became.

I learned from another sale experience. I had purchased one of my father's original Herefords, and although she was old and looked awful, she gave me two fine calves. She was ancient for a cow, and I decided not to chance her living out another winter. This cow, it was obvious to me, was going for hamburger prices too. By this time I was sixteen or seventeen, and I thought I knew something about livestock and that I could judge them as well as anyone. There may have been some small justification for this. My old, skinny cow came into the arena, and two men whom I knew to be tops at evaluating stock both stopped their conversations. Now that was something of note, because the last thing these men wanted was to betray any interest they might have. My old cow took some concentrated study to see what she really was. Then they bid her up, far past hamburger prices. I knew then that I had made a mistake selling her, if Rod McKenzie was going after her like that, but I was also proud to have owned her. It was obvious to those men bidding against each other that this cow had the blood to produce calves like those I had gotten from her, and that there was a good chance she would do it again, at least once again. I went home that afternoon realizing I knew substantially less about livestock than I had thought that morning.

28 Camping Out

It might be surprising that I love the outdoors as deeply as I do. After all I worked outside in sometimes unpleasant circumstances with my critical unforgiving father and often was cold, wet and miserable. Perhaps exploring the countryside and hearing stories about the old days from both of my grandfathers had an effect.

I was fascinated by the Indians I read about, and tried to duplicate their hunting gear. Vine maple had strong limbs and trunks which bent without breaking. In secret shaded areas where they grew, I tried to choose an appropriate branch to fashion into a bow. It took some time to cut vine maple, even when I brought a hatchet. Back at the barn I used a course-toothed cross-cut saw to square the frazzled ends. Dried this wood was like steel, so the notches for the bow string were best cut when the wood was green. A plant appropriately called arrow-wood grew with straight vertical shoots, and I collected these for arrows. Arrow-wood ends notched easily but the shafts were prone to splitting. Pieces of red cedar left from post-making also could be used for arrows, and these left splinters in my bow-hand as they shot by. I fitted 30-30 shell casings over the ends, and the arrows struck rocks and barn walls with satisfying thunks. I stalked squirrels and birds with my ragged outfit, but nothing I aimed at was in danger. The arrows flew in various directions, and I was impressed by the Indians who could make this stuff work — and they had not had even a pocket knife to help them.

My father kept some Indian artifacts on a high shelf with an old hunting knife and two boxes of bullets that fit none of our rifles. There were a few arrowheads which

I greatly admired, two sandstone club-ends, and a large pipe-bowl that came from eastern Washington with my grandfather Waterman. The pipe-bowl was a grown-man's handful of smooth dark-brown volcanic stone and was perhaps as ancient as the Indian occupation of that country. The rich surface seemed to resonate with the past. I imagined a long carved pipe-stem with a few feathers hanging down. This image must have come from Western movies. George Miller was an Indian who lived on the main fork of Four Mile Creek; he was big and heavy and strong enough to hold the pipe. My father told a convoluted story involving whiskey and George Miller sitting in a tent cradling his balls after being visited by some ladies. I didn't quite understand the story, but I thought my imaginary pipe belonged with George in that canvas tent.

Some large rocks stood on a hillside near Frog Creek below our barn. Some of the less-solid fragments could be split into flagstone, but the attraction for me was climbing. One rock 20' by 30' stood tilted up like a giant's shoe coming to earth. I could just climb the low end, and had adventures on that rock, many of them imaginary. Below the big rock were two almost square boulders, about 15' square and 3' high. The tops were slightly concave, perfect places to lay out my bow and arrows.

I lay with my back down on the rock, watching the sky, daydreaming. When I could get some of my mother's home baked bread, I built a little fire and toasted it, holding the bread over the blaze with green willow branches. Another large vertical boulder across the creek had a ledge I climbed down onto to lay above the trail. There I was an Indian or a hunter, but never did I believe I could stay quiet and still enough to see a deer. Only in my dreams of wilderness.

A set of books sat on a shelf in the living room. Published in 1910–1914 by the Outing Publishing Company, the Arts and Crafts design of these 4 1/2" x 7" books had an overlapping line of ducks along the top, fish leaping over and under each other across the bottom, and in the center was a linear series of tree trunks locked together by a line of earth below and branches above. They had belonged to Frank Lockart and covered a variety of topics: *Practical Dog Breeding, Taxidermy, Practical Dog Keeping, Backwoods Surgery & General Medicine, Tracks and Tracking, Packing & Portaging*, and *Winter Camping*. My father forbid me to touch the books which just altered the times when I intently studied them. Now dogs I liked but knew as much about dogs as I wished to, taxidermy was entirely beyond me both as a concept and as a skill, medical matters were of no interest although I liked the sound of "backwoods," but the last three had an impact. Reading about tracking deer, I didn't learn much I didn't already know (unless we could produce some more snow!), but even those sections were full of hunting stories. Other animals including birds were covered, all with the idea of making the reader a better hunter. The book on packing was a revelation, 133 pages of camping details, camping using canoes, horses, or even on foot. The author for example recommended a 72" x 78" all-wool grey blanket weighing 5 1/2 pounds. This bedding he "found sufficient until "the weather grows cold enough to freeze streams." I decided I was in great need of a frozen stream, imagine walking on solid ice instead of wading! The book on winter camping went even further: "A sixteen-pound bag, or the same weight of blankets, exclusive of cover, is enough for cold weather." These last two books were consciously aimed at outdoor recreation without any more motivation than of escaping urban life. Chapter 1 of *Winter Camping* is "The New Sport." Sign me up!

If I had to be shut in the car for a couple of hours, as soon as I was home I got out and ran down one of those steep hills screaming with relief. And I wanted nothing more than to be an explorer. What was it like to be the first person in a new country? Country that had not been logged out and the fishing ruined. Where were the snow-covered ridges my grandfather Waterman had hunted for mule deer? And those mythical rivers, the McCloud and the Madison, where my grandfather Payne had fished?

The closest I could come to exploring was camping. My mother knew nothing about the outdoors, and my father did nothing with me that did not involve ranch work. So I tried to make it up on my own, but the Outing series was of no practical use to me. My grandfather had a canvas tent in his barn, but it was rotted out by the time I got to it. Still, it was a real tent! I guess that he had it for their trip across Oregon in the wagon, or perhaps he even camped in it at the Bandon beach when it took a half-day to go one way.

Eventually I obtained a boy scout's cooking outfit, one of those aluminum cooking kits with a fry pan and plate and knife and fork. Somewhere I did get a little tent, likely from my grandfather. I tried cooking with my gear, and it was impossible to clean the burned-on food from that thin aluminum. Shredded-wheat cereal in those days came with cardboard inserts between the layers of cereal, and on those inserts were diagrams of elaborate things you could make outdoors with a little twine, a knife, and some sticks. Of course they were just an artist's daydreams, and not a few bushes died in my futile crude attempts to duplicate what I saw in those drawings.

I did camp out down by our creek a few times, and it was great sleeping there. My cooking was always a total failure. If anyone had shown me about making coals and cooking on them, I might have been more successful. However, I was so impatient that I doubt that I could have been helped. My brother did anything I did, and we ate my so-called baked potatoes, which had a charcoal outer shell, a thin ring of cooked potato, and a raw center. One night I chased away a raccoon that was gnawing on the end of our sleeping bag. That was the highlight of the outings.

My aunt Leora's boys visited my parents during the first two summers they were married. There was no bed for the boys, and they slept in the barn in the hay loft. They simply pulled the loose hay over themselves and slept. The second summer my father had a sleeping bag that he had purchased for his shearing trips. My mother told of the fighting between the boys about who would get to use the sleeping bag. She solved it by having one sleep in the bag until midnight, and then switch with the boy in the hay. The instinct for camping equipment apparently goes deep.

29 Home Grown

Every spring when it was dry enough to work the ground, we spread wagon loads of manure over the one-acre garden plot. The manure accumulated in large mounds where all year we shoveled it out of the barn windows from the horse and cow stalls. Cow manure made much better fertilizer. In order not to harm the plants, the manure had to be at least a year old, and it was pitch-forked off the piles in layers. This was the next step after a winter of heaving shovel loads of fresh shit into the brutal south wind. I kept on the lookout for deposits of earthworms, which I hoarded in quart cans or gallon buckets for the day when I could escape to spend some time fishing.

After the manure was spread over the garden, the ground was plowed, disked, and finally a sturdy sled loaded with heavy rocks was pulled over the area. I liked riding that bumpy sled, hearing and feeling the clumps of earth resist and then break down. Clod busting. Our two draft horses, Babe and Bill were used until we bought the John Deere. The tractor speeded up the entire process and once again I preferred the old way of doing things.

The ground was still rough, and we hoed and raked it until the earth was ready for planting. Everything except tomatoes was planted from seeds: carrot seeds carefully sifted between thumb and forefinger into shallow lines, corn seeds dropped into deep furrows, chunks of potatoes tossed in behind a shovel pushed full into the soil and tilted ahead. We planted long rows of vegetables essential to our life: carrots, peas, beans, corn, tomatoes, cucumbers, squash, pumpkins, potatoes. The tomatoes required the most preparation. Deep holes were dug and partially filled with manure, then a layer of soil, and finally the seedling was planted. To complete the job, the seedling was covered with sort of a paper hat, weighted down by dirt clods or small rocks so it would not blow away in the wind. This last step was to protect the plant from the weather and keep it warmer.

And the weather was a problem. In country where seventy degrees Fahrenheit is a hot day, it was difficult to get everything to ripen. There was no water for irrigating the garden; the plants had only the moisture in the soil, hence the importance of planting early. My mother hoed and weeded, and I helped sometimes. I disliked gardening and anything related to dirt farming. I would rather have been riding a horse herding stock, so I received little pleasure from gardening. It was just a job.

Deer jumped the fence and ate the plants. Raccoons helped us harvest corn. Against these transgressors we waged war, shooting the deer and trapping the raccoons. These activities interested me much more than the growing of vegetables. One of the most troubling things I have done in my life happened in that garden. My father was away, and because raccoons had been in the corn which they shucked and ate, I went out at night with a flashlight and the .22 to see if I could shoot them. I crept to the garden and flashed my light down into the corn, and there were eyes shining in the night. I took aim and fired, and then a deer bounced out of the garden. I ran down through the rows, and there was another deer whose eyes I had mistaken for a raccoon's. It was hit in the lungs, and was dying rapidly. I was extremely upset.

"Never point your gun at anything you do not intend to shoot," that was my father's motto and I had violated it. Worse than that, I had shot the wrong animal.

The sound of that wheezing animal in those rows of corn with long rasping dry leaves is still with me. I went to the house and talked to my mother about what could be done. She had no suggestions; this was beyond her boundaries. When I returned to the garden the doe had died. I was unsure of my ability to butcher the deer and pulled it up the slope to the fence. I managed to get it under the woven-wire, and it slid easily on the short dry summer grass down the hill to Frog Creek. My mother stood high above me on the bank and held the light while I caved a bank down on the body. Rocky soil thumping against the doe's ribs, dust in my nostrils. My father would have shot that deer himself, so it was not out of line with our life.

The fact that I did not know what I was shooting upset me a great deal. My father brought up this incident at any public occasion when he thought it would embarrass me. I did think of telling him that at least all I had mistakenly killed was a deer, not a friend like he had, but I never said that to him.

When a vegetable was ripe, we picked it and my mother went to work, canning with her pressure cooker. On a warm summer day, this was hot work on the wood-burning stove. It made her house smell wonderful, and nothing was better than the preparation of jams and jellies with that sweet pungent gummy scum from the cooking which I got to taste. Corn, beans, tomatoes: they all had special aromas carried by billowing clouds of steam. "I put up beans last week," my mother said. "If this good weather holds up we'll do tomatoes soon."

Shelves on the back porch filled with jars of canned vegetables which saw us through the winter. The potatoes, dug up with the same six-pronged pitchforks used to shovel manure onto the garden, were forked into burlap sacks and stored in a cool corner of the barn. Just before the fall frosts, tomato vines were pulled up and laid out by a garage window so that they could finish ripening.

These crops were crucial to our getting by, and we did not buy much food except flour, salt, shortening, and sugar. My mother received deep satisfaction from gardening and canning.

We had many apple trees, as every homesteader planted an orchard with many varieties. There were some that were perfect to pick off the tree and eat right there, that had no other use. Others were special for pies and applesauce. Gravensteins did well and are a great all-around apple. A certain tree bore apples that kept well all winter in that musty corner of the barn. Late in the spring, my mother announced that she was making the year's last apple pie, and she peeled little shriveled-up fruit which you could not sell today. One-hundred years after the pioneers planted their orchards, some of their trees continued to bear fruit. They had not been pruned for eighty years.

There was always a milk cow on our ranch, a cow bred by the Hereford bull gave birth to a calf which was raised for meat or sale. The calf got some of the cow's milk, and we drank the remainder. From my earliest memory, it was my job to milk the cow morning and night. That involved bringing her in from the pasture, feeding her some grain and hay, washing her bag, sitting down beside her on a stool and milking into a big tin pail held between my legs. Only farm boys have that way with cows. Milk cows are almost all belly, a huge volume of stomach hung from backbone, wide hips, narrow shoulders, and held in place by ribs and taunt cowhide. I listened to the cow digest her food while I leaned my head against her warm flank, the squirts of milk ringing into an empty pail, then slashing through a rich foam. Evening light came in through south-facing windows which were crusted with dirt and dried manure; brighter morning light was strained through that same filter. We always had barn cats which got some milk slopped into a dish. Sometimes I squirted milk to the cats, and they went wild trying to catch the white stream arcing midair. Then I turned the calf in for his share. Unless all the milk is stripped from the cow, she will go dry and then there will be no milk until the next calf is born. Before I sent the cow back out to pasture, I wiped off and smeared her teats with Bag-Balm, a medicated Vaseline which came in a handsome green tin.

One cow is difficult to forget. She was a Jersey and beautiful, if you know milk cows. It soon became evident why we had gotten such a good deal on this animal. She was incredibly jumpy, and it was difficult to milk her without having the pail kicked over. I was determined to succeed with this cow. The least noise or motion, of mine, of a cat, of the wind, and bamm, the pail was struck by a hoof. She was so agile that, when I was fast enough to get my left hand across to grab her hamstring above her hock, she could kick *over my arm* and slam her hoof down into the pail. After a few successful days of getting milk, my brother sneaked up outside and flung a rock. Bang, the milk was lost again. Finally I was rescued by some advice from a visitor, someone who had been around dairy cows.

"There are two ways to go," he told me in the summer twilight. "First try this: you get a piece of rope and tie it snug around her so that the rope goes in front of her bag on the bottom and just behind her hipbones on her back. This will work. She cannot kick then; she just cannot get her feet far off the ground. The rope shuts off that big vein that carries milk to her udder, and she may not give any milk. But I guarantee she will not kick the pail over. If this does not work, the other thing to do is to get a big stick and beat the hell out of her every time she kicks the bucket over."

I listened carefully and thought about these options. I was not mean to animals like some people who hurt them for pleasure. But this cow had pushed me pretty far, and I found that I was really angry at her. So before I tried the rope method, I went in and milked her like I would any cow, and she kicked the bucket over. Then I got the three-foot-long stick which I had leaned up against the manure-splattered wall, and I beat the cow, crying while hitting her. I confess that it made me feel better. When I tried the rope method the next night, it worked perfectly, and after that I could milk the cow and be relaxed. I never again saw the man who gave me such good advice.

Doing the milking usually included feeding horses and perhaps other livestock, and I enjoyed forking hay down out of the loft into the mangers. There was another less pleasant job of shoveling the manure out of the barn windows. First of all, you had to fling it pretty far, or manure would pile up and block the window opening before spring came and we were ready to haul the manure away in the wagon. The stalls were on the south side where the wind and rain came in the winter. After the initial cedar shingles proved ineffective against the brutal winter storms, my father re-roofed the barn in bright aluminum so that the south-facing roof I milked under rang and clattered in the rain and gusts of wind. The manure shoveling was into the wind, and some of it came back in my face. The cows often had loose manure and shoveling that required balancing the shovel so the stuff didn't run off. Horses had more well-behaved manure, and I often let their stalls go for a week or so and then had a layered mess of manure, urine, and straw to launch against the weather.

Our milk was never pasteurized, something I did not hear of until I went to school and encountered a white fluid which tasted so different from what I knew milk to be that I was amazed. I carried milk down to the house in the pail, poured it through cheesecloth into big stainless-steel bowls, porous white gauze straining off foam flecked with hayseeds. Then it went into the cooler, or after we had electricity, into the refrigerator. Overnight the cream rose, and cream it was, thick and clotted. It could then be scooped off the milk and put into a cream bowl. In the milk bowl, there remained a delicious ring of crust dried to the side where the cream had collected. Running a finger along the ring collected dried cream with a counterpoint of heavy white liquid. The cream was made into butter, used in baking or just served in a green pitcher that my grandmother Waterman gave to my mother just after she was married.

"Here, take this. You will need a pitcher for cream."

My mother used that pitcher sixty years, but after the cows went, the pitcher held only thin store-bought milk. The real thing would not even pour out of the pitcher, you had to spoon it out, and it came with distinct clots. The cream I buy in the supermarket seems about equal in butterfat content to the skimmed milk I drank on the ranch. My mother used cream to great advantage in her cooking. She made various cream pies and cream went into all cakes. But best was a frozen custard she made in her freezing compartment. It was not technically an ice cream, but had ranch cream and eggs. A piece of her warm apple pie topped with two or three scoops of that ice cream ...

The eggs that went into the desserts came from our flock of Rhode Island Reds, a breed of chicken which does double duty for meat and eggs. They were kept in a chicken yard later, but at times they ran free. Skunks and weasels sometimes killed them, so for protection they were kept in a tightly fenced yard and went at night into a tightly built chicken house. Skunks and weasels can get through extremely tiny openings. Feeding the chickens was such easy work that it didn't count, just a few minutes spent tossing grain about and checking the chicken house for eggs. We kept around twenty of these birds. Then some years my mother ordered chicks. We fed them, trying to keep them from pecking each other to death, until they reached fryer size and could be slaughtered. My job was to kill the chickens. They were laid across a chopping block, held by the legs with my left hand, my right hand swinging the axe. The ability of the chickens to wildly thresh about with their heads cut off — even to walk crazily down the road — impressed me a great deal. I hated cleaning chickens: the odor and the stubborn pin feathers. But they were tasty. My favorite pieces of chicken were the neck and wings, parts for which I had little competition. In 1929 the "singing brakeman" Jimmie Rodgers sang:

> *I ain't got the blues,*
> *Got chickens in my back yard*

The second line was delivered with emphatic satisfaction. Only a person who had lived in the country during hard times could have composed and sang as Jimmie did: "chickens — in my back yard." And as always Jimmie also had something else in mind.

30 The Brush Eaters

One summer my father brought home a new animal from the Willamette Valley, a truckload of Angora goats. This was a wonderful idea. Our ranch was covered with bushes and trees that we had to chop and burn to keep the land in grass. The new animals would eat the brush that was the bane of our ranch, and they would in addition produce angora mohair, long silky curly mohair, that sold for over a dollar a pound which was about three times what wool brought. The wethers—castrated males—ate brush too, so we would keep them all until they died, every goat young and old happily eating brush and growing hair all the while. The herd would explode in size while the brush was destroyed. This was it; we had solved a big problem; we had it made.

I was impressed with this new venture and eager to learn about goats. Somehow I had come through ranching liking animals. They behaved in interesting ways, and you had at first to concentrate on them or you would just say, well those (you fill in the blank) are really dumb, they don't act like I think they should. And by the age of twelve, I knew who was being dumb. Well, bring on the goats!

And the first thing my father did was to shear them, just why I do not know. Perhaps he was anxious to begin cashing in on his new money machines. But shearing a goat is an activity that deserves a book itself. Angora goats are not limited like sheep; there is no way to position them and have them just sit there. Shearing goats is like handling an agile high-school wrestler who doesn't want to be pinned. They have horns, small curled ones on the females and long spirals on mature males, and these horns give the shearer a handhold at least. My father, shearer extraordinaire, had a hell of a time with these Angora goats, and for once catching the animals and tying the cuttings was easy. The difficulty was separating the goats from their hair, and as must be clear by this time, Ray was a stubborn man. The work went so badly that I spelled him at the shearing machine, and I found myself with a shearing head vibrating in my right hand and a bouncing goat at the extreme tugging end of my left hand. We spent a couple of days testing whose will was stronger, the goat's or Ray Waterman's. Fortunately the goat hair came off first. My father would have lost a longer contest.

Then we turned those creatures out to feast on the brush. Everyone has heard the saying, tough as a goat. Yes, but not in Oregon, at least not on the Coast. Those critters were accustomed to hot dry climates and not to cool foggy air. In our summer, the naked Angoras promptly caught pneumonia and died. About twenty-five percent survived. Amazing, I thought as I pulled them off to a remote location to decay and feed the turkey vultures, just amazing. Many years later I learned that this was a common occurrence when the goats are sheared in wet conditions. It was usual to leave a strip of mohair along the backbone (a so-called cape) or to use raised shearing combs which leaves hair all over the animal. Either my father did not bother to learn of these techniques or he just ignored them. To the goats it was pretty much the same thing.

Male Angora goats are the worst smelling animals I have been around. The males or billies wet their belly hair when they urinate, and the combination of goat hair with urine is a potent one. A herd of wethers can be smelled for at least a half-mile when the wind blows from them to you.

My father was not likely ever to say he had made a mistake, or even to reconsider. He brought over the next truckload and did not shear this batch. Most of them died anyhow, probably just to show him they were boss. I had a lot energy at this time and thought that we had paid for some expensive hair. I cannot blame my next actions on anyone but myself. I took that little John Deere tractor to where the goats had died, and I tied a rope around their various horns. I pulled as many dead goats as I could tie to the tow-bar of that tractor. They had been dead a day or so, and were not bloated too badly yet. I dragged them down a half-mile of dirt road to the barn where the shearing machine was set up. Then I set to work. The damn things didn't get up on me this time, but it was a long smelly job, shearing a dozen dead goats. Then I towed their naked dead bodies to a remote gully where they drew in buzzards for miles around. It did occur to me that in many ways I was not so different from the father whom I hated so much. You have to pick and choose what to be in life, but not everything is in your control.

This episode did not stop the flow of goats onto the ranch, and they were nice to have around. The billies had long spiraling horns, and they fought in the fall. I sat on the hill and watched them run and crash their heads together to see which one got to breed the does. And I fell for the baby goats that came from all this drama. I even took one that would not have survived and nursed it for weeks on cow's milk. A farm boy has to be tough and should have learned early not to give his heart to an animal.

The goats didn't make a dent on the rapidly growing brush, and they slowly disappeared from the ranch, never becoming acclimatized to the damp air. My father went silent at any mention of goats, angry at his failure.

31 Trout Fishing

I was born with the trout fishing gene, there is no other explanation except genetics. Somewhere far up my family tree there is a very dedicated fisherman. According to my mother, I was happily dropping a line into Four Mile Creek at two-years-old. She would bring me back up the hill to the house, where I continued fishing in the largest mud puddle I could locate. My grandfathers talked about trout fishing in the old days, in large clear rivers, and I was an addict. Tell me more, take me fishing! And whenever I was allowed or could sneak away, I fished in Four Mile Creek which was basically a hatchery for coho, Chinook and dog salmon and sea-run steelhead. There were rainbow and cutthroat trout living in the stream year round too. The best fishing was in the winter when the high waters receded between storms. I caught small trout, many of which should have gone out to sea, but no one thought of that then. No one cared at all.

My equipment was a small stiff pole with which I could hardly cast. My lure was an earthworm dug from our manure piles. I flipped the worm into the current and let the drift do the job for me. This is a way to learn where fish live and how currents flow and how those two things are related. Just the surface of a trout stream can quicken my heartbeat. It did then and it does now. I love streams and rivers and how the currents and trout move in them. Smaller can be better. Oceans, lakes and even large rivers become uninteresting abstractions, because I am unable to see the currents, to imagine the contours of the bottom, to know where to cast my line.

A few magazines came regularly to our house: *Ladies Home Companion* and *Farm Journal*. Less common were copies of *Outdoor Life* and *Sports Afield*, magazines that fueled my fantasies. They contained *trout*: brown trout, brook trout and arctic char, all new to me; cutthroat trout and rainbow trout in sizes larger than I had ever imagined. Fish such as bass, perch, tuna and marlin were featured as well, but although those fish had their abstract appeal, my intense focus was on trout. It is possible to catch bigger fish in exotic places, but trout remain my first choice. Trout beside a rock in clear water, waiting for food to come with flowing water. Trout spawning in fine gravel in the late fall, red-spotted sides flashing to the world. Trout dependent on stands of uncut timber and clean cool water.

The stories that went with the pictures of trout were about water and fishing techniques which I could not understand. Dainty flies cast over eastern streams were beyond my comprehension. It was at least twenty years before the water and fish of the West began to receive their due from this crowd of angling authors, although there were articles showing huge browns caught in Yellowstone. I went over and over those pages, memorizing the fish and wondering about the fishing. My conclusion was much the same as that I had reached about ranching. They were just trout and they lived in water that flowed by them and they ate bugs. If I could get to one of those magic places with my pole, I would find some worms or grasshoppers, drift one in, and see what happened. I could take it from there.

My fishing was almost always done on the move, and I rarely just let the bait sit on the bottom of a pool waiting for a fish. Instead I drifted the bait down the currents. The stolen hours I spent on my belly watching trout in clear summer pools convinced me that they took their food from the water flowing by them. So I let the current carry the stiff line into the pool, hoping to see it move from a fish taking the bait. That is an art, sensing when an almost invisible line has moved from a fish and not from the currents. When one took the bait, I instantly jerked the line up as hard as I could. I had no concept of playing a fish and with the heavy line there was no necessity of it. Finding a fish in the weeds after I flung it over my shoulder was often as hard as catching it had been. Usually I caught nothing and was on to the next fishing hole. Part of the allure of fishing is the prospect that the next pool contains a nice trout and that next pool can be turned back, from pool to pool, as long as the stream and the day last. It is simultaneously exploration and introspection: the pools are always new and what you know about fish and water goes into the cast and the drift and when to pull the lure out sky-high. On a rare day you connect with a beautiful silver fish whose ancestors swam the same waters for millennia. When I escaped to fish, I found it almost impossible to concede the end of the day, and instead rushed ahead to fish just one more pool, just one more pool.

In addition to worms and grasshoppers, I used caddis nymphs for bait. They crawled on the underside of rocks inside tubular constructions which incorporated sand and tiny twigs. I tore the casings and put the white naked nymphs with their black heads onto my hook. The smaller periwinkles had hard spiral shells and were not obtainable for bait. I heard a story of trout with stomachs full of salmonberries that sent me into a fantasy. I pictured myself on my horse — for that is where I usually ate salmonberries — eating berries and catching trout on my hook baited with the same berries. The fish must have mistaken the orange berries for fish roe. Indeed the roe from a salmon or steelhead could be cured with borax and used to bait a fishhook. We would no more have eaten fish roe ourselves than we would have eaten fish guts.

Logging and ranching almost destroyed the fish population of our little creek. Cutting off the timber lowered the water table and made the summer drought more severe. My grandfather Waterman understood this very well. His intuition about the ecology of our country was correct, and he had never heard the word ecology. He could have lectured to biologists, in his faded suspenders and patched jeans. So he and I were in pain over the decline of the creek and of the world around us. My father wanted to succeed and not to be ashamed, and he saw no merit to trees unless he could sell them. It was an odd generation skipping, and it made my grandfather and me close. I caught a 19" trout above the Wilson falls, the largest of my Four Mile catches, surely an immature steelhead stealing eggs. It was a dark winter day, not quite raining, and I bounced the silver-grey fish up a steep slope of slick damp river-smooth stones. The fish came unhooked and I sprawled onto the rocks to keep it from escaping. Then I ran to my grandfather's house, the trout swinging from a forked willow branch. It was a long run to his house, but he was the person I wanted to share my catch with. He stood me in front of his house and took my picture.

In my first years my parents restricted me to the Cox Place, our home ranch. That stretch of the south fork of Four Mile Creek flows inside me yet. From the property line with the Wilson Place: water dark and dangerous in winter floods, blocked by new fencing in summer. Each run, each pool, each land-eating bend. I walk it, leave my steps molded in damp sand, rattle gravel, scatter minnows. Salmon rocket downstream along the long cut-bank to escape, frantic torpedoes half out of the water, flinging spray, leaving uncovered spawning nests in fine gravel, unfinished business.

Past the swimming hole with its mossy granite island. If it is summer I launch a flat stone across the surface, hoping for four skips, happy with three. Finally a last wade to the big turn above grandfather's Place. His streamside pile of rocks softens this boundary; someday he'll take them down to his house on a horse-pulled sled. I'll ride along.

My dream was an unruined watershed. The idea I had was that if an entire watershed could be saved from the power saw and the bulldozer, it would be a paradise. I constructed the landscape as I was falling asleep under those tight eaves in my room, building it like I would a gate, sawing and nailing and bracing. I tried to be original, after all Four Mile was already a disaster, sliding away into the creeks, its springs drying up, its salmon trying to spawn in mud. So I tried my best to construct a new place. Many of the slopes and gravel bars of my imaginary world had a definite similarity to those I knew. But I looked in magazines when I could and took images from them. I had adventures there, catching fish in deep clear pools and then realizing I should take care not to ruin my own creation. I hiked up the rivers and along the ridges. My wilderness had our little blacktail deer and the big elk that once ranged our country but then had been shot out. I could camp where I wanted and see the animals, which were not hunted. Little did I know Aldo Leopold had the same concept in the 1920s and had invented the American wilderness area. Today I know well portions of the Gila, America's first wilderness that Leopold established when he was living in New Mexico. It is far beyond my childhood dreaming in that way reality often has of outdistancing fiction.

My father fished twice with my brother and me on Four Mile Creek. He had a long telescoping steel rod, and he moved along the creek ahead of Charlie and me and lobbed into those holes Colorado spinners with a worm behind. This combination worked, and he caught fish. I watched him, trying to learn for myself what he was doing, so I could try it if I ever had the chance. He never offered either of us a turn with his equipment; in fact we never fished a hole he had not already drug his spinner through. Once we took a day off and went to Sixes River. We had no luck at all except when out of a scum of river foam I popped a ten-inch fish which immediately fell off the hook, and we never repeated that adventure. Except for deer hunting that was the only time out from work he ever took with me. Once after I was in college, my brother learned of a place on the Coquille River above Powers. It was a rough river there, crashing down a steep canyon, with nice pools among big boulders. My father must have been fifty, and the outcome was different from the days when he had swung that long steel whip. My brother and I both caught fish this time, and of course we found it much easier going, leaping from rock to rock. He didn't say much about the trip for years until in his old age memory softened his recall of that day.

In my early years, salmon and steelhead ran up Four Mile Creek in multitudes to spawn. They spent years at sea, exactly where no one knew (we were even taught this fact at Langlois Elementary), and during summer and fall schools of salmon and steelhead cruised off the Oregon Coast. Catching and canning salmon was then a thriving business, and some of my classmates spent their high-school summers working the fishing boats. Fish came up Four Mile Creek when there was a freshet in fall and winter. There would be some early steelhead and then there were fish after every good storm. You could see them when the water was going up, especially if the rain was not too heavy and the water ran clear to steel-grey, but in big heavy storms the fish were concealed within the dark flood waters. It gave me a good feeling knowing they were there. They dug beds in the fine, clean gravel for the females to deposit their eggs. The males sent clouds of sperm—milt—down the current to fertilize the eggs, and they fought each other for positions in front of spawning beds. Roe and milt. I crawled up in the cover to watch them. The females twist in the water as they deposit their eggs, their silver sides flashing in the dim light. That is one of the most sensual and beautiful sights I have witnessed, that pulsating flashing. Immature salmon — jack salmon — came in too with young steelhead, and they positioned themselves downstream eating the eggs that floated by. The whole process is not always so romantic. The salmon decay in fresh water and are dying even as they spawn. The fish come in from the sea silver-bright and shining. In the creek, their color dulls and then sometimes becomes bright-red and orange. White spots of decay appear, and fins and tails almost rot away. Fallen alder leaves, themselves bright with autumn color, sink into the water, and in still shallows they turn almost black. The banks could have decaying fish on them, and the low water might contain fish that could hardly move. Any predator that ate fish fattened up during salmon runs. There was a hurdle which these fish crossed which fascinated me. Four Mile Creek flowed through the sand dunes into a long narrow lake which paralleled the ocean. Other small streams fed New Lake which had no consistent outlet, so each winter the fish had a confusing pathway to reach the riffes on our ranch. This splendor came to an end with clear-cut logging, and by 1960 there were only a few salmon and steelhead left alive to return to our stream.

After I graduated from high school, I had more time and freedom. I took up steelhead fishing and fished for some time without catching one. The standard rule is that if you fish enough you can expect to catch one fish your first season. Steelhead are not easy game. Then one rainy evening up the Elk River, twenty-five miles from Four Mile Creek, I hooked a fine bright fish, fresh from the sea. It moved out into some shallow flats and repeatedly leaped out of the water. Rain was drizzling and hissing on the open river, and my beautiful fish was jumping, shining twisting silver, arcing in the fading light, crashing back into the river.

32 Pointing Guns

My father woke me before dawn on the first day of hunting season. It was the fall of 1954, and I had turned twelve that summer. I had no idea that I was going hunting, and had never shot the old 30–30 he placed into my hands with some mumbled directions about how to use it. I had absolutely no idea how the lever-action gun worked, and his incoherent muttering wasn't going to do the job at 5 AM. Some other men were there, and we ate breakfast and went hunting. This was my first experience of that intense world of men gathered before daylight preparing to go out into thick darkness. It was as compelling and mysterious as that of my mother's friends The Girls, and apparently I might be able to belong to this one. I wasn't put anywhere that a deer might go. That was just as well, I wasn't sure how to operate the rifle.

The one recreation my father encouraged was deer hunting, why I am not sure. Perhaps he enjoyed hunting himself, but that is hard to believe after all those years of shooting deer for the family meat. Or he considered it work and hence wanted to get as much out of me as he could. He was indifferent to the small game I shot with the .22 rifle, but he set me to hunting deer. And he was a fanatic on gun safety: "Never point a gun at anything you are not willing to shoot." That is valuable advice. It explains why pistols are so dangerous: the barrels are short and it is hard to control what they point at.

I carried that old rifle as if it was about to fire at any moment that day, as I did every time he sent me out hunting, if you can call what I was doing hunting. It was quiet in the cold morning air, and I saw a few deer and other things like dew and birds and bugs. One day I decided that it had gone on long enough, and I sat down on an old log and took a close look at the gun. I had not been sure if the rifle was ready to fire by simply cocking the hammer back and pulling the trigger, or whether I had to lever a shell in first. There was a tube that held the extra bullets which the lever fed into the chamber. OK, I decided, it won't shoot unless there is a bullet in the chamber. Carefully checking where the gun was pointed, I levered it part way and saw that as best I could tell the chamber was empty. Then I levered a shell into the chamber. The hammer was up, ready to fire. I eased the hammer down. Then I levered all the shells through the gun which flipped them out onto the ground. I tried pulling the trigger on an empty chamber. It made a satisfying empty click and gave me confidence. I wiped the bullets on my pants to clean them, reloaded the gun and then learned how to get a shell in and out of the chamber. Now I had it.

Then I became interested in getting a deer. I saw a couple bucks, too far away for me to shoot, and that was exciting. My favorite places to hunt were the Sis Mitchell orchards. Deer came into the orchards to eat apples, and after I failed to get a deer, I could eat an apple too. This was a nice arrangement for the deer and for me. The cold air was full of the decaying, musty odors of fall, and while our leaves were never bright, they had some color. It was nice to be out, and I could avoid working fence while out "hunting."

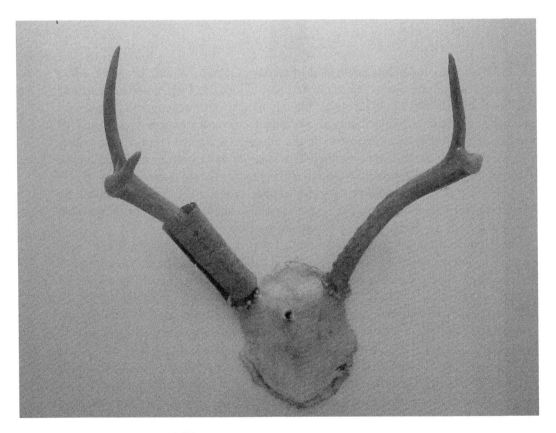

On the last evening of season, my father went with me to the lower Mitchell orchard. We were coming back to the car when a deer walked out in front of us, where Sis Mitchell had her little house. My father had a 30-06 with a peep sight, and he raised it and started blasting away. I stood beside him thinking that the deer must have horns if my father was shooting, although I couldn't see horns. (I needed glasses and that explained my difficulties.) My next thought was that, if my father was missing, it must be a difficult shot. So I just aimed at the biggest part of the deer and pulled the trigger. The bullet struck the deer in the middle of his body, where I had aimed. That is less politely called a gut shot and is to be avoided. The deer started running, and I shot ahead of his white tail as he ran into the trees. I made an excellent shot that time, bringing the deer down. My father had been blazing away, unable to see through his sight, just pointing and guessing, trying to kill the deer before I did. My hands were shaking so violently that I held my grandfather's old 30-30 under my arm with my hands thrust into my pockets. The beautiful little buck was a forked horn with two points per side and was actually legal. We hauled him back to the barn and butchered him. My life as a hunter had begun.

Just why deer antlers had such a pull on me I do not know, but their geometry alone could have done it. Bifurcation was the law of costal blacktail antlers, the youngest bucks with spikes and then forked horns. (This was pronounced "fork-ed," just why I have no idea. And we used horn and antler interchangeably, although horns are permanent and antlers shed annually. Cows have horns and deer have antlers. But we said fork-ed horn and never fork-ed antler.) Three-points were what I later learned Easterners called eight-pointers: a long point added to a deep fork made it a three point to us and we did not include in the count the jutting eye-guards near the skull on each side. Easterners counted everything on both sides with a point, and while this seemed to me a bragging inflation, I secretly would loved to have been able to say "I shot a four-point," instead of a forked horn. Older bucks could have four points, a deep branch branching again so there were four points on each side, not counting the eye-guards. But sometimes antlers were damaged in their yearly growth or there was just a tweak in the developmental process, and then points could go any which way. I was fascinated by this variety, astonished, abstracted, and absorbed by it. Finally the colors: young buck horns were usually ivory, pale and austere. Older deer had horns stained a rich rusty earthy brown which tugged on me. I loved wild, and I loved deer with their graceful branched magnificence.

In my second year of hunting my father told me to "go get some meat," and I killed a deer on the steep Mitchell hill. Gutting a deer looked easy enough; I had for years watched my father make short work of it. But alone on the downhill side of a doe, it no longer appeared to be such a routine job. The knife finally penetrated the tough layers of hair and hide and fat and muscle, but it also punctured the gut releasing a blast of complex odors. A chilly frosty morning; I shed my coat and rolled my sleeves up and wondered what to do next. I recalled the way my father slipped his hand inside the belly, and then I was able to hold the gut away from my knife as I made the slit up to the breastbone. Internal organs are built to stay internal, and while some intestines spilled out, it was necessary to go inside with my knife and cut stuff loose.

Sweating now, I was in over my elbows with an armload of guts and blood, trying to make sense of what I was doing. I recommend this experience to all meat-eaters; killing a deer or cow is the easy part, no matter what your morals are. Finally I made no more progress and discovered the existence of the diaphragm which had to be cut from the ribs. Then the heart and lungs came out after I reached far into the body cavity and cut the windpipe. I was left with the large intestine leading to the anus. This gets tricky as the urine sack is right there too. Finally finished with the job, I cut the heart and liver from the offal and tucked them back into the body cavity. Then I tried to wipe the blood off my hands and arms onto grass and the moss on a nearby tree. The substantially lighter-weight deer pulled easily to the barn by a rope attached to my saddle-horn. At the barn, the deer was skinned and hung from a rafter using a block-and-tackle. Skinning deer or sheep should be done with great care not to get hair or wool on the meat which will taint it. Cattle do not require so much fussing. When the skin is opened up and turned down at the rear of the animal, the hide can be pulled down easily, especially if there is a good layer of fat between the hide and muscle. As the skin comes off the fat and flesh, there is a dry sound like the tearing of newspaper. It was at this stage with a skinned naked animal hanging vertically that I felt a kinship, the shoulders and back and hips could all have been covered by human skin. I identified my body parts with those of skinned animals. The deer hung for a week or so, covered with a burlap wool-bag to keep off the flies. The meat the day the deer was shot was too tough to eat. But that night my mother prepared heart and liver in her cast-iron fry-pan along with mashed potatoes and home-canned green beans. We ate the vitals of that deer: sweet chewy cross-sections of heart; complex musty soft-textured slices of liver. It was delicious.

Homesteading was hard work. Forget falling all that timber, just keeping the cleared fields free of brush was difficult enough. Then there were the wild animals, weasels and skunks and hawks which ate chickens, raccoons and deer which ate corn and other vegetables, bears and mountain lions and bobcats and coyotes which ate sheep and cattle and horses. Bald eagles flew off with lambs; ground squirrels and mountain boomers dug up the hills; and beavers dammed the streams and flooded the fields. The pioneers shot everything that held still for it and a lot that was running away from them. Deer were the only wild animal they saw any reason for, and they cleared out the wild animals with the timber. In my days, we were still at it. The mountain lions and bears were much less frequent, and we trapped the coyotes that ate our profits. If it was alive, someone shot it. Once when looking at an old elk horn in the hills, I spoke my wish that elk still lived on Four Mile. "If them elk ever show up here again, I'll kill them quick as I can," my father snapped at me. I was amazed at his reaction and asked why. "They'd eat feed and break the fences, raise all kinds of hell."

Late one fall my father's appendix almost ruptured, and I rode the range alone that winter, spending every daylight hour I was not in school feeding and checking hungry stock. One dark grey day with the clouds just above my head, rain lashing the sodden ridge, a pair of dark-antlered bucks crossed below a collapsed barn. I wished for a rifle bulging in the scabbard against my cold leg, but it was a winter without the usual strong salty jerky.

I had mixed feelings about hunting. I loved being out. It was nice to miss a little fencing. And I liked the excitement of shooting a deer. The hunts when people came out from town were less pleasant. My father sent me with others through some patch of brush, and we were to drive the deer to someone at a stand on the other side. He stationed himself behind us where the most clever and experienced deer, slipping by the drivers, came out the back way. He killed some large deer that way. For some reason, I didn't like to take part in those drives and was not careful to do a good job of moving the deer. I much preferred hunting in solitude. One group came from Bandon to hunt the Moore Mill land my father had burned and seeded to rye grass. It was thick with tall grass and deer. Walking out one of the logging roads, someone loading his gun let it fire, and the sound struck me just before some mud hit my back. I thought I was shot and was considerably relieved to learn that I had only discovered a new way to get dirty. I stayed low and out of the lines of fire after that.

Along with the lesson about pointing guns came the way to approach a down deer. We always came to it from the back so that if it were not dead we would be safe from its hooves and horns. Only a rifle barrel touching a wide open eye was convincing evidence of the animal's death. Trained in this way, I found the cowboys in the Western movies silly; they would bring down a man with a six-shooter at some amazing distance and know instantly that he was dead. That and all the galloping about they did made me a skeptic, although I still enjoyed watching Westerns.

A nice buck lived on the hill above where I had chopped alders, and as I knew the ground there as well as I knew anything, I thought I might have a chance at him. I got up in the dark and walked up the logging road eating cold biscuits which my mother left out for me. Inevitably the buck and some does heard me, and I sometimes saw horns silhouetted against the early morning sky as the deer topped the ridge and escaped. Some nights dense fog lay heavy in the valleys, and the sun expanded it, sending fog streaming by me. I was clumsy, and the deer always heard me moving in the fog. Invisible, they snorted a few times, stomping their feet. Then they ran away with high jolting bounces. So I huddled behind a log in the damp air, waiting for the sun's warmth and light. One day I was day-dreaming, and a buck and doe walked up the opposite slope. I decided to shoot when they reached a certain distance from me, but they smelled me first and ran off with that tall bouncing jarring gait. I feared wounding a deer and not killing it, and was very cautious about taking a shot. On the ranch I learned sheep, cows, and trout; sometimes I could predict what my father would do next. But I never really learned deer. They remained almost mythic creatures, especially the bucks with their marvelous horns, creatures occasionally I glimpsed on skylines and at the edges of the timber and during the rut.

Deer lived in the thick timber adjacent to the rich bottom land of the Lower Place, and in the dark nights they fed in our hayfields. People from town and hard working Okie loggers hungry for venison came up the short road from Highway 101 and spotlighted deer out in the dense fields. Sometimes we found the offal from a butchered deer; more often we found a murdered sheep or cow, mistakenly killed and then left to spoil. Why people would steal game animals and not take the stock they killed was a puzzle to me.

One night I was visiting my grandfather during hunting season. "They're coming in here at night, getting the wind-fall apples. Why don't you see if one isn't a buck?"

I went out with a rifle and a flashlight and caught a heavy-horned two-point in the beam. My grandfather asked if I had seen one, then asked why I had not shot it. The reasons included legality but for the most part I was staying away from my father's marked territory. He killed deer at night; I did not. It never occurred to me that my grandfather might have had a a stake in it too, that it might have mattered to him that his grandson take a deer off his homestead orchards with his 30–30. It was one of those events that was more complex than I could make out at the time and didn't understand it for many years.

About the time I started high school, I began to wonder why we should shoot, for example, a red-tailed hawk sitting on some remote snag. It did not make sense to me, killing those wild creatures, and my reluctance to keep up the shooting drove another wedge between my father and me. Cries of hawks seemed valuable, and I did not know enough to make the argument that hawks and predators kept the ground-squirrel population in check. Instead we shot the squirrels too, and they became wary beside their mounds of earth. After I was in graduate school, my father sent a hand-scrawled note with my mother's regular letter, something he did only two or three times in his life. The bald eagles were taking lambs, he wrote in block printing. "Eagles are killing Clydes Shorts." This furnished me with a cartoon image of the eagle flying off with his claws in the underwear of Clyde Short, Clyde dangling and shouting, and my father trying to decide if he could shoot the eagle and miss Clyde.

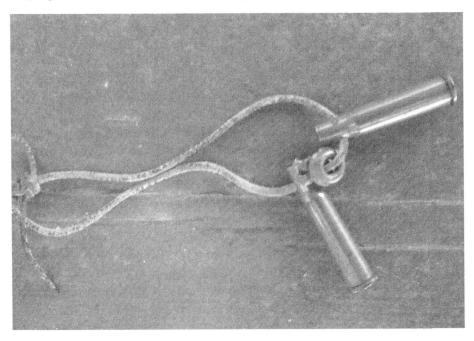

I shot a few more deer, some after the season closed when the bucks were in the rut to breed the does. The meat could be smoked, and I loved to eat jerky. One fall I legally killed a beautiful buck on the Walker Place. I took the two shell casings from my Mitchell Place first deer and the spent bullet from the Walker Place buck, and I made myself a good-luck piece, drilling holes in the objects and stringing them on a piece of leather twine. I wanted to believe that carrying that charm would bring me good fortune, but it did not seem to although I still have it today.

33 Working in the Woods

I will not have it," my mother screamed at my father. "I will not have dust from log trucks all over my house! No!" My father had to change his initial plan to cash in on timber from the recently purchased Wilson place. A road was built down the south fork of Four Mile Creek, and each year a road was bulldozed down the creek bottom. The so-called environment was unheard of in those days, at least on the Oregon Coast, so there was no concern about blocking water flowing down the creek. The truck drivers hated to open and shut the stock gate, so I was hired at twenty-five cents an hour to stay by a gate and keep the livestock in their pastures. This was incredibly boring for an active boy, and I hope I kept most of the stock in place. My mind and sometimes my body wandered. But eventually I was paid fifty-cents per hour that I recorded I had watched the gate. I had a lot of time to look down into the creek, and I saw in those muddy pools the beginning of the end of Four Mile Creek as a salmon and steelhead hatchery. The next winter brought heavy storms, and the stream ran mud for weeks. So we killed the little fish in the creek, and we muddied up the spawning grounds to stop the future fish from spawning and hatching. Some few fish survived, but logging destroyed the native runs of salmon and steelhead. I saw it happening and I became a conservationist before I knew the word. There had to be a better way, but that would require landowners to stop acting like they were the first pioneers in the country. If my father was any example, that did not appear too likely. The races of trout and salmon in Four Mile Creek did not go extinct, but their genetic variety decreased drastically.

The fish shrank to a tiny population, a narrow bottleneck, as did the buffalo on the American plains, and only the genes of those lucky few were passed along. Although muddy water is not as dramatic as rifle fire or barbed wire, it is just as deadly.

At the end of World War II, returning soldiers married and started families. Home construction boomed and brought money to the Oregon Coast which was like a third-world country with natural resources to sell. Actually it was more subtle than that. In the fifties, many sawmills and plywood plants processed the logs into the products that builders purchased. Large companies such as Georgia Pacific and Weyerhaeuser had plants and mills, often located in Coos Bay where the port was crowded with ships full of plywood and lumber. Coos Bay was said to ship more lumber than any other port in the world. Smaller companies like Moore Mill grew with the market and had thriving businesses. At the bottom end were the gyppos, tiny marginal operations which survived from job to job, usually not getting ahead.

This need for labor brought in itinerant workers. Most of them were Okies and Arkies, people who had been driven from their homes during the Dust Bowl and had not found a place in California or anywhere else, twenty years later. Okies were our foreigners, and the derision reserved for Blacks, Asians or Mexicans elsewhere was heaped onto these people. They were the Blacks of the Coast, along with a few Indians. Many of my classmates spoke with the accents of Oklahoma and Arkansas and Texas.

The usual pattern of our ranch purchases was that the timber was already sold before we bought the land. When we got the logging slash burned, timber prices had run up more, and there was usually a batch of timber that had not been profitable to sell in the first cutting. Then a gyppo came in, cut the timber and hauled it out. When gyppos logged that steep stand of timber above Sis Mitchell's house, they wanted to live there, and not to drive in and out each day. They camped in the open on a flat area below her wreck of a house, assembling an array of beds and stoves. When the logging ended, they left it all behind. I walked with my grandfather Payne through their old campsite on his last deer hunt, and we made our way around a stove with brush growing out of it. My parents thought those gyppos were degenerates. Imagine the fun they had, cooking on a wood stove in the open, eating at the table, watching the wood-smoke drift across the valley, sipping whiskey and waiting for the deer to enter the orchard. And a little later climbing up into a bed with a rusty iron frame and springs. The squeaking bed, the cricket's chirping, the owl's hooting, it was all-American music.

A more positive experience for my parents came with Ken Rogge, who had moved to Oregon from Minnesota with mill experience. He and my father made a deal, and Ken set up a mill beneath a stand of timber on my grandfather's Place. This went very well, and Ken went on to build a good-sized mill on the Coquille River and become a leading citizen of Bandon. My grandfather was still alive and did not share in the proceeds. At least he kept Ken and Ray from cutting the last old-growth fir tree on our ranch which stood down by the creek.

After my father's back went out from shearing sheep, he turned to falling timber to produce the cash necessary to keep the ranch going. Working in the woods was what logging was called. Falling timber had the right features: the work was solitary, and it could be done whenever my father wanted, just so long as he kept ahead of the crew pulling the logs out to the trucks. The first job he took was up Two Mile Creek, and after a few weeks, he asked me if I wanted to come along. "There is some chittum to peel," he said. Dried chittum bark could be sold in town, eventually to be used in a laxative. This just like skunk glands used in perfume seemed exotic to me, but if someone paid for this stuff it must be true. I knew Ray by this time, and if he was doing something for me (and some cash and a new view were something) he wanted something from me. So away I went with my best knife up Two Mile Creek. The drive was over several miles of rough recently built road. The logging site was high up on a ridge so that, although I headed downhill a few times, I never reached the creek that was down there somewhere. My hidden motive was to locate some water, water that contained trout, and then to sneak in some fish line and hooks. The chittum trees had been bulldozed out of the way and were in a tangled half-buried pile beside the logging road. I started out on the trunks. It was nice enough work, cutting bark around the trunk in two places, not too far apart, then cutting a line between the circles, and finally the hard part, peeling off the bark. The fact that the trees were dead or dying did not help. I probably needed a tool; I found a rock that worked OK. The first day ended with my father coming back to the car after his day's work, and we drove home bouncing around on the raw road. He even asked me how it had gone peeling chittum. I was on alert.

The second day I got tired of peeling, and my hands were skinned up and sore. As with anyone who has done work like that, I realized that I wasn't making much money. By the time those ragged pieces of bark dried they would weigh almost nothing. Still I thought I might get to that creek if things went right. Again that evening my father asked about the bark. Then he revealed his motive.

"How'd you like to come out and give me a hand?" he said next. "Markin' logs and choppin' limbs."

I have no idea why he tried to be clever. I always tried to do what he told me, if I could figure out what he was talking about. Maybe he was working up to this with my mother who, if she had known the danger of a lot of what we did, might have stopped it. But my mother completely ignored what happened outdoors and was not stopping anything. Or the environment of working out around other men could have affected his behavior. I am sure that even then it was illegal to have children eleven- or twelve-years old working in the logging woods. Years later I earned a man's wages doing the same job, but then I was not asked to chop limbs, the faller cut them off using his power saw. When I started to chop limbs, he stopped me, saying, "That's what we have machines for."

My father's task was to fall the timber and to buck it. Bucking is cutting the fallen trees into lengths that can be pulled out of the woods and loaded onto the log trucks. I received a nickel per tree the summer of 1953 to chop the limbs off and to use a steel tape measure and mark with my axe on the tree where my father should make his cuts. I learned a lot on this job. In the beginning it was not easy. Before he brought me out, this is what he did. He fell a tree. Then he set the point of the tape measure into the trunk and walked along the log, holding the power saw and tape measure in one hand and swinging a single-bit axe at the limbs with the other. His contract required the bucked logs to be limbed. He did fine with the red-fir, but he had come to a bunch of white-fir that have notoriously tough limbs. You can dull the blade of an axe if your hit a limb wrong and your hands sting from the handle. White-fir have a smooth grey bark, mottled with white spots and scattered with large blisters full of sticky pitch. The sawdust stinks like it is rotten, and then gallons of fluid can come gushing out of the largest trees, sometimes killing the power saw's engine. They were called piss-fir by the loggers, and the logs sank in any mill pond. No one liked logging piss-fir.

So I started on those hellish piss-fir limbs, with branches I had difficulty chopping off, on logs I could hardly walk without falling. My father had a pair of Currins logging boots, calked boots (pronounced cork boots), and he looked the part of a logger with the bottom of his pants cut off and frayed. Stagged pants they were called. This is done so that a logger will not hang up in the bushes at a bad time and be killed. And there I was with my leather-soled farm shoes which I cut up with my axe, trying to swing and keep my balance on the log at the same time. I do not understand how I managed not cut my foot or chop a toe off, but I never hurt myself with the axe, just ventilated those shoes. When the trees struck the earth, sections of bark were sometimes torn away, leaving white surfaces wet with sap. They were slick as ice to my shoes while my father's nailed boots gave him even better than usual traction. This was reversed when a loose piece of bark remained on the log. Then nailed boots could anchor the bark like a skate. In the beginning, I could not get the limbs cut off in time to measure the logs. Eventually we came to some red-fir, where the limbs cut more easily and pitch, if there was any, was white, solid and dried, like crumbly spun honey. I even became a little better at walking a log. Now I was working in the woods.

Brushing out around the next trees to be cut was part of my job. Sometimes this was just cutting some ferns; other times there was a clotted tangle of undergrowth to clear out. Swinging a straight-handled double-bit axe, I put to good use lessons learned from my grandfather. While a tree was being cut, the air filled with the whining revving roar of the two-cycle power saw engine and the fumes of the oiled-gas exhaust. The cutters of the power saw's chain ripped out mounds of white sawdust from the innards of the tree, and sharp resin spiced the exhaust smell. We fell a group of trees, bucked them, and moved on the the next ones. I lugged a tool box, a big gas can, a small oil can, wedges, axes, lunch, and a gallon glass water bottle from site to site. Destruction was wedged into the forest, piece by piece. In the morning we walked along raw new roads gouged into the earth, passing by mangled terrain. Some piles of sawdust remained stump-side, the top crust already weathered to a dark yellow.

Pitch stuck to hands and tool handles. The remedy was find a handful of rich forest loam, and rub those sticky hands and tools. The fine soil bound to the sticky spots, making patched friction-free surfaces. My mother had a concept of "clean dirt," and I figured dirt didn't get any cleaner than what was out in the woods.

Marking logs was satisfying when I finally pieced together from my father what the job was. He couldn't explain anything, but as usual I got clues from what made him angry. I already had practice at this inverse interpolation. The basic idea was that the lumber was to be cut at a mill into usable lengths, from 8-feet to 18-feet long, in multiples of two-feet, but the lengths 12-, 14-, and 16-feet were preferred. If a log is 11'11" long, then almost two feet of timber is wasted. So we added a few inches for imperfect cuts in the woods and in the mill. I measured down a log to the first cut as soon as possible, so that my father was not waiting while I cut limbs. I chopped neat notches into the log to mark the locations for bucking. A length might be 30 feet 8 inches, made up of 14'4" + 16'4". The total length of the tree mattered as it all should be cut into logs of reasonable lengths for the cats (bulldozers). Short logs wasted their time; long ones were impossible to pull out and wouldn't go onto a log truck. Also if the tree had a crook, a break, or some rotten spot, I had to account for that from the first cut, and eliminate those defects. I liked doing this and became skilled at sizing the situation up, even accounting for good places for my father to stand while he was bucking. It is hard to cut a log that is twenty feet off the ground. It took a month or so to catch onto this work. Then I could confidently stride down a Douglas-fir log, tape measure in my left hand spooling out its ribbon of metal, double-bit axe in my right hand swinging at dead limbs, feeling the tight grooves of eighty-year-old bark through the thin soles of my farmer shoes.

Logging was far easier work than almost anything we did on the ranch. And it didn't take a genius to see that it generated more money than the sheep and cattle did. I knew my father was paid in dollars per thousand board feet, and the estimates of board feet were made whenever two loggers talked, so his wages were not a secret.

One afternoon a man came out to the logging woods to see my father. Whatever brought him to the end of the dusty road I have no idea, but there he was calling out during one of the brief times the saw was turned off, climbing over the log-littered ground to join us. He brought with him his son who was perhaps a year or two younger than I was. I expected to have some conversation myself, but I glanced away and the boy disappeared. I walked up and down my logs, nonchalantly trimming and tidying up while in fact I was trying hard to locate the vanished kid. Not a sound, not a sign. When the conversation with my father was concluded the man called his son in with a sharp whistle as if to a just-trained dog. The kid reappeared as instantly as he had disappeared, and I went back to work humbled by my meager woodcraft.

Much white lichen or any fungus growing on the trunk of a tree and we knew it to be riddled with rot, not sound and white and vital. Such trees were more likely to be problems to fall, and they were laid down in whichever direction they leaned. Sometimes dead snags stood among the live timber. It was useful to get them down for the safety of the chocker setters, but it was long, hot work cutting them down for no pay. Instead my father aimed the timber he fell at the snags in hopes of knocking them over. We placed the undercut at the proper angle and watched the tree fall toward the object of destruction. Flying squirrels lived in snags, and they launched themselves at the last possible moment, when the falling tree was sure to hit their home and all hope was lost. They stretched their front-and-back legs out and sailed on the wind toward timber and safety.

The radio played country music for the loggers, and there was a catchy musical ad for McCulloch chain saws:

> *You're in luck when you got a McCulloch chain saw.*
> *You've got power by the hour in your hand.*
> *You're in luck when you got a McCulloch chain saw.*

In those days, Japanese power saws were sold but were still inferior to American brands. Our big McCulloch chain saw was a bright optimistic yellow. Power by the hour.

The real dangers were not from falling off a log or from my axe, but from almost everything else. Logs are laid down in a tangle of destruction in front of you, behind is the virgin forest. The timber faller cuts a notch in the tree he plans to fell, and the notch points the way of the tree's path if he has it right. A lot can go wrong. The tree can lean the wrong way or wind can push it. Then the tree can fall onto or away from the saw. That smashes the saw or at least the bar (which is the saw blade). Trees can be coaxed by inserting a wedge in the straight back-cut and hammering it in while the cut is being finished. The tree can sit back on the saw blade, which creates a large amount of swearing and wedge pounding. It is a lot better to have that wedge in there if it is going to be needed. There were light-weight aluminum wedges that my father would insert after I chopped the bark away from the cut. The saw-teeth could cut the metal, and the ends of the wedges became elaborate with gouges and scallops. Some-how the texture of these wedges was profoundly satisfying to me with their bent-over hammered ends and front edges grooved by the saw teeth. When things went right, my father shut the saw off, yelled "timber" or "down the hill," shoved the saw behind something to protect it and finally he ran for cover himself. The wood between the under-cut and back-cut creaked and broke in the sudden silence from the power saw being turned off, and the tree crashed to the ground, sometimes bending limbs of nearby trees which could break and fly back to injure a person or the equipment. Limbs called widow-makers hung in trees, waiting to crash down and kill us. We wore aluminum hats — tin hats — which were dented by these limbs. A small limb falling fifty feet could kill you.

A song written by a Coast logger became a local hit that was played that summer. At least that was the story up Two Mile Creek. (Johnny Cash recorded a version of this song.) A whistle punk was a worker in high-lead operations where the logs were hooked to cables and winched to the landing through the air. The whistle blasts were to signal what the operator of the engine should do.

> *It's one for stop and two for go,*
> *Oh, why I'm a whistle punk, I don't know.*
> *I was told this by a logger named Ray,*
> *Don't you cut timber on a windy day.*
> *Oh, why I'm a whistle punk, I don't know.*

This good advice to timber fallers was to prevent the trees from falling in unex-pected directions, pushed over by gusts of wind. The widow-makers fall more often on windy days too. There was a set number of blasts of the whistle that meant a man had been killed; maybe it was nine for dead but that wasn't in the song. Even high-balling reckless fallers stayed out of the woods on a windy day.

While then I thought that I hated country music, this is where my love of it began. The loggers, amazingly even my father, played the radio all the time they were not running equipment. Merle Travis, Roy Acuff, Hank Snow, Maddox Brothers and Rose, they were part of logging.

Bucking was the most dangerous work my father and I did. I watched logs shift and drop, and limbs snap back after a cut. Everything was in a tangle and under great stress, and you had to watch everything not to get hurt. We lost some equipment but were never injured seriously ourselves. I stayed as much out of the way as I could.

The next summer my wages doubled to ten-cents per tree, and one great day we fell thirty-one trees. $3.10, a magnificent sum of money! That summer we fell a couple of old-growth firs, glorious trees that were seven and eight feet in diameter. It took time to plan the direction the tree would fall and to be sure that it would not be shattered and ruined when it hit the earth. Some logging operations took a cat out to dig a level trench for the tree to fall into. Old-growth logs were valuable for making plywood. We called them peelers, and I saw them spinning in my uncle Ben Payne's plywood plant, their growth rings peeled off to be glued onto cheap core to make plywood. I decided that my uncle's business of making plywood was doomed, because it was obvious to me that Oregon's peelers would soon run out.

It took most of a day to cut down one of those big trees. The power saw seemed puny compared to the tree, and it even sounded differently, embedded into the thick cork-like bark under the high canopy of the tree. Once we had to cut a notch and insert a springboard for my father to stand over empty space while he cut the tree. (Many years after my greatgrandfather Charlie Waterman was frightened by a tale of cutting on a springboard and dodged the logging camp at Cutthroat Bay, Washington, there we were seeing what he had missed.) Finally, late in the afternoon after hours of cutting, the tree imperceptibly began its long fall to earth, and the saw was turned off. The amazingly long new silence was punctuated by loud creaks and pops, which eventually increased in frequency to a constant roar, until the tree broke off the huge stump. Then after a few silent seconds in free space, the giant with its ancient gnarled limbs crashed to earth. I climbed onto the log using the deep furrows in the bark and walked along it. I made little money the few times we cut old growth but it was to me an epic adventure.

My father told me that the old growth timber had been logged out by early steam-engine loggers. Some old growth were out of the reach of the cable rigging, he explained, and that's why a few remained. I tried to imagine those old-time loggers with powerful steam donkeys to handle the heavy cable in their high-lead operations. Then one day I realized that the second-growth timber we were cutting was 80 and more years old, pushing the date of the early logging operations too far back to be possible. This country had only been settled a bit over 50 years. I didn't upset my father with my conclusion, and forty-five years later when I read my grandmother Mabel's diary of crossing Oregon in 1911 in a wagon I had the answer to my puzzle; she wrote of the terrible fire of 1854 that killed most of the timber in this region.

34 Living Off the Land

There were a number of foods that grew wild and we harvested them. If there was something you could eat, you gathered it in and ate it. Sustainability was a word for another century. In damp shaded mossy areas, sheep sorrel sprung up. I loved the tart, sour flavor and ate clumps of it whenever I had time and opportunity. My grandfather Waterman taught me to eat sorrel which I thought was a plant exclusively for children.

There was a variety of eatable berries. At the top of the list is the small wild blackberry. Today people think they know what this means and that they have tasted this berry, but unless they were on the Oregon Coast in the 1940s and 1950s, it is doubtful. It has almost entirely disappeared. This plant was small and hugged the ground, and it was easy to miss altogether. It grew in and around logged off land. It was prevalent in my time there, especially the early years. The small, white blossoms transformed into tiny white berries that successively turned light-yellow, to red and yellow, to black and red, and finally, to a juicy ink-black. My mother said she would pick blackberries on her way to visit my grandmother Waterman, and that I would pick a few for grandmother, and then announce that I would eat what I had. They were delicious, that tart-sweet delicate blackberry flavor with tiny seeds which did not stick between your teeth. Eaten off the bush outdoors, in a bowl covered with thick cream, in a cobbler, and best of all in a pie. If I but think of them, I have pangs of desire. The down side was that the little vines had small sharp thorns, and that the berries were so small that it took a mighty effort to collect a gallon. No one who tasted them ever doubted that they were worth it. We had silver gallon pails into which my berries thumped.

There is a larger blackberry that grows wild; we called that invasive plant Himalayas and scorned them. Still, I ate them along the creek banks. The berries were large, and became ripe and sweet, with large seeds. When we bought the Wilson Place, there were banks of these berries, walls of big thorny bushes loaded with fruit. This was too much food to waste. We took ladders to push the thorny vines back and then climbed up and picked gallons of berries. My mother squeezed juice from them and we drank canned juice all winter. A big glass of blackberry juice with one or two scoops of her ice cream was a favorite treat.

Other berries were not gathered by our family. Tiny wild strawberries growing on creekside hills were almost invisible; I was amazed at the explosion of flavor contained in those red dots, although it took a good deal of searching to find a gritty red berry and patience was not among my natural talents. I ate huge amounts of thimbleberries, a deep-orange berry that formed as a cap over the end of the twig. The seeds made the eating of these dry berries crunchy and satisfying. In the same category of trail-side eating were the even more prevalent salmonberries, a lighter-orange berry with a classic berry shape. The flavor was weak but pleasant. I pulled the bushes down and ate them as my horse passed by. Finally there were two types of huckleberries, one with a dusted dark-blue berry and the second of a light-orange. I liked them both, but it took so long to pick enough to get full that I seldom indulged. They only grew on one corner of the Stonewall Wilson Homestead because of the sandy soil there. Later on when I was logging and living in my grandfather's house, I made a pie of the pale huckleberries.

Elderberry fruit hung in clusters from the ends of the branches of shrubs with long green leaves, and although they were reported to be used for jellies and even pies, we never ate them. One type had blue-black fruit and another brilliant red fruit, and the fact that they were left to the birds (who did relish them!) seemed to me to indicate a great abundance, so much so that I mistrusted the information that they were not poison to humans. There were also gooseberries and serviceberries.

Spring and summer, bees were everywhere, at fragrant balls of clover, at berry bushes, at wild roses, at anything with a flower. Despite my allergic reactions to their stings, I was fascinated by bees. My grandfather Waterman possessed a thick volume The ABC and XYZ of Bee Culture (1908 Edition) with a gold bee on the faded black cover, and I spent hours reading this tome, learning how bees lived and how people raised them. My keen interest, started by my love of honey of which I could not get enough, grew as I learned about the complex social behavior of bees. My grandfather had raised bees earlier in the century, but by my time the hives and equipment were just dusty litter scattered among old empty whiskey bottles. Stories were all he had to offer me then, how he had done bees. A red-cedar tree cut down for posts and shake bolts contained a wild-bee hive, and I tasted some of that hard-won honey: it was fantastic — vivid dramatic flavors rang and echoed in my mouth. I had to have more and made a quest of finding wild-bee hives. I looked up BEE-Hunting in the book, and read of elaborate strategies to determine a "bee-line." The whole enterprise had an elegance about it, and I would find honey to boot! This was perhaps my first encounter with the gulf between theory and practice, as none of my bees "lined" back to their hives.

Finally I found a way to make them more visible. I caught bees on clover with a glass jar which I up-ended and added a dollop of flour stolen from my mother's pull-out flour bin. Shaken and suitably whitened, the bee was released. The creature inevitably spiraled away from me, never tracing that required straight line. I was never able to satisfy my lust for wild-bee honey.

From the age of seven when I was given a firearm, I shot rabbits, quail and grouse. The rabbits were fairly easy to collect, but I had to shoot the heads off the birds, something that gave them a good chance to live. I was not told to go shoot something, but a couple of grouse made a meal. No one suggested that these animals might be conserved or managed, and I certainly did not hit on the idea for myself.

And I caught trout at every opportunity, which was not nearly often enough for me. But I could have spent full time trout fishing and not tired of it. The trout twisted and curled as they fried, as vitally as they had when they were alive, slow-motion versions of their silver speckled aerial displays. I loved the crunchy tails and ate the smallest fish whole, bones and all.

Every fall flocks of ducks and geese arrowed by far overhead, never landing, not even on the Lower Place during high floods. There were tall tales of rifle shots bringing down a goose, its head neatly shot off. But those wild birds did not give us a glance; we could neither feed nor harm them.

Our main source of protein was venison, the meat of the Coast blacktail deer. For years my family did not eat the meat we raised on the ranch for sale, unless the animal was so defective that it could not be sold. The livestock brought in cash needed for running the ranch, paying down loans and making the down payment on the next ranch. So my father tried to shoot one deer per month on average, something that was illegal. My conservative parents, about as faithful as citizens can be to this country, ignored the fact that they were not following the rules. It fits into the Western ethic of live-off-the-land, you are ruler of your own property. The American relationship between public and private rights regarding wild game had been worked out not many years before this. There were a few tight situations, as when a game warden acquaintance dropped by, and my mother had to wrap a deer carcass in sheets and hide it in a closet while the guy visited away with her and later with my father. But all in all, my father just went out and shot what came by. He used the old Model 64 30-30 that my grandfather brought across Oregon in the wagon, and for some reason he later bought himself a single shot .22-hornet, one of those wildcat cartridges that people like to make. It has a small bullet mass ahead of a lot of powder. Later when I learned more about guns, I found that it is a poor bullet for brushy country. And it was a single shot. But once he made it pay: he came onto a herd of deer and managed to kill three with one shot. Knowing about that cartridge, I realize he couldn't have hit any bone to allow the bullet enough energy to pass through two animals and still kill the third.

"I didn't have to hunt for two months," he said with relief that fifty years later was still palpable.

My mother made fried steak and roasts, but as anyone who has cooked game knows, this meat without fat in the muscle comes out very dry unless great care and skill is applied. I liked the canned venison my mother put up with her pressure cooker, a preparation that gave the meat moisture and took away the strong gamey flavor.

In this category of subsistence hunting, I locate my father's fondness for night hunting which we also called spot lighting. He continued night hunting in later when we were no longer hunting out of need for the meat. Ray had learned to night hunt in the hungry days of the depression. The idea is that deer will stare at a light at night and that they can more easily be shot. They often are caught crossing a road in the headlights and just freeze. Night hunting has never been legal for good reason. Out in the country, it is difficult to drive rapidly to where the deer are eating apples and then blast away from the car. And deer are not helpless at night. Until that light catches their eyes, they — not you — can see, and they hear incredibly well too. So the strategy was to take someone carrying a big light, and yourself carry a smaller light to fit along the side of the rifle for aiming. Then try to slip up to a high point without detection by the deer. Lights come on and perhaps a deer is shot. I hated these ventures. There was always a possibility of getting caught, although we never were, and there was the tension of never reading my father's mind, not knowing what he wanted. I never got the details right. My father did like to night hunt, and he was good at it. It produced meat, even if he did have poor help.

The last source of wild protein was salmon. In the forties the salmon and steelhead runs were still substantial, and many fish came in from the sea to spawn, and in the case of salmon, to die. Coho, chum and Chinook salmon ran up our stream, and the Chinook were larger, sometimes weighing thirty pounds and more. The steelhead have the more attractive option of living to return to the sea. In the fifties, the runs took a nose dive because of the watershed damage from logging. We made a number of meals of these fish, but many fewer than from deer. Fish was a less regular resource. They were taken in this way: my father got his gun and sent me to the barn for the six-tine manure fork. Then we stalked a riffle where salmon or steelhead were spawning. My father positioned himself for his shot. These fish were spooky and anything could startle them; whenever that happened, I might as well have caused it because I received the blame. If the setup was successful and a shot was made, my father started shouting and swearing at me to pitchfork the fish. Otherwise the fish could recover enough from the shock to escape into deeper water. This was tense work which contained none of the deep pleasures I found in trout fishing. For reasons unknown to me my father considered all but the steelhead to be tainted and not eatable, that the salmon were already rotten, and we never kept any salmon to eat. But those shining twisting silver steelhead straight from the sea and who knew what travels, still crawling with sea-lice, wild with the slight taste of salt water in their flesh, those were the most exciting, the most exotic fish I have ever seen or eaten.

Excess venison and fish were smoked, and I loved smoked game. The venison was sliced into thin strips with no fat as the fat quickly becomes rancid. Then we salted it down in a crock for a day or two. There were minor variations on this theme, valued and hoarded in inverse proportion to the innovations which included: adding brown sugar, adding white sugar, including minute amounts of saltpeter, drying strips before smoking, using un-ionized salt, and most radical of all, parboiling until the meat turns grey-white and then drying. We had a smokehouse, a eight-foot square building about twelve-feet high. There were mesh racks high in the smokehouse, and we made fires of alder or apple-wood, fires that just smoldered along putting out strong, intense smoke. After the coals were going, green vine maple branches could be laid on top of the coals. The idea was to smoke-cure, not to cook the meat with heat. One way to make jerky is to produce dry strips that are cardboard in your mouth. This is the traditional Indian method, and their jerky will last forever. We made moist, chewy, tasty jerky which we kept in a warm cupboard by the fire to prevent mold. On a cold rainy winter day, riding along a ridge checking the stock, jerky was comfort food. I usually had an apple or two to balance the flavors.

My favorite was smoked salmon. Salmon is very easy to cure with heat, instead of smoke. That is a mistake. The best method is to pipe the smoke to the fish from a distance to cool the smoke as much as possible. Most people who smoke fish commercially make a dry inferior product. We did not cut slabs of salmon, but cut it into steaks as if for frying. We cured the fish for a few hours in salt and then put it in the smokehouse with very low coals. Then there is a critical fifteen minutes when you can go out to the smokehouse, reach up and pry a piece off the mesh and eat the warm juicy oily fish, full of intense smoke and salmon flavors.

35 Grade School

My introduction to school was traumatic. My mother left me in a bare-clay yard full of screaming children, and I had no idea what was going on. With no experience around other children, I did not learn very fast. As we were herded into a room, I was totally confused about what was expected of me, a condition which did not improve for years.

In a few weeks, my teacher sent a message home that I was far behind the class. An ex-teacher, my mother was upset and set out to make things right. Amazing to me now, she had not read to me as a child so I had no introduction to reading, nor to arithmetic. She made cards for the letters and sounds and for arithmetic, and drilled me each night. Apparently I did not learn my sums properly, and in frustration she made me eat one of the flash-cards. Years later, she thought that I had looked more deeply into those simple tasks and that explained my difficulties. I doubt it; I did not know what it was meant on the simplest level. But full of flash-card, I did learn my sounds and sums, so much so that in a few more weeks, my mother received another note from my teacher: I was now ahead of the class and would my mother please stop whatever she was doing with me?

My barrel-shaped battle-axe of a teacher disliked me from the get-go, and she taught my class for three long years. Certain children ascend to the top ranks of school, and in my class this was Janice Boice who, as we went through twelve years of school, was cute, then pretty and finally beautiful (or so we thought then). Her mother dressed her to make certain we all understood just how special Janice was, and everyone including our teachers knew it. Her handwriting was perfect; in contrast, mine was terrible. I never saw the point of much of what we did in school and didn't attend closely to what were to me mysterious rituals. Once I made a passably legible attempt, and on the third-grade bulletin board, our teacher posted my only slightly smudged page. Janice who dominated in the posted-work category walked primly up and looked it over.

"Why," she sniffed, "that is just awful!"

"Oh yes, it is," the teacher answered with a sigh, "but you should see what he usually turns in."

The months of school were mostly months of rain, and I often walked the half-mile to the bus stop in the rain. It could get cold in the fall and winter, and then the mud-puddles froze so that I could try to fracture each one and still catch the bus. A few times each winter it snowed but seldom enough to last more than a day. More often, snow stuck to the highest ridges to the south on a ranch we called Vanderworkers where in eighteen years I never saw one human. Snow was a disaster for livestock on the open range, but I never thought about that on the way to school. My sinuses became infected each winter as soon as the rains started, and my nose continuously ran day and night. In the morning, all four of my pant's pockets, front and back, contained clean ironed handkerchiefs. I came home with those pockets stuffed with damp crumpled cloth. The flow would alleviate in summer, but most of my school days were spent blowing my nose.

The school cafeteria served globs of tasteless food, slapped and slopped onto our plates. I hated most of it including the milk which was pasteurized and tasted weird to me. I ate as little as possible, except when once a month in huge containers we had peanut-butter-and-honey which we spread onto thin slices of white bread. This was my favorite food at school, big hunks of peanuts in the peanut-butter like gravel on a sand bar with rich deposits of honey.

In the third grade I had an experience that changed my life. I was reading a book at a big table in the winter afternoon sunlight, and I entered into the book so deeply that I forgot my surroundings, going into a trance. The book was a biography of Daniel Boone, opening with a dramatic clash with the Indians. Then the narrative described his childhood, his love of the woods, and his skill barking squirrels which was shooting into the tree next to them so they would fall to the ground stunned with no meat lost from the bullet. This would not work with our digger squirrels which did not climb trees. And we didn't eat squirrels, but I imagined myself creeping in the forest barking squirrels. Then the book came to Boone shooting a bear after which he started his own hunting company. At 15 years old! The battles of the French and Indian War were interesting but I was more engaged in his life after his marriage when he kept moving westward to explore new county. In the book he had just discovered the Cumberland Gap when my teacher with some difficulty brought me back to the Langlois classroom.

This profound experience gave me a hunger for more escapes. I read everything that I could get my hands onto. Unfortunately that was not much. When I could take books home from school, I read them on the hour-and-a-half bus ride I endured each trip to and from school. But when I was allowed check books out, I quickly read all the books that my schools had in their libraries that were of any interest to me. I seldom looked words up; I guessed their meaning from context if I could. As a consequence I knew the meaning of many words I had no idea how to pronounce correctly. My family possessed only a few books, and I suffered from not enough to read for the entire time from learning to read until I went to college. Books seemed an impossibly valuable resource; I day-dreamed of having enough books to read and the time to read them. I worried that there might be too few books in the world, that like our red-cedar logs or old-growth firs they were too finite to last a lifetime.

Each morning was the Pledge of Allegiance with "one nation, under God," God being introduced in 1954. The Pledge was as mysterious as everything else, and it was years of chanting it before I wondered what the words meant. Flag-republic-liberty-and-justice-for- all, it was actually delivered in one long run-together phrase without taking breath or pause. From the hallway it must have sounded like nests of wasps behind the classroom doors.

Recess was a generally unpleasant experience. For me the ball games were impossibly involved, and even when I learned their rules, I was inept at them. The skills of riding, shoveling and chopping did not translate from the ranch to school. And my general approach to anything, evolved for dealing with my father, was to try not to be noticed and not to make an effort in public. I was usually among the last chosen for any game. One recess activity I did enjoy was marbles. In spring after the rains stopped, we drew circles and ovals into hard-packed yellow clay with our broad-bladed jack-knives, and then each player carefully placed his stake into the ring. The click of striking marbles, the studied disinterest of spectators waiting their turn, I now see that at marbles I might have developed my love of gambling. Other things took place at recess. Boys who did not pass even one test in the classroom recited long obscene poems in the bare-dirt playground, something which impressed me very much. If they were so dumb, how could they remember all that?

Sometime in the early years of school, we took an IQ test. I have exactly one image from the test. A man in a suit and tie wearing a derby hat waiting at a crosswalk for a light. I had never seen a traffic light or a crosswalk in my life, and the men I knew wore Stetsons or tin-hats. This was so mysterious to me that I had no idea what to think. I wish I could say that I sat there imagining asking that little man questions about sheep and cows and grass and logs, or that I had wondered what he might do if I galloped my horse straight at him, but alas no such mutinous thoughts came to me. Instead I was struck dumb by the image. There is no chance that I answered the question correctly, and I suspect the test was written for affluent white children from the suburbs. This day circled back to find me when leaving high school I was interviewed by a man from Oregon State.

"You will do well in college," he said confidently, "with your IQ and the grades you have, you obviously have very, very good study habits." My grades were really not so good, so my IQ score must have been "very, very" low.

The atom bomb intruded into our classroom, and we were shown mushroom-cloud graphics and then drilled on getting under the wooden desks. I had some experience dodging rams and bulls, and knew a desk would not save me from them, let alone from a rifle bullet or from a blast of the dynamite we used for road building. I didn't put much stock in crouching under my desk with my hands over my head and didn't take the end-of-the-world talk seriously.

I flunked flutaphone. My family was not musical; neither of my parents even played the radio to hear music. My mother was indifferent to music; my father despised it. In grade school, I was forced to take the mandatory class in flutaphone. I thought it was dreadful, and as usual I was totally confused. After not passing the first year, I was sent through the class again with the two or three other flutaphone failures. That second spring I was playing at a median level, sounding the correct notes in time and feeling superior to the new crop of failures. I was relieved to end music class, although to my surprise I missed it.

FIRST GRADE

FIFTH GRADE

SIXTH GRADE

LANGLOIS GRADE SCHOOL

Langlois, Oregon

Student Body Card

1954-1955

The Langlois school system had a strong stake in music with its director Charley Jensen. There were substantial investments in musical instruments and concerts for the schools and the public. I was immune to the attractions of those nicely rounded smooth notes and to that message of an avenue of escape from the Coast, but others were not. Without rock-and-roll with its brash and irreverent noise that arrived when I was in high school, I would have gone through life without music. Looking back on it I wish that Charley had thought to bring in the works of Miles Davis or John Coltrane to the windy Oregon Coast, even some Charles Ives. Their harsher sounds might have reached me.

All grade school students took a hearing test. After other such measured events, including classroom examinations, I was always astonished at the high achievements of the other children which they related in the recess playground. What they knew, how high they could fly! So I decided I could fake the hearing test, just to be in the same elite group as my classmates. It required a response at regular intervals until one could no longer hear the sounds. I thought I had done fine, that is that I had successfully faked it, when I was kept back with a few others for more testing. After a bit I panicked: if my fake was substandard I must be going deaf! So I faced up to it and only responded when I could actually hear something. Soon I was released into the schoolyard where I heard tales from kids who had heard something at every interval. It was my first glimpse of how much and how well people can lie, and a small hint of my gullibility.

In our fifth-grade year, the Brown girl went to the bathroom one rainy afternoon and did not return to class for a few weeks. She had two huge brothers, brutes who bullied me and anyone smaller than they were on the bus. They twisted my arm until I cried, tore off my shirt, threw my hat out of the window, an assortment of mean things. I hated those guys almost as much as I hated my father, although at least they could only get at me on the bus. It turned out that they had fathered a child with their sister. While I knew how farm animals created babies, this event caused me to think hard about human babies and the possible details of making them. Given the mysteries of the human activities around me, it seemed to be complicated. Still the Brown boys had managed something, even if it was unspeakable.

Generally school improved as I grew older. The expectations became more evident, and the benefits of school slowly became apparent. It gave relief from the irrelevance and embarrassment of being young. Not long after this being young was viewed as valuable, superior. But we carried the opposite labels and to gain some ground each of us referred to our father as "the old man." My father planned his jobs so that he could get as much out of me as possible, and I rode to school on Monday in an exhausted stupor. I paid no attention to the classroom until Wednesday or Thursday, when finally having enough rest, I shrugged myself out of lethargy to tune into what my classmates had been doing all week. That gave me a day or two to catch up, and neither I nor my teachers found it remarkable that I could in a day or so accomplish a week's schoolwork. Fortunately for me examinations were private affairs, one sat at a desk and wrote answers to questions without being observed by others. I was at my best when alone, unobserved with a task in front of me.

Although I did not relate well to children my own age, I was able to carry on conversations with adults. Often I was the last passenger on the school bus, and I got to know my bus drivers well. The bus ground up and down muddy roads, and I sat up front in the nearly empty bus, chatting with the drivers. Often they were men who were too worn down to hold a job in the logging woods or even in a saw-mill. In a conversation about life and what it held in promise, one of those men told me that adult life consisted of dull, repetitive work, and that the major task of youth was to learn acceptance of that dreary truth. I thought about the adults I knew and saw that he was correctly describing most of their lives. Except for my grandfathers, the men around me were just grinding along like old transmissions, doing tiring and boring work, hoping to earn enough to live on and not to be killed or injured. Both my grandfathers had satisfying lives, and neither of them sat down in submission. Riding up the winding road that rainy afternoon, I vowed that I would not live a boring life. It had to be possible to be interested in what might happen the next day.

At times my class had sessions on current events, and I seldom had any idea what was being discussed. It was in the same league as geography lessons about the cities, climates, and products of foreign lands. My family only discussed matters outside our lives when the price of livestock went down or the price of fencing or taxes went up, and then they complained about the government. What the government was or what it did was unclear to me, but my parents strongly objected to it. I did know Canada was to the north and Mexico to the south, and pictures of fish in the sporting magazines gave them some faint reality, but the rest of the world outside our bit of Coast might not have existed for all the thought I gave it. The brush I chopped and the lambs I cut tails from were real even if I might not much like it, while the U.S. Senate and the principal product of southern Chile were completely irrelevant to me. I had no idea why anyone cared.

Mathematics seemed the dullest possible subject, and I was surprised when in the sixth grade we began to do story problems. Story problems combined arithmetic with reading in a neat way, and there was a little suspense in sorting out what bit of simple arithmetic it took to solve the problem. My classmates, who probably could not read too well, foundered on these new problems, and it was the first sense I had of being different from other children in a positive way. About this time I wrote a few short stories, heavily influenced by the cowboy author Will James. Some Westerns sat on our bookshelf, and my uncle George loved cowboy stories. Will James even drew sketches of the horses he wrote about with such love and accuracy. My own stories were about pioneers and western explorations, and I cannot recall that anyone was interested in them except for Bertha, my grandfather's third wife who wondered if we couldn't sell them. That was obviously ridiculous: you sold cows, sheep and logs. Not stories! Later in high school, one of my classmates recalled listening to me read my stories in class and how impressed she and everyone was.

"We were writing about Jane and Dick," she told me, "and you came out with those marvelous tales. We sat there amazed." I had no clue even that my work was different from that of anyone else, and I let my writing lapse.

In the seventh grade I had a wonderful teacher, Mrs. Churchill. She was my first teacher who possessed any curiosity about the world. She had red hair, and I now suspect, a sharp, dry wit. I heard my mother telling The Girls that I had a teacher who liked me.

"And Mrs. Churchill says he has such a good sense of humor. Of course, neither of them has a sense of humor," my mother laughed in that superior disparaging way she had.

I found this fragment of conversation remarkable: just exactly what was a sense of humor and why did I find so much funny which was unnoticed by or just irritating to the people around me? Much later I realized that much of what was considered humorous on Four Mile involved ridicule. Some animal or person—often from town or Oklahoma — fell down or did something considered stupid. My mother sometimes added with a condescending chuckle, "Well, I'm sure they just didn't know any better." Humor was used to hold what ground these people had gained. Irony would have been much too risky, and laughing at themselves was unthinkable.

At the close of a school year, infinite summer loomed ahead, horizon after horizon, like the rings of an old-growth fir stump stretching beyond sight. Haying, shearing, building fence, setting sheep upright to find them down again the next day. Summer lasted forever. I was never sorry to see school end, but I was always glad finally to see summer close down so I could once again get some rest from Monday to Friday.

In the fourth or fifth grade, we were asked what we planned to be when we grew up. "A rancher," I answered, "I guess."

I did not wish to continue what I considered an awful and boring life, but I could not see what alternatives I had. My mother tried to make my going to college a given by mentioning it often, but other than going away to school, she did not provide me with any clues as to what I might study there or do after. Then in the seventh grade I exploded. That year I received a huge, extravagant Christmas present from my mother, a Gilbert chemistry set. It was the next-to-smallest model that Gilbert made, and I was thrilled with the bottles of chemicals and the precise equipment, all neatly enclosed in a wooden case. It set my brain on fire. Just why did things have their forms and properties? What made one thing sticky and another smooth? Or one salty and another sweet? And just how did two unrelated chemicals mix to become a distinct third? That there were explanations for such things was astonishing! There was no one to ask my questions, and I found an old book that referred to valence. Mrs. Churchill knew no science, but she urged me to look to the high school, where in one of the set jokes of lousy American high-school education, I was sent to the coach who taught science. Of course, he had never in his life understood valence, but after my short lifetime spent listening to my father, I could quickly distinguish utter confusion from an explanation. I decided I could not get the story then, but vowed to sort it out as soon as I had the resources. I set off, mixing everything I could find, systematically recording the results. I knew that I was just cataloging observations but I hoped understanding was somewhere nearby. The varnished plywood walls, floor, and ceiling of my room became splattered with chemicals from my experiments. My father hated this new passion, but I was accustomed to his scorn and anger at me doing anything that was not ranch work done in exactly the way he'd been doing it for years. The enthusiasm I possessed somehow made both him and the ranch smaller. For the first time, I could see out over Four Mile to another place. Somewhere people truly understood chemical mysteries; somewhere there were people called chemists who had jobs that employed that understanding. It was a revelation. Finally I had a goal. I would become a chemist and live in Chicago, a place so far away that it might have been on the moon.

I have no idea what became of Mrs. Churchill, but I owe her a great deal. She like my mother's friend Aloma Gamble encouraged children to be curious and to follow a lead. I did not become a chemist but did learn some science on my own. More importantly I learned to dream outside the watershed of Four Mile Creek. And Mrs. Churchill taught me to trust my own sense of what was funny.

36 On Vacation

My mother wanted to see the world and my father did not. Bessie applied pressure to go to different places, but she could not budge Ray from the only place on earth where he was comfortable, Four Mile. She could not have been less interested in anything than a rodeo, but that is the only thing my father would do. My mother allowed her husband to ground her totally. If she had been able to choose a trip, where would she have taken us? It was by 1950 far too late to know that. So we went to the rodeo on the two vacations we took in 18 years, to South San Francisco to attend the Grand International Rodeo at the Cow Palace.

On the way to San Francisco, the City, we took more time to see the redwoods than my father and I had when trucking sheep past the same trees. At one place you could pay a small fee and drive the car through a redwood. I thought it was terrific. Then again, I was ready for almost anything new. And being inside a car that was inside a tree was new to me. Imagine: men had cut the heart out of a tree that was standing when Jesus Christ was born, cut out a slot of two-thousand years, and we drove right through it.

We stayed at a little motel in San Francisco. This time my father was challenged to find his way about the city, not that he asked directions or ever admitted that he was confused. When he finally found a route to the zoo, say, he never varied his approach. The same meandering loops were duplicated each time. My job was to sit in the back of the car and keep my mouth shut, something for which I had been trained. Most often we went to the rodeo.

In the beginning I loved watching the events in that huge arena. We didn't have much else to do, so we attended most days. Barrel racing, calf roping, steer roping, bull-dogging, bucking-horse riding, bull riding: these events cycled and recycled before us. My favorite cowboy was Casey Tibbs who won the all-around championship. What a name for a cowboy! Casey Tibbs had slim hips and broad shoulders, and he could do anything on a horse. (He makes a brief appearance in the best rodeo movie ever made, Sam Peckinpah's Junior Bonner.) The acts spooled on and on until the finals, and then we were done with rodeo for another year. Rodeo had little to do with my life on a livestock ranch except for barrel racing and the cutting horse contests. Although I was in awe of the athletes, I became less and less of a rodeo fan as I grew older. John Sinclair who cowboyed in New Mexico in the 1920s put it well: "I was absolutely bored to death. I saw those acrobats coming out and riding those bucking horses and getting bucked off, and I saw wild-cow-milking contests.... I was just bored stiff. Livestock appealed to me, but rodeo didn't appeal to me at all."[1]

We went to the zoo a couple of times, and I was fascinated by the animals. My family's favorite animals were monkeys, and my father laughed at their antics. I preferred the grazing animals, the zebras and antelope of the African plains, and tried to imagine their home country. I placed them into a huge grass rangeland that was our Indian Allotment greatly expanded.

I was curious about the different people and wanted to know what they did, how they lived. I saw Blacks, Chinese and Japanese people, for the first time, and I heard another language spoken for the first time. We walked into Chinatown down Grant street, and it was much like today, full of tourists and natives alike. Ducks hung in shop windows, covered with flies, and I had not even tasted duck meat. Would those glistening birds taste like the wild ducks that I knew people shot and ate?

On our first family trip to San Francisco we visited some people who lived in a massive Victorian house. We must have been ordered to go by my grandmother Payne, as the woman of the house Fairy had been married to her brother Ira who had died. Fairy's current husband was a prosperous minister whereas Ira and Fairy had traveled the Nazarene Gospel circuit and had no money. In that room filled with heavy dark furniture arranged on acres of patterned carpet, the tension was as stiff as my new jeans. Our reluctant hosts were formally dressed, and apparently viewed any relationship with the likes of us as an unfortunate accident, to be forgotten as soon as they could get us out of their house. There were long painful pauses in the conversation, and I heard my mother sigh with relief when we were going away down the walk.

Having idolized the incredible Golden Gate Bridge from my livestock hauling trips, I was in love with the City. The bridge, the zoo, Chinatown, the steep streets. Sutro Baths was my favorite spot in San Francisco. Adolph Sutro made a fortune in silver in Nevada's Comstock mines, and he spent it in San Francisco. Religious about water and bathing, as soon as he became rich Sutro had a portable bathtub which traveled with him for his daily bath. In the early 1890s he built Sutro Baths out where the Pacific halts the City. In its heyday, Sutro Baths had seven pools and over 500 private dressing

1. *A Cowboy Writer in New Mexico*, 63–64.

rooms, all under a vast glass canopy. When I saw it, there were no pools and no dressing rooms. Instead only a dingy skating rink and some exhibits were open. The building's glass cover was dimmed by sixty years of weather, and it was a damp, dreary place with marvelous light. That only sounds like a contradiction; this huge structure was a great many things. There were exhibits of dolls, of a carnival model made by prisoners from toothpicks, of mummies, of ancient instruments of torture. These objects were amazing to me. My family did not possess the concept of museums, we did not even know the De Young existed, but Sutros was a museum, bizarre as could be. I studied a Ferris wheel constructed of toothpicks and knew that those prisoners were more bored and confined than anything I could imagine on Four Mile. Such intricate work! And the torture equipment was almost beyond belief. How could human beings treat each other like that? The strange exhibits, the light, the eerie nature of the place; Sutros was absolutely tops with me. It burned down in 1966, "a suspicious blaze." Today you can see the crumbled, ruined foundations sloping down to the ocean. Imagine the Grateful Dead playing that rink. Imagine gays and 500 private dressing rooms.

One trip we also went over the Sierra Nevada Range to Virginia City and Fallon in Nevada. The mountains I saw outside the car window seemed abstract and unreal. Some relative of Aloma's had a little roadhouse outside Fallon in what I then thought to be desert, the heat and the sand and the lack of green. Little did I know I would come to love that spare landscape. Al ran the roadhouse and cooked. His menu was steak and hamburger, and he prepared a meal for us. My father obtained a truth about fine dining from Al which he often repeated. "Eat 'er while she's hot! Old Al said to eat 'er while she's hot!"

Once after the rodeo was over we went to Los Angeles, a huge shapeless city. There was nothing to appeal to a child in love with San Francisco, something many San Francisco boosters today echo. The goal (or excuse) for an excursion so far south was to see the Lockharts, more relatives of Aloma Gamble who sometimes came to Bandon. They lived in Pasadena, and I was bored with the palm-lined streets. We did go to Hollywood, and it was commonplace, even to me. At home I listened to a radio program, brought to you from Hollywood and Vine. Well, I was standing at Hollywood and Vine, and there wasn't a radio program in sight. It did not look to me as if there ever had been.

On the vacation when I was eleven, my brother was almost seven, just about to start school. He had not yet learned to count to ten, something which worried my mother the former teacher. He had not reached the number five, and the road to four was not reliable. Charlie only ate hot-cakes on the trip. He found something restaurants could cook that he could eat, and he stuck with it. Late in the evening, a short-order cook came out to see the little boy who insisted on hot-cakes or nothing at all. He looked at Charlie for a bit and went back into his kitchen to mix the batter. My mother even tried the "Learn to count or no hot-cakes" routine on him, but Charlie was long past being bribed by food. It was an event for family history when, at the end of the trip during which he had said even less than usual, out over the evening hot-cakes came an unexpected chant.

"One-Two-Three-Four-Five-Six-Seven-Eight-Nine-Ten."

37 Dying Off

Birth and death came and went with the seasons. Lambs were born in late January and February, and calves were born in February and March. We sold animals for slaughter, the sheep in August, the cattle in September. We shot deer in October. Late fall and winter salmon came in silver-bright from the sea and then rotted in the fresh water of Four Mile Creek. Ewes died giving birth, and at any time an animal could die from disease or an accident.

Our livestock had a difficult time surviving the winters. Blacktail deer had it much worse. Some deer died of starvation each winter, and many died in the most severe winters. The rains came, the sun was not seen for months, and the forage was consumed. Deer that had been in prime condition in October were stumbling and falling, unable to jump a low fence to escape us. Their bones were visible; no flesh seemed to remain on their skeletons. Shooting a deer out of season when it was in good condition, and making mincemeat and jerky out of it, was an alternative to the animal dying in a muddy ditch. Even the coyotes did not get much food from deer that died of starvation. I found the animals that struggled and died in ditches remarkable. They did not protest their cruel fate that in the fall they had been fat and healthy and here they were starving to death. They lived entirely in the present, so it seemed to me. I remembered the pleasant autumn days, I anticipated the warm, sweet spring to come, I rebelled at the present damp, cold winter. The animals around me, domestic and wild alike, had their entire existence in the present, a nowness which I found both compelling and frightening. They were completely there, not saving up to buy land or waiting until they were eighteen to escape their circumstances. The eyes of those starving creatures were awful to look into: they looked by me or through me, the animal they had feared the most, to see something else in the distance.

It was not surprising to me that my grandfather grew old, then became sick enough to commit suicide. Animals and men wore out, bones broke, teeth ground down to the gums, winter came. I cried for my grandfather in my room which he had helped to build, but my eyes were dry at the public funeral where I sat with my family under a tarp at the Bandon cemetery and listened to a dreadful sermon. Some relatives came for the occasion and tried to steal his best cribbage board. (Snooping in their luggage, my father found it and stole it back. He couldn't let something like that leave Four Mile.) I vowed never to attend another burial, it all seemed so remote from the warm man I had known. For many years I refused to visit his grave-site. I had listened to his stories for my entire life, and I sat with him at the end when his memory of them failed and they were shattered into fragments. What could some preacher tell me about Charlie Frank Waterman? What was there to be found at the location where they tossed his dead body in a hole in the ground and covered it up with dirt and flowers and a silent gravestone?

I heard that suicide was illegal and that I decided was nonsense. Laws against killing other people, deer, and even fish made sense to me, even though I might not always have obeyed them. But a person's life and what they did with it was their own business, including ending it with a hunting rifle, as my grandfather had done. The law is not coming after a successful lawbreaker, that is for certain.

God was held in high regard by my parents, or so they said, although this had no noticeable effect on our lives. We worked as hard on Sunday as Saturday, and while I was taught the Lord's prayer, even saying grace at meals was reserved for infrequent family holidays. I puzzled over the line in the Lord's prayer: "The Lord is my shepherd I shall not want." Failing to put in the comma, I found this odd beyond comprehension: if I was not to require the shepherd, why worship him? The very notion of sheep that would hold in herds day and night seemed pretty far fetched to me, judging by our Four Mile stock. I did pray a few times for petty things such as a present or not being found out for failing at some task assigned by my father, but the results seemed far from miraculous. Besides, praying appeared to me to be begging which didn't appeal to me at all. God was as remote and as intangible as Chicago or the Chinese language, all of which I could safely ignore. Religion did not provide me with any basis for understanding what was happening all around me.

During my teen years I developed a keen desperate anxiety about death. People often say that teenagers have no consciousness of death, that they behave recklessly as if they were immortal. Not I. I had a sharp sense of myself, of my identity that I carefully separated from the rest of the world by my skin. The dirt and pine tar was not me even though it stuck to me; the inside of my body seemed to contain my self that was bounded by my skin. I could see that a man who lost an index finger in the fan belt of a tractor remained the same person, but obviously it was a threat to who he was. Cut too much off and he would die, I reasoned, so it was getting close to what defined a person. The thought that I would die and no longer exist was deeply troubling and terrifying to me. It was impossible to find my way around this: death was staring me in the face. These thoughts kept me awake some nights, and occasionally I walked the roads and ridges of the ranch in the dark trying to calm myself. Other times I would be absorbed in something, and the sudden fear of my death would strike me in the stomach like a blow. That I would not exist and that the world would go on without me was obvious, inexplicable and totally terrifying. What about me? What was I?

Nothing I read helped me with this, but I decided that not getting killed was one of the few things I could do. "Wake up and die right," my father had growled at me. I wanted to wake up and live longer; in fact I wanted to live forever and knew that I would not. In the logging woods where I worked setting chokers, the cables and winches created dangers which were beyond my experience and intuition. I tried to manage this by constantly watching and concentrating on what was happening, but limbs and logs flew in every direction and I was often paralyzed by indecision as to which way to run. The terror I felt in the logging woods developed into undiagnosed stomach ulcers.

My grandfather Waterman seemed content with his life and fate, and I believed he had committed suicide with acceptance and grace. There I was writhing about like a raccoon caught in a bear trap. I wanted to ask my grandfather how it was done, but he was gone and could not walk up this road to show me how to chop down this mass of tangled brush. The conclusion I came to was that my only hope was, as I became older and lived out my life, that I would be satisfied with that life and could accept the inevitable end of it. Perhaps like the wild animals I would lose my fear of this earth, and even more, leave it content that I had lived.

38 High School

My eighth-grade teacher Mr. Flood moved with us to small Langlois High School. He taught both science and English, and as always he had difficulty with discipline in his classes. Mr. Flood had won a gold medal running in a relay in a world Olympics, but by 1956 he was a troubled alcoholic. He beat kids who irritated him as he tried to maintain quiet in his classrooms. Once he was hitting a boy with a ruler and the brass edge flew off hitting a student acorss the aisle. I had some influence with him, and ran his science classes. He sent questions to me, and I decided what we studied next in the textbook. "Go ask Mike" was Mr. Flood's usual answer to student questions. I knew little science that was not in our shallow book, but at least I could understand the book and apparently no one else bothered to. My mother told of my returning from the first day of high school deeply disappointed, saying the science book was "for children" and that I began writing my own book which was to contain what I knew about science.

I loved fiction but had little to read. My mother possessed two books by John Steinbeck, one of them *The Grapes of Wrath*. I did not miss the point that many of my classmates were from Oklahoma, Arkansas and Texas, just as in that book. Twenty years after the dust bowl, these people were still wandering, looking for steady work and a home. But I could find no other books by Steinbeck, and soon read everything in the library of our little school that was of any interest to me. In our English class, we had a book of essays and stories, and I read them the first week after being issued the book. It included a story "I Catch a Pig" by someone named Thoreau. It was the funniest thing I had ever read, and recommended it strongly. Mr. Flood assigned it, and no one else found it amusing. My currency in English fell after that, but I maintained my high opinion of the writer Thoreau, whoever he was.

My mathematics teacher at Langlois High School was Billy Nan Kolibaba. From California, she knew in depth the subjects she taught. I was instantly captured by algebra: the symbols saved me from the dull labor that I associated with arithmetic, and the manipulations were much more interesting now. I finished the year's work in less than a half-year, as she let me go ahead at my own speed. Mathematics was the one subject for which I did not yearn for more material. Billy Nan watched my progress and kept me going.

I played basketball on the freshman team, and we did not win a game all year. I played basketball because I was tall, but I did not have much talent for the game. It was just another game with a ball. My parents did not see the point of buying me special gym clothes, and for the first time I was humiliated by my clothing. The legs of my white underwear kept falling out from under the bright team shorts, and I could not keep them rolled up out of view. I envied my teammates for their trim athletic supporters. The basketball coach gave us some advice in that tight Langlois locker room.

"Boys, when it comes to the girls there's just one thing I want you to remember and don't you ever forget it: keep it in your pants! That's all there is to it, just keep it in your pants and you'll save yourself a world of trouble."

Our losing streak started a trend. Even though we consolidated with Port Orford, the district to the south, and for the next three years had a substantially larger pool of talent, no football team and no basketball team won a game during my four years of high school. I had so little interest in baseball that I am not sure we had a team. We were losers, even beaten by the tiny Ophir High School south of Port Orford where all five boys in the high school played on their basketball team. At least they could not field a football team, because the five of them would have surely won those games too. One of those nights as we were showering off our sweat of defeat, Roy Mollier discovered that if we put our fingers in our ears the drumming of the shower was a joyous rumble. Cleaning up from yet another rout, we were tripping on water rapping our skulls.

In Langlois one of the students I did not know was killed in an accident, and a ceremony was held for him at school. Chairs were set up in the gym, and class was dismissed for a half-day. Walking by with an older student, we had the idea of putting tacks in the seats. There is no way to see now why it seemed to be a good practical joke, but it did. We placed a few tacks, five or ten or fifteen, on the seats and saw mental cartoons of people startled to their feet by our clever prank. By that evening on the bus ride home, it seemed much less clever. Thankfully the tacks were found before the ceremony, and I was expelled from school for a few days because of that stupid thoughtless act. Amazingly my father did not punish me physically, and I was sent to the old barn to rub the sprouts off the potatoes stored there. I was familiar with a world where a mistake could have serious ramifications. Men or livestock were easily killed; I had grown up with that. Sitting in that musty old barn rubbing those white and slightly obscene sprouts off wrinkled potatoes, I realized that the mistake of not seeing what our stunt did to the parents and friends of the dead student was serious.

A boy moved from Los Angeles and joined our freshman class. The rumor was that he had been expelled from schools in Los Angeles, and his parents were trying to get him away from the bad city influences, although today I doubt the story. Jon Cox was cool, wearing stylish clothes and walking with a swagger. He was a nice person, and I got to know him in my classes. When he was interviewed by the school newspaper, he named me most-likely-to-succeed. I was surprised as I was not optimistic that I would even escape the ranch. I heard a popular and attractive girl express her amazement that Jon would think that I would be a success. Agreeing with her, I thanked Jon for naming me. He told me emphatically that he believed it, and that I would have a different life in a larger school, where I would be in the math club and would take part in interesting things. I had never heard of a math club and by this time did not join clubs, but Jon gave me a different sense of myself and the potential of the world.

Langlois High had four years of students. My freshman class had twenty-six students and the remaining three years had forty-three students for a total of sixty-nine students. We were just in front of the baby boomers, and our small building was inadequate for the future. Our district consolidated with Port Orford, and Pacific High School was built between Langlois and Port Orford. Pacific was a three-year high school, and we were the first sophomore class. The first year Pacific had one-hundred-and-forty-five students, and it seemed large to the Langlois students. The teachers except for Kolibaba remained dreadful, and the library was still small and inadequate. The state library circulated wooden crates of books to our new school. A shipment came in, and the books were put on a special shelf for three weeks. After that they were sent on to the next rural school, and a new crate arrived. Unlike the anemic books in our permanent library, the books sent out by the state included some substantial volumes. I read everything they sent in the categories of fiction and science. I do not claim to have understood everything I read, but I checked the books out and turned every page. It opened up worlds to me, including the plays of Eugene O'Neill and modern physics.

My mathematics teacher Billy Nan first lent and then gave to me *You Can't Go Home Again* by Thomas Wolfe. It was a force of nature describing a whole new world the South with energy and appetite and passion. A perfect book to read while young and rural, it blew me about as if I were standing on an open ridge during a violent winter storm. The main character's relationship with an older woman, the distancing from family and home....

The new school brought new students, and I made a real friend. Donald Price, a curly-headed juvenile delinquent, was smart and never studied. He had the quickest mouth in class and a reputation for being fast with girls. The music of Bill Haley and then Elvis Presley, Fats Domino, Chuck Berry, The Coasters, Buddy Holly, Bo Diddley, Carl Perkins, Patsy Cline, and Jerry Lee Lewis flooded into our small community late at night over dim-and-distant California radio stations. We all instantly made it part of us, music so immediate and vital that it was searing, unforgettable. I loved Fats Domino with an intensity I cannot explain: that New Orleans boogie piano, that tenor sax, that sweet resonate voice, *I found mah thrill on Blueberry Hill*, it seemed to come from some distant enchanted place. I had no television set, but that did not matter. Rock-and-roll was here to stay, and we all knew it. After all, it was impossible to live in our dirt-roads logging-and-ranching community and not have breathed in with the dust songs of the recently deceased Hank Williams, who was singing rocka-billy before anyone called it that. (Soon the Everly Brothers were singing teened-up versions of Hank's songs.) In this energetic outpouring of music I first heard "Cotton Fields," "Matchbook," "Easy Rider," and "Midnight Special," all looted from the supply of American roots music.

Don Price was rock-and-roll and cutting school and riding in a car with the wind blowing on your face. We called driving up and down the main street of Port Orford "cruising the gut," and there was no better person to ride with than Don. Out on Beach Loop Road near Bandon, with a beer in my stomach, flying down into that deep dip in the road, hitting the bottom and then the road and the car's springs propelling us up into another world. Don's caring parents were mystified by their son who remained in so much trouble. They were building a motel on the bluff south of Port Orford in anticipation of the tourists who were to come twenty years later. After all, Highway 101 went down the hill below their unfinished building and turned at Battle Rock to become the main and almost only street of Port Orford. The winds came so hard in the winter that the pounding surf churned the sea into foam that blew up that steep sandy slope, across the parking lot and then up the main street. Dirty clumps of foam on a cold lonely blacktop road was not a tourist attraction. Not in 1958. Don and I played records in one of the bare unfinished rooms; we played Little Richard screaming over the wind and the waves and the loneliness of Port Orford and the sweet pain of being fifteen-years old. Don danced that music like no one we had seen, a limber shaking all over, spasms in perfect rhythm, a beautiful boy in a trance. The girls loved him, at least those who were not too proper. Who could blame them!

I discovered girls and took them to movies and dances when I could get both the nerve and the car. Beer was as attractive as girls, and we drank Olympia and Rainier whenever we could get a six-pack. Like reading, getting a little drunk allowed me to transcend my ordinary life. There was a pleasure in the yeasty smell and taste of beer (which was seldom chilled when it reached me). Girls and sex were an exciting but remote prospect. I prepared for these outings by shaving and splashing my face with that cowboy standby, Old Spice Lotion. Late one afternoon sitting at a table, one of my teachers in her early 30s rubbed her knee hard on my leg. She had a wimpy husband who came and went from California. I was not confused at what she intended, at least I thought I knew what was happening, and to her evident irritation, I ignored her. Looking back, I wonder the effect if I had let that woman introduce me into sexual worlds. It certainly would have given me a perspective which I lacked, fumbling about in back seats with girls my own age.

My senior year I noticed a sophomore from Port Orford, Vicki Buss. From a logging family, she was bright and attractive. I took her out and continued to date her after I went to college. She lived in an unfinished house on a dirt road in Port Orford. Her father was a gentle man who spent his life logging on the Oregon Coast. He was always working in the woods, taking care of his garden, or fishing for salmon and steelhead; before I met him he had played Hank Williams songs on an accordion. He taught me to fish for steelhead, something I did not have time for until I started college. My instructor could feel the bottom of a Coast stream with his okie-drifter — holding his rod at ready to strike with a calm abstracted look on his face. Vicki's mother was ..., well her mother just sat there among dust and piles of newspapers and disorder, and didn't seem to do anything. Apparently she was an alcoholic, but I didn't have a clue. She certainly was a deeply depressed woman. My future marriage and its long, slow wreckage was there for all but me to see.

Our school was built on the costal plain, back against the hills in scrubby logged-over land. My new classmates started a poker game which fascinated me. One short almost white-haired boy called Six-Foot had a deck of plastic cards, and he ran the game. We went up eroded logging roads into the brush behind school where I am certain the teachers thought we were smoking cigarettes (and some of us were). Six-Foot had a piece of aluminum roofing which he stashed in the brush and was used as a portable card-table. The thick, flexible plastic cards made a satisfying rattling sound as they struck the aluminum. The smell of those cards when removed from their dark hard plastic case was almost intoxicating. I learned various poker games and began to play. Poker took concentration, and we had noon-time hands with pots that totaled over a week's full-time wages for me. We played various versions of poker, and I learned to mistrust the appearance of abundant luck that came with the "two-eyed-Jacks are wild" style games. Instead I much preferred the lean precise elegance of five-card draw with its neat hierarchy of hands from two-pair to full-house to straight-flush. I made some money at that game and greatly enjoyed it. I was impressed at the amount of effort it required, tracking the people and the cards.

Aloma's son John received the monthly magazine *Boy's Life* which was produced by the Boy Scouts of America. Sometimes I read it at Aloma's and once saw an article about a summer program in mechanical engineering for high school students at White Sands Proving Grounds. It sounded amazing to me. Eventually I learned how to apply for it and took a long written exam in Coos Bay. I was the only person taking the test and I believe I did well. But I had entered that I wanted to participate in that specific program at White Sands. So there was no offer for my junior summer but one came the next summer for the Navel Test Station near DC. I had mononucleosis and did not take the opportunity. Later in my life I had a strong interest in computational number theory, and a pioneer in the subject Daniel Shanks was at that location. Going there would have changed my life.

My senior year we had a delicious crisis. Our coach had not won a basketball or football game for our new high school, but that was not what got him fired. He and the home economics teacher had a secret affair, at least it was secret from us. In addition to teaching female students how to make pies and to keep their future husbands' houses neat, she became pregnant. Scandal in our community was a curious thing. Somehow Langlois wanted to think of itself as a hot-bed of racy behavior, and the community was smug about its minor sins. As far as I could make it out, a rancher would take on a housekeeper after his wife died, and eventually the housekeeper would be discovered scrubbing the rancher's back while he was in a bathtub. That is how the community gauged the progress of an affair: when it got to the bathtub stage, the rancher married the housekeeper, and that was that. But our coach was not a rancher and might not have wanted to marry the home-ec teacher. They were both unmarried and stuck in a boring remote rural location with a cold damp climate, but that did not matter to the school board who fired them. They both left at mid-year without any explanation to the students. But the word was out that the coach had knocked her up. I thought that the young woman surely had some good advice about birth control for her classes, but she was not even given a chance to say good-by to them. These were days before contraception was openly discussed. Condoms were kept behind the counter at pharmacies, and I can tell you from my experience, it took courage to ask for them and even then they might not be handed over. The coach, who taught English too (another joke!), carried on until a Ph.D. student from the University of Oregon came down to fill out the year. My new teacher was the third good teacher I had after Billie Nan and Mrs. Churchill who had taught my seventh-grade class.

Nothing like Jerry Crandall had ever been seen in our schools. He was full of cynical enthusiasm as only a Ph.D. candidate can be, and he analyzed the texts we read, demanding us to learn from how they were written and from exactly what they said. He didn't have much to work with as most of his class was destined for the sawmills (which themselves were destined for oblivion), and many of his students would not read anything much more complex than Life Magazine for the rest of their lives. Still he ranted and taunted and pushed his classes, and I for one loved it.

I was running around with the Manicke boys then. Forest had graduated and was driving a log truck. Richard was in my class and Bruce was a year older. They lived in a shack which the wind blew through, with chickens in the living room laying eggs on piles of newspapers beside oily dismantled power saws. They cared for themselves, and it seemed to me that they often did not get enough to eat, but that was their business. They asked for and accepted no sympathy. Bruce Manicke regularly drank beer with the loggers at the Langlois tavern, and he bought me six-packs of Oly when I asked. Bruce had played inspired basketball, sinking beautiful, exuberant jump shots from the corners of the court, and then he got extremely drunk after the games.

I liked these bright energetic children who had a fierce vitality in them which many of my classmates lacked. One night Bruce, Richard and I showed up at the Crandall's home in Port Orford, a rental filled with books and papers. Everyone was drinking, we the beer we brought with us and the Crandalls drank brandy, and I may have been the only one not smoking cigarettes. I heard Jerry Crandall's frustration with me come out as he lamented to the Manicke brothers about people (like me) who were narrow scientists ignorant of the humanities. I knew that, other than Jerry Crandall himself, I had read more literature than anyone in Pacific High School, faculty and students. But although I had just finished Paradise Lost by Milton, I was far from knowing what it was about. And I hardly knew any science either. This caused me to step a bit back from the situation. I could see the patterns we traced that pleasant evening, the smoky spirals weaving in and out: brandy and beer, teaching and setting chokers, books and oil-soaked newspapers, and yes, poetry and physics. I wondered where they would lead us in the next few years; what then would be revealed in the smoke-filled air?

39 Gyppo Logging

During the summers of my undergraduate years, I returned to the Coast and worked in the logging woods and mills. There was no financial help from my parents, and taking out a loan looked like the start of a long slide to the bottom. I lived in my parent's house the first summer. After I married, I lived in my grandfather's vacant house. I did no ranch work and looked for a job where I could accumulate wages. My first employers were the Letsom Brothers, two guys from the Willamette Valley who ran a little mill on the Eisenhauer ranch. I showed up, had the job explained to me, and the mill cranked up.

My first years of college were full of catching up, and it was not in my background to exercise to stay in physical condition. I doubt that a body builder would have been ready for my job though. I was OK stacking the 2" x 4" and 2" x 6" lumber into the required stacks. I had handled enough lumber not to screw that up completely, but I was unprepared for the the resaw cants, timbers that were 6 inches in depth and from 4 to 12 inches in width. This was green lumber and heavy, and I didn't know how to handle it or exactly how wide or deep to stack it. That first morning was a nightmare. I dropped timbers between the stack and the rollers, and couldn't retrieve them. Fortunately for me, the mill broke down and we had to quit early. I came back the next day concerned that I wouldn't make it, but I survived the day. It was Friday. My muscles had stopped hurting so badly by Monday, and I improved a little, just keeping up and wondering if the stream of timbers would ever stop falling off that screeching saw blade. By the second week I could do a fair job, although I still didn't understand the dimensions of the stack of resaw cants.

Let me explain a little about the Letsom's operation. They had one man in the woods who cut the trees down and bucked them and who also set chokers, those loops of cable put around the log and hooked to the bulldozer or cat (for Caterpillar) to pull the log. One brother ran the cat back and forth, building roads and pulling the logs to the mill. Then they had a man Tex who cut the logs into the lengths to be sawed; he ran a collection of machines called the loghaul. The second brother, called RA, ran the saw. Then the person at the receiving end of the resulting lumber was the off-bearer. He pulled the slabs and boards out of the mess that fell off the saw's cut onto live rollers, and he sent the slabs down a set of rollers to the sawdust pile. Then he quickly stacked the lumber if it was 1" thick, and he sent everything else down to the next guy, that was me. The off-bearer had the hardest and most critical job in the whole operation, other than the sawyer. It didn't take the brains that being sawyer did, but it was by far the hardest work. Finally, there was a truck driver who drove the lumber to town. There were operations like this all over western Oregon.

The Brothers kept talking about someone named Red. If they could just get Red, then they could make some money. We were sitting on the lumber stacks on a break the morning Red showed up. He roared up the steep hill, slid his beat-up old car into the yard with a cloud of dust, leapt out the battered door screaming at the top of his lungs in an Oklahoma accent. He was six-foot-four, freckled, with an uncut mass of curly red hair that made him look even taller. He appeared to be a wild man.

"Highball, RA, HIGHBALL! You bastards ain't gettin' nowhere just sittin' 'round. Start that damn engine up, and let's get some work done!"

Well, I had hardly kept up with the previous off-bearer who apparently was Red's inferior. That guy quit because the job was too difficult for him. Red never stopped talking or moving, characteristics I came greatly to admire, but right then I was just hoping I could keep up. I was worried. No need, this guy did his job as if he was the world champion. Seeing me fumbling around, he ran down to show me what to do and then raced back on top of the stacks of resaw to recover from the tangle of boards that accumulated by that huge relentless screaming saw blade. No one else who had that job could have pulled that off. He was a worker and wanted to show me how to get my end of the mill covered, so we could really saw lumber. Indeed, I became good at the job, learning how to handle the lumber, never lifting it directly. It helped to know how many board inches wide the cant stacks were supposed to be, and that board inches and real inches were not identical. Actually there was another part of my job, and that was to trim the ragged ends off of all lumber that wasn't square. That meant taking a little power saw and cutting the lumber the correct lengths, and if it was a 1" board, I had to push it back up to Red when he had a second to stack it. Eventually I was on top of things enough to carry that lumber back myself and stack it while Red did his job. This became enjoyable and easier, so later in the summer Red motioned me up and showed me how to do his job. We were friends.

The Brothers got an order for railroad ties, a special order that required specified numbers of specified lengths of 8" x 8" timbers. That meant that RA cut some 8 x 8's, and I was to keep an account and cut the numbers and lengths needed. They told me later that I had one tie too many or too few in one length, and that it was the first time anyone had come close on an order. It was nice to be told, and it was enjoyable working there for $2.10 per hour.

One day when things had really been moving, logs falling onto the carriage just right, the lumber coming off the saw in stacks, we finally took a break. The shriek of the saw ceased, work stopped, and Red bounced on his toes, sawdust falling off him, then he jumped onto the nearest lumber pile and came down it toward me.

"RA got dollar signs in his eyes!" he shouted. "Sure thing, ole RA got dollar signs in his eyes today!"

Red made a big impression on me. I was amazed that he worked so hard, was so good at this work, and that he had so damn little to show for it. He was a little older than I was but not yet thirty. He was married, had a couple of little kids, and lived in a rented trailer with a washer and dryer that he was buying on time. In other words, he was exactly the kind of person that my parents felt so superior to. I knew for certain that I wasn't better than this hard-working, bright, good-natured man. Like my school-mates who flunked classes and knew endless dirty stories, this guy was as smart as anyone I knew in college. I asked Red about the appliances bought on time, saying that when the Brothers went back to the Valley, wasn't it going to be hard to keep up the payments? He answered that of course, the store would come and get them after a few missed payments. But he loved his wife, and she had a hard life and that anything he could do to make her life easier, he would do it. Now, while he could work like this. But that would not always be the case, and then.... Well, who knew what would happen then? I hope his future held more than he assumed it would.

During one of these summers my cousins from the Willamette Valley, sons of my father's sister, came by the ranch. Like their father they talked easily, voluminously and seemingly endlessly, but never seemed to say anything memorable. Except once when one of them puffed up when he heard I was working in a mill. "Time and motion studies," he said. "I could come and apply time and motion studies." This was something he had learned in a class in college and he went on at length explaining this wonder. Apparently all the Letsom Brothers had to do was to bring in someone with this guy's insights and their mill would run with much greater efficiency. I had never heard of anything like this and I gave it some thought. There wasn't much the Brothers could do; their worst problems were men getting injured and the old equipment breaking down. But the egotistical audacity of that soft cousin who had never in his life worked even one day as hard as Red, and the notion of such stuff being taught in a classroom I found remarkable. I wanted to have whoever thought it up come and show Red how to be an off bearer or show me how to stack resaw cants. Now that'd be a real study in time and motion!

Although I was going to college, I came back to the Coast to work in a gyppo mill to make summer wages. I did not even apply to a large company. All the people I worked with felt superior to the pampered union workers at Georgia-Pacific or Weyerhaeuser. One summer there was a big strike, and a guy who had a combination bucking/chocker-setting job at one of the big companies came to work for the Brothers while the strike lasted. This man was not skilled at either of his jobs, and he was not a hard worker either. This just cemented my unexamined belief that working at a lower-pay no-security job with no benefits made me superior.

Our faller/bucker/chocker-setter drove the wreck of a van called a crummy and told stories about his days in the woods. To work for a gyppo outfit like Letsoms, you were either inexperienced as I was or you were at the end of your days of high-balling dangerous logging. Our crummy driver was on the downhill slope. He had been busted up working for some big outfits, and he had in fact worked the logging show out on Eden Ridge near Powers where my grandfather Payne had built track before and after the Depression. His favorite story was about a married woman from Powers. They drove out in his Chevy Coupe and parked high on a lonely bluff overlooking the Coquille River. They made love in the car, and he became enthusiastic talking about her orgasms.

"She like to pounded my head through the top a that little car. She'd come, over and over, and I thought my hair would wear right off the top a my damn head. Them were the days, yeah them were it."

The next summer the Brothers did without the man Tex who ran the log-haul to cut the logs into lengths for the saw. Instead they bought a larger power saw and had me buck the logs on the landing in my spare time. Then I used a little forklift to place the logs onto the rollers to the saw. I fitted this into my full-time job of the year before and in effect was doing both jobs. Here was a time-and-motion study case study: eliminate one job and get someone to do both. Of course the trick was finding the person who could handle two jobs! I missed the Texan who had run the log-haul the previous summer; he and I had long conversations about country music, country Jimmie Rodgers, Hank Williams and others. Tex recommended the Carter Family and told me not to miss Ernest Tubbs, good old ET.

"When ole Jimmie sang 'good mornin' shine,' he weren't meanin' no sun. No sir! When that sun come up it hit a Negra workin' man and he was a shinin'." I had sweat enough to know what he meant.

Letsoms raised my wages to $2.35 per hour. I was happy so long as I got in a full days work. During breakdowns we were not paid, so nonstop operation was what I needed.

Then something wonderful happened. When I rode that school bus all those hours, I had regularly been tormented by two huge brothers who lived on Lower Four Mile Road. Those bullies had a sister in my class, a large girl who had a miscarriage in the fifth grade, fathered by one of her brothers. They viewed me as something to pass their bus time torturing. I deeply hated them and dreamed of the day I could shoot one of them. Or both. And now on this landing was the new hire of the Letsom Brothers, one of the Brown boys. Now I had my wish: I was bigger than this guy now, I was in far better shape, and I was a lot smarter. He thought it was great to see me, and I was asked to teach him my job. Wonder of wonders. I just savored the situation for a few days. The possibilities were delightful. I could get him out of sight of the others and beat him up, and I could do that as often as I wanted. I could easily maneuver him into a situation where he would break a leg or arm. I could even get him killed, but that was no longer such an appealing idea. I still wanted revenge, and there he was, standing waiting, grinning stupidly at me, completely unable to understand how to measure and cut a log, let alone remember it 20 minutes later when the next logs were pulled into the landing. Even if every log had been the same length, he couldn't have coped. Another way to go was to tease and humiliate him day after day after day. That had appeal. Finally after a few days, I decided that he was so dumb that it would be like hurting a rabbit — there could be no pleasure in taking revenge on somebody so stupid. Burdens I still carried from those earlier school days evaporated, so it did me some good. I moved to the off-bearer job, and the Brown brother went back on unemployment. They never found anyone who could handle the dual-job I had been doing.

Even after I was in condition I never completed eight hours as off-bearer without almost collapsing in exhaustion. The job required strength, dexterity, speed and endurance. And either courage or stupidity. The saw screamed as it tore the hearts out of fir after fir. There was a heavy leather apron which I never wore; it was just too hot. And no amount of protection would have saved me from the explosion of wood that came once one summer and twice the next. If the pieces of those shattered logs had hit me they would have torn my head off or gutted me out. But all three times I was left frightened but intact, missed by the wooden shrapnel.

After two summers, I left the Letsom Brothers mill for a chocker-setting job where the landing was solid blue-clay. Landing is a term that came from high-lead logging where the logs are brought through the air to a central location. Our logs were pulled in with a dozer. This landing of ours was solid until it received a bit of moisture, even one of the heavy Coast fogs, when the entire surface became so slick we couldn't even walk across it in calked boots.

"You can't even spit on the son-of-a-bitch," one of the men said. "You be damn sure you piss on the downhill slope!"

One step and the nails of our boots dug into the clay, and on the second step the layer of clay now on the boots met the new clay. Down we went, swearing and laughing. We were out a day's pay because of the damn fog and the damn blue-clay, laughing at ourselves falling in the mud. There was a joy in this rough dangerous work which I had not experienced in ranching. It was the men I worked with. Here we were in it together, we shared the labor and the accomplishments and the damn blue-clay.

Riding to work in the crummy, one man told us that an absent co-worker's wife was pregnant.

"The thing is," he said, "is that he is sterile. He shoots blanks."

Apparently the couple was divorcing as a result of this turn of events, and the man never returned to work. I was reminded of the old country joke about circumstantial evidence which sometimes is very strong, such as when there is trout in the milk. The point is that the farmer stopped the wagon on the way to town to scoop water from the trout stream to add to the milk so he could be paid for water.

One summer I was setting chokers for another small gyppo outfit and had taken the job because of fifteen cents more per hour, longer hours, and a safe cat driver. Well, they put the safe cat driver on another job, and I was working behind the owner's brother, a bastard who didn't care about anything and whom we could not get fired. Fortunately I had a partner, an older guy who was an alcoholic. You could smell booze on his breath at 5:30 AM when we rode in the crummy to work. I liked him and was in good condition, so I always told him I wanted to do the early work myself. This let him recover before he did anything. We got along, and he showed me how to set chokers. The work wasn't as physically demanding as being off-bearer, but dangers were everywhere and I wasn't a natural at recognizing them. One day when as usual I offered to set the first turn of the day, he said no. I said, really, no problem. "Look," he told me, "this is a bad situation and you'll get hurt in there. Look how that bastard has it set up." He was referring to a hassle we had the night before about which logs the cat driver would pull out and when. I watched this man, this alcoholic who was hurting badly and shaking a little, take the cables, and I watched where he moved and what happened. I probably would have been killed, at least seriously injured, and I knew it when he came back. Take those over there next, he said, motioning to some logs, and he went off to rest.

One early morning a new person showed up to work for a couple of days. He was splendid in his logger clothes, especially the pair of White boots on his feet, and in addition he was a great athlete. This guy was too good to stay working for this tiny outfit up Bear Creek, but I envied him his gear. No way could I even afford Currins boots except for a broken-sole pair cast off by my father, but I lusted to have a pair of Whites on my feet.

I worked two summers setting chokers up Bear Creek in the blowdown from the 1962 Columbus Day storm. The full crew was less than ten men. This included the two cutters who really couldn't be called timber fallers as the entire forest had been laid down by the wind. They had souped-up red Homolites, the saws from Japan that had eclipsed the powerful yellow McCullochs my father and I had used ten years earlier. Sawdust flew as they bucked that twisted timber. They went fast, making big money until one man's leg was smashed by a log that sprang back, one of the dangers I had learned in 1953. During my time on Bear Creek, two men were killed on the landing. One was decapitated when a cable snapped, his head just barely attached to his body by the skin of his neck. The other was crushed when a log fell off a trunk onto him, the log rolling up the hill a bit before it came back down onto his already dead body.

"You get that ed-u-cation and don't you spend your life doin' this," the men all told me. "Find yourself a better way to make a livin'."

40 Crossing the Divide

Rugged 5000-foot mountains are a barrier between the Oregon Coast and the rest of the world. The Willamette Valley and the Oregon Coast were grooves and to move from the Coast to the Valley required substantial effort. I had no idea what was required to escape the Coast groove.

My first choice was between Oregon State College and the University of Oregon. They were the only schools I considered, hovering out there at the rim of my known universe. Oregon State was reputedly the school for practical studies; it then was my obvious choice. What was I but practical? I also decided on a physics major. My mother's superintendent at the Coquille schools had somehow become the head adviser for the School of Science at OSC, and she and I made the trip all the way to Corvallis to consult him. He advised me to major in engineering.

"It is always easy to go from engineering to physics but not the reverse."

I still have no idea what possessed him to advise me so, perhaps he thought I aimed too high with a physics major, but I did as he suggested and enrolled at Oregon State as an engineering student.

The college had almost ten-thousand students, and I was amazed by their numbers and dazzled by their sophistication. Registration seemed a chaotic process to me; it took place inside a large covered gymnasium where I lost my sense of direction. There was no geography to the place, and no sky. I wandered randomly, standing in long lines which sometimes were lines I needed to be in, and eventually I was registered as a freshman engineer for seventeen credit hours.

Then wonders began. I attended only twenty-seven hours of classes and labs per week, an amazingly small number it seemed to me. Beyond that I was left entirely alone. No one required me to work mornings or nights, and my weekends were unscheduled. I could not believe such luxurious freedom.

Soon I discovered the library in an elegant old building crammed with more books than I had thought existed in the entire world. My fear that there were not enough books on the planet to last me a lifetime seemed childish. I was stunned. The problem turned out to be deciding what to read in that lifetime. How could such riches be coped with; how could the most important and exciting books be located in the endless aisles? As the loggers said when someone married a pretty woman who had some money, I thought I'd died and gone to heaven.

My first term I lived in a dormitory. This was a shock to a boy who knew fewer people than lived on one dorm floor and who was used to night sounds of wind and animals. It was interesting too, although I didn't sleep well cramped up with all those people. One Sunday I was looking through a newspaper and saw my first Andrew Wyeth reproduction. Printed in color on cheap paper was one of Wyeth's precise stark masterpieces of a working man standing by a window in a plain room done in faded wallpaper. He was about sixty years old, wearing an old worn shirt, sleeves rolled up showing his muscular forearms with veins standing out. This guy had worked hard all his life and showed it in his stance and his build and his look at the painter. He made me think immediately of my grandfather Waterman who standing by an upstairs window in his house would have looked just like that. I tore the picture out of the newspaper and taped it to my dorm wall. I told someone that men like that were the backbone of our country. Later I heard this repeated to the amusement of the listeners. I was not embarrassed; I had said it and I believed it. It was years before I understood this incident. Those soft boys from the suburbs were right to laugh. The industrial revolution had already occurred, and our entire century was an exodus from the farm, one that continues today. So hardworking Charlie Frank Waterman was a hundred-and-more years out of date, something for an artist to represent and for the image to be purchased by people who made their living from factories.

A common dilemma for college freshman is balancing partying and drinking with studying. I had little money for beer, but had to balance recreational reading with studying. I feared that I was not bright or hardworking enough to earn a college degree. Whatever the case, I was having an experience for which I was grateful, flunk or not. And I studied as much and as hard as I could, with less background than most of my classmates.

Many of my fellow students like Don Campbell from Portland had the advantage of attending a high school with college-prep courses. Don also greatly impressed me at dinner with his ability to eat any piece of chicken without picking it up in his hands. Don Campbell was truly part of the outside world I had wondered about when I was a child. He was as natural and true in it as I was when wading Four Mile Creek above the Wilson Place bridge after a good rain. I was a clumsy visitor to Don's world, and he became my friend as he did everything from engineering to girls, all as smoothly as graphite.

One looming horror was the swimming requirement. We suited up and had to try to swim the length of the pool and back. On the ranch I had taught myself a dog-paddle stroke which did not get me far. So I took remedial swimming, which was where I got to know Don Campbell who had faked failure for an easy first-term PE class. I became relaxed in the water and developed an efficient backstroke. Throughout the two years of PE requirements, I avoided taking classes involving games with a ball. I even took weight-lifting which like swimming turned out to be a great class.

After completing the first term, I went home exhausted. My father had saved the heavy jobs for me, just as he had collected them for weekends when I was in grade school and high school. Needless to say this further sharpened the divide of the Coast Range. I anxiously waited to see if I had passed my courses. My GPA was 3.24 out of 4.00, something which also surprised the Dean of Engineering who taught my beginning engineering class.

"However did you do that?" he asked, and I answered that his class was my lowest scoring subject. Actually that was not true; I had received a "C" in PE.

The weather in Corvallis put me slightly off-balance. I knew that it rained less than on the Coast, but that was not quite it. Then one day it came to me that rain in the Valley fell down from the top of the sky straight to the earth. On the Coast the south wind blew the rain in sideways. The Valley was an entirely different place.

Two years of Reserve Officer Training was required of all men attending land-grant institutions. We were issued an M1-rifle, heavy brown uniforms and uncomfortable black shoes we were taught to spit-shine, and then were put to marching about the Armory where the grounds contained piles of horse manure left from riding shows. I was not a natural at marching and unlike swimming did not soon discover its rhythm.

Spring term I was taken aside by the commander of the OSC-ROTC. It is unlikely that this position was on the upward arc of a military career, but his attitude toward me was one that I myself had taken toward problem livestock.

"I can get this poor creature to do what I want. See here, it's easy."

The unfortunate man found our session as frustrating as I did, the platoons marching smartly around us. In spite of myself, by the spring of my second year I could march well enough not to be singled out. There were classes as well: in field-stripping an M1, shooting, map reading, and military history. When we shot a small-caliber rifle for a grade, I approached the firing line with confidence: here was something I actually knew how to do. The rifle shot in a scatter pattern, and when I held the gun up to the light and looked down the barrel I realized that the rifling was shot out, it became a private joke to me. I quickly fired the remaining rounds and finished the minor ordeal. I saw my first contour map in an ROTC class, and it was the best moment of ROTC, those lines resolving into mountains, rivers, valleys, and cliffs while we waited for class to begin. We were taught military history by a Japanese-American, Capt Takasumi. He had a dry sense of humor and brought the subject alive with men who became frightened when shot at, who swore, and-so-on. It occurred to some of the class for the first time that people just like us were sent to fight wars. Abruptly the Capt was removed from the class early in 1961 to become a military adviser in Vietnam. This was the first I had heard of that country and that war. One frozen winter day in the early 1980s in Washington DC, I walked along that magnificent black gash into the earth, searching for his name on the tragic list. To my relief the Capt apparently survived Vietnam.

While in the dorm my first term, I made friends with Lowell Euhus from Clatskanie. He was the son of an itinerant preacher, and we had a lot in common including being on the social fringes of university life. We both had visited fraternities and had simultaneously rejected and been rejected by them. We were good at science, loved literature, and had little money. Ma Hamer had an eating house on the edge of campus where she fed sixty boys well for a reasonable sum. Lowell and I took a cheap room in the attic of a decaying house nearby, signed up with Ma and were much happier. This was a few years before being out of the system was fashionable, but we had found our place at OSC.

My second-term English-composition teacher gave us a method to structure our essays. The first paragraph was to contain thus-and-such, the next paragraph this-and-that and so on to the prescribed end. It made essay writing a form of fill-in-the-blanks, and our essays were more coherent than they had been first term. I memorized this "little-boxes" formula and followed it without difculty. Unfortunately I cannot recall one detail of that carefully crafted method, and when struggling with some topic that refuses to be pinned to the page, sometimes I think with nostalgia of the nimble writing abilities I possessed the winter term of 1961.

Lowell and I had a hunger for books which our meager funds could not satisfy. We haunted second-hand bookstores, going as far as Portland to collect stacks of old books scented with decay and ammonia. Tennessee Williams and Erskine Caldwell, warm-weather writers, huddled on Portland's cold shelves. The OSU bookstore was well stocked, and several of us began to steal books from it. The winters were damp even in the Valley, and books slipped under a coat were held by the pressure of an arm. Everyone was bundled up, and we were not caught. Copies of Hemingway, Steinbeck, and then Faulkner disappeared under our coats. Our interests widened further, and Joyce, Flaubert and Balzac found themselves thrust into the warm darkness of an armpit. Our thefts were spiked by adrenaline at first, but greed kept us going back. After I moved away from Ma Hamer's I stopped stealing books, but one of my friends continued. He stole a world atlas on commission for a fraction of the face value, an atlas that was as wide as his back and several-feet long. The heist involved a loose raincoat, but it was hard to believe that even he could have pulled it off. Fred Krogh was a graduate student in mathematics living at Hamer's, and he heard of this feat. Fred threatened to turn my friend in unless he returned the atlas. Using the raincoat again he did so, and Fred checked the bookstore to be certain that the deed was done. Then my friend swiped the atlas again, this time keeping quiet about it afterwards.

The second year of college I specialized in electrical engineering, then the most abstract branch of engineering. I enjoyed learning mechanical drawing and many aspects of engineering, but especially in lab I was driven mad by the emphasis on "make it work" rather than on "why it works." My ranch life had taught me the value of being able to do things, but that was just the point. I had come to college to learn the why of almost anything, otherwise I would have been ranching. It was not, as I had been so confidently told, so easy to transfer to physics, and I transferred instead to mathematics, my easiest subject. It was a huge relief.

I got married that summer. It was not unusual for the times, and in the rural logger culture I had grown up in, early marriage was normal. My wife Vicki from that logger life worked that summer in a bank, but when she got to Corvallis she just sat at home doing nothing (so far as I could tell) except a minimal amount of housework. Our apartment with its dirty chaos reminded me of her parents' home. It was a crisis for me—my ideas of soul merging and endless sex disappeared and instead I was facing personal disaster. A few years later and a divorce might have been the solution. Instead I was slowly pulled into a deep despair. At the term's end I received my grades, the only time my average sank below a 3.0. This shocked me into realizing I could destroy my life by failing in college. My resolution was not to let that happen, and at some cost to my self-image I rearranged my priorities. My grades never fell below a 3.5 again.

Much of the time I was able to ignore my dying marriage. The university occupied most of my thoughts, but when it was time to visit Four Mile my mood would rapidly fluctuate. On the way over the Coast Range I was increasingly apprehensive about seeing my family. No one there said anything positive about what I was doing. Instead there was overwhelming and silent criticism, perhaps generated by my strong desire not to become a rancher. They disapproved of my marriage, and Vicki was a silent and non participating guest in their home. But on the way back to Corvallis, leaving the Coast behind, driving the curving roads, I was overtaken by waves of optimism, optimism that with some attention my marriage would turn out well, that I would learn many new subjects, that I would find the path to permanently escape Four Mile.

Don Campbell and I were bored in linear-algebra class, and I decided that we should invent a student. Jack Rice was the superintendent of schools at home, a hollow, formal man with a job that seemed to me to have no duties other than showing up. A couple of homework assignments bearing his name were turned in, and Jack Rice took the first in-class exam. Perhaps I should have used the name of a child of my childhood invention Mrs. Bonney, but that never occurred to me. Our instructor was Frank Wyse, a never-to-finish-his-Ph.D. fixture of the Mathematics Department. Disheveled and disorganized Frank Wyse tried to locate Jack Rice.

"Apparently he enrolled late ... but ... he is doing fine ... but he hasn't picked up the midterm.... Really ... he is doing ... actually doing very well.... Anybody ... anybody who sees him ... tell him to see me."

Jack did not do as well on the second in-class exam because there was one difficult problem which took up *our* time. But Frank Wyse then became even more desperate to locate Jack Rice, and I began to wonder if I couldn't get Jack a student loan and send him all the way through college.

My new schedule allowed me to take more electives. I mixed physics and chemistry with an increasing number of courses in literature, philosophy and religion. Along with many others I was led by J.D. Salinger to Zen Buddhism which launched me into trying to understand what religion was. (Sadly Salinger wrote himself into a corner and fell permanently mute. We never heard from him again.) Professors Warren Hovland and Nicholas Yonkers were extremely patient and encouraged my wanderings in philosophy and religion. I even took a graduate seminar in Advanced Existentialism, a title I thought to be very funny.

Literature was my deepest love. One of my professors was H.E. Childs, a crusty older man who was tolerant of honest effort and opinions but who became brutal even at a hint of fakery. He had done his Ph.D. thesis on Sinclair Lewis.

"Among other things I demonstrated that he made grammatical errors," he said with a sigh. He demonstrated a good deal more that that, but picking out his own weakest point and revealing it was typical of the man.

He was fondly remembered in the autobiography of William Kitterage, who was raised an eastern Oregon ranch. I wonder if there are not a bunch of us rural children with literary bents who were influenced by Childs. Once I disagreed in class with Childs about the famous Hemingway story, "The Short Happy Life of Francis Macomber."

"You are wrong," he said.

"I don't think so," I replied.

"Well you are," he said firmly, and carried on with his lecture.

Later I went to his office and showed him what Hemingway wrote, and then told him what my assumptions were and how my reasoning went. "I see what you mean," he said. There was a long pause as he sat behind a desk covered by books and essays. "You know, you are correct."

He began the next class by recalling the incident from the preceding class and then corrected his interpretation. What a man! Years later I was pleased to see in print essentially the same analysis I had made.

I took my first graduate-level class in mathematics when I was a junior. Professor Jim Brown used Tom Apostol's famous book in analysis, and the material was a shock to me. For the first time I could not just glance at the text, practice a problem or two, and get an "A." Fortunately I was also enrolled in a course that used Suppes' text in symbolic logic, so that I was learning what precise language and logic were. When in high school, a new OSC-graduate Jim Green who taught science told me that I would flunk out of college. I suspect that I provoked him into making this pronouncement, but I was pleasantly surprised to see him in the back of the analysis class. I scored at least one grade-level higher than he did all three terms, but the course was so difficult for me that beating Jim Green was not the sweet satisfaction it could have been. I felt lucky to pass and wished that I better understood the material.

I tried my hand at writing fiction, and the once-a-year college literary magazine published my story "A Clean Feeling." I was informed by a young woman in one of my philosophy classes that she was on the selection committee and that the committee had chosen my story because they could not understand it. This seemed to me a strange reason, especially as I thought the story was transparent. I did not find the drive, talent or time to do much more fiction writing. When I was finishing my B.S. degree, I considered going to the University of Oregon for a masters degree in English.

"Don't do it," Childs told me, "You are going on in science, now or later. Don't waste your time on side moves. You can always read and write." I saw that he was probably correct and took his advice.

I stopped going to movies and listening to popular music in 1960 and did not return to those things for many years. They seemed a waste of time. Instead I read and increasingly listened to folk music. The foundations of the rock-and-roll I loved in high school were found in Mississippi, the Appalachians, out in the margins, and by 1961 this roots-music was being widely distributed for the first time. Woody Guthrie was a dust-bowl refugee, and his songs had the texture of sand and rusted barbed-wire. He invented Okie-rap, just take a listen, he called it the talking-blues. (This was an adaption from the talking blues of the Blacks.) When I heard Bob Dylan I sneered that he was just a Woody Guthrie knock-off, and for some time that was close to the truth. Then Dylan's huge poetic gift became obvious even to me. Leadbelly, Robert Johnson, Blind Lemon Jefferson, Jimmie Rodgers all came back to life on reissued records in those days. Miracles happened too such as Mississippi John Hurt found alive and singing in "Avalon, [his] home town." I discovered the high-lonesome sound of Bill Monroe in a 95-cent bin in a supermarket. "In the pines, in the pines/ Where the sun never shines." Along with jazz, bluegrass is another incredible American musical invention.

October 22, 1962 I was walking home in a healthy wind. Limbs were breaking and falling out of trees, although I could not see why such things should happen in the brisk but mild wind of 55 mph. It would hardly have stirred limbs on the trees on the Coast. I moved out to the center of the street and proceeded carefully. The Columbus Day storm blew over 120 mph on the Coast, and although the Coast Range cut by half its speed, it was devastating and blew trees down and roofs off all over the Valley. It laid down mountain-sides of timber on the Coast, and I logged for two summers in the blow-down from that storm.

The civil-rights movement was in full force, and my parents were strongly opposed to it. My mother referred to *those* people as Negros, the then acceptable term, while my father never used *that* capital-N-word. I was foolish enough to argue with them about civil rights, and finally my mother played what she considered her strongest card.

"How would you feel if your own brother married one of *them*?" For once I did not have to search for an answer. "I would be proud of him if he did, but I doubt that he has what it takes."

A TV signal had finally reached our highest hill, and a ghostly picture flickered on their screen. This brought an immediacy to current events that they had not previously possessed. Who could ignore Martin Luther King when you could see his passionate face, hear his cadences, watch the crowds roar their response? When later in the early 1970s I heard that my parents enjoyed the hit show "All in the Family," I found it hard to believe. But I should have guessed. My mother identified with the long-suffering Edith, while my father laughed with each of Archie's racial-and-class slurs-and-insults. They completely missed the heavy-handed brutal satire. It gave the show new meaning for me.

There is an afternoon of November 1963 which is almost frozen. I am living on 9th Street in a small cottage, and outside the leaves have already fallen from the trees. Dusty slabs of late-fall sunlight angle into the room which is furnished with an old spring-broken couch, an oil heater and stacks of papers and books. Jim Spoerl, whom I had corrupted in the back of a differential equations class with Haiku poetry, had gotten me the cottage that went with the huge boarding house his parents ran next door. (Jim began in physics, switched to mathematics in order to understand physics, then to philosophy in order to understand mathematics. He ended up studying religion and became a minister.) Jim is at the door out of breath.

"Have you heard Kennedy was shot in Dallas? He may already be dead."

We turn on the radio and it is true and probably John Kennedy is dead. I had only been eighteen in 1960 and therefore was unable to vote for Kennedy, against Nixon whom instinctively I disliked intensely. Kennedy is dead and the motes of dust in the yellow light move infinitesimally. There is no traffic on the normally busy street, we hear instead the quiet roar of empty space.

The old tale of returning to a childhood home to find it much smaller than remembered never happened to me. The ranch remains the size it was when I grew up there. But twenty years after leaving OSC, some young faculty knew of my work and invited me to visit and give a lecture. It had become OSU of course. To my surprise, OSU was much smaller than I remembered OSC from my student years, and I walked around the campus in amazement. In a way OSC was the location of my intellectual childhood. Not so many years before my attendance OSC taught plowing, and I saw photographs of students behind teams in the fields. At my OSC there were new acreages to explore: the equations of modern physics, a system of probability formalizing years of bad crops or low prices, ferns that fling their sperm into the winds with catapults, the Hindu religions with their many-armed and sexual gods, Joseph Conrad fighting his way up a steamy jungle river, Haiku poetry with fourteen quiet and potent syllables. Each of these began as an unscaled world of its own which then created its particular system of measurement. These new territories were mine for the wandering, and I would not have missed those explorations for the largest ranch in Oregon.